Overlay
A Tale of One Girl's Life
in 1970s Las Vegas
The first of the trilogy

by Marlayna Glynn Brown

ISBN-13: 978-1475200355
ISBN-10: 1475200358

Dedication

I dedicate Overlay to the four luckiest hands a woman could win: my children Ryder, Ever, Waverly and Asher Brown. You will forever be my biggest wins. Knowing you has brought joy far beyond my wildest childhood expectations. Loving you has healed me on every level and I thank you for allowing me the pleasure of sharing your childhood journeys with you.

I wish to thank the beings that helped me learn the most difficult lessons in childhood. We often grow immensely through pain, and some beings were more skilled at delivering the important lessons than others. Thank you for your participation.

Marlayna Glynn Brown

Overlay – A Tale of One Girl's Life in 1970s Las Vegas

PART ONE

(1970 – 1972)

Overlay – A Tale of One Girl's Life in 1970s Las Vegas

Overlay – A Tale of One Girl's Life in 1970s Las Vegas

Prologue

Overlay: A good bet where you have a distinctive edge over the Casino.

"I will never drink or smoke," I announce to my mother, pausing for what is most certainly a dramatic effect. I snap my mouth closed and wait, sitting comfortably cross-legged on the shiny bathroom countertop to watch her apply makeup.

The elegant tips of her fingers circle the liquid black eyeliner around her eyes. Her concentration on this delicate act is fierce. Her small frame is bent forward from her trim waist as she weaves the tiny black brush between her long lashes. Although I know each minuscule movement of her hand brings her one step closer to leaving me, I am transfixed by the mysterious process of makeup application. I sit solemnly, watching as she carefully peels twinned lashes from the white plastic container and presses them to her upper eyelids. Her mouth creates a dark O as she blinks with every deliberate stroke of the mascara brush. The result of this process is a secret face, not unlike a distorted view through a dusty window. The face now beside me in the mirror isn't the real face of my mother at all. Gone is the everyday face with large blue eyes and Pond's cold-creamed skin and long dimples that frame an often hesitating yet perfect smile.

"Good decision!" she remarks, clearly impervious to my philosophical underpinnings. Perhaps she thinks I am only four years old, and what could I possibly know about the world and its vices? Perhaps she agrees. Perhaps she thinks nothing about my thoughts at all. Perhaps she didn't even listen. I can never tell what my mother thinks. She is silent, serious. Ungiving. Inexplicable. Her inner nature is like a puzzle to me and I seek ways to learn her secret thoughts through announcements designed to fire up conversation or create a reaction. Seldom am I successful in this constant gamble for my mother's love and attention.

"Butterfly kiss?"

She hesitates, then leans in so close I smell her perfume – Tabu. She once told me that Tabu means a secret thing considered to be against the rules and I like that idea very much. She blinks her long feathery eyelashes up and down against mine, tickling. Sometimes if I am feeling especially lonely I demand, "Eskimo kiss," close my eyes and rub my nose softly against hers. Opening my eyes on this night, I pull away at the transformation of her face to another. My mother was my mother, and now she is someone else – a painted sort of thing.

Turning to the mirror to gaze at my own face, I twist my white-blonde hair around my fingers and stare into the blue abyss of my own eyes. Tommy Jenkins from down the block, or The Red Headed Hamburger as I call him, told me that the pupil of your eye is really just a big black hole into your brain and that you can stick a needle straight through if you want. I believe this because I haven't yet learned that people can say things that are untrue. Moving back from the mirror, I view the smattering of orange freckles across my nose that I've earned in my four summers under the burning Nevada sun. Faces are an endless source of fascination to me. They convey the stories that words and gestures often do not. If you just study the faces, you can learn a whole lot of things about the people around you even if no one says a word.

"What are you doing?" My mother laughs and paints my lips with quick, darting strokes of her tiny pink lipstick brush, applying a frosty glaze to match her own. I smack my lips together the way I see her do, spreading the color evenly across my lips. I know lipstick is the final stage of the process and she will be leaving soon. My heartbeat speeds.

After a parting glance in the mirror, she gives me a quick kiss on the top of my head and leaves for the Casino where she will serve Drinks to people who are thirsty. The front door snaps shut, and the heavy silence settles across the house as it always does. I run to my bedroom window and pull the lace aside to watch the headlights grow smaller as she backs the car down the long driveway.

When she has gone, I join my dad in the living room where he spends his evenings lying in his black recliner chair, watching black and white television. His glass of water and whiskey rests on the table next to him. His cigarette burns down between his fingers, the smoke twisting into curling purple plumes above his head. I try to sit still to watch television with him but he tires of my attempts to engage him in conversation and eventually ignores my questions or takes so long to answer that I stop talking. Gathering my courage, I run down the darkened hallway to my bedroom before the monsters at the end of the hall can pounce and shut the door against the smoke and the sound of the television. After a time the television hisses from the living room, signaling that my father has fallen asleep in his chair. I say this to myself even though I know he hasn't fallen asleep in his chair but Passed Out, a frequent occurrence.

The television programs end at what is considered to be a reasonable hour. I assume most reasonable children are asleep in their reasonable beds by the time the last show of the evening draws to an end. These other children probably never get the chance to see the five colored bars that appear on the television set after the programs are finished. We are an unreasonable household with unreasonable hours, so I am gifted with this colorful view when I creep out of my bedroom and peek at my father.

Although my father doesn't wear makeup, like my mother he harbors a secret face. I stare at his secret face, so unlined and slack against the black leather of the recliner chair that he looks like someone else entirely. The shifting colors of the television set are free to create craters and hollows on his pasty skin. I turn off the television and run back down the long hall toward my bedroom, again escaping the monsters who live in the shadows at the end of the hallway.

I lay in bed and wait for sleep to come. I try not to look into the corners of my room because it's dark. If I look long enough I will see the monsters who hide there take shape, grow larger and more menacing. I know it's best not to look. I know I am alone and there is no one to protect me. I look anyway. I look fixedly at those monsters, silently daring them to step out of the safety of their darkened corners.

We are at a standoff, those monsters and I. They remain looming and massive in the four corners of my room. I remain resolutely in my bed.

I know I have the overlay - the distinctive edge of being real.

Chapter One

Face Cards: The Jack, Queen and King of any suit of cards.

Sitting on my bedroom floor, I pull out one of my many books from the little yellow bookshelf my mother painted for me last summer. My mother likes to shop at the Second Hand Shop and bring home Unloved and Unwanted things and fix them up like new. My bookshelf is one such thing. We found it collapsed on its side, and my mother lifted it and set it right and brushed the dust from her hands and proclaimed, "This will be perfect for your books. I will paint it Yellow." She made it happen that night, and I fell asleep with the chemical smell of varnish and paint in my nose, gazing at the proof that my mom could Make Things Happen.

My mother taught me to read shortly after I turned four, and filled my yellow bookshelf with books of stories and poems. One of my favorites was Mary Howitt's The Spider and The Fly. I run my finger under the words as I read, trying not to pay attention to the illustration on the facing page of a tall Spider dressed in a suit and holding open a red velvet drape to entice the Fly to walk into a room called a parlour. I'm not entirely sure what a Parlour is, and this word joins some of the other things I don't yet understand about life.

Take cousins, for example. When pedaling my Big Wheel up and down the sidewalks of Flamingo Road I always stop to watch when cousins arrive to visit the neighbors. Reversing the pedals, I slam to a sliding sideways halt to watch as they tumble out of wood-paneled station wagons like Weebles after a long and unsteady drive. As I might have imagined, one day I see that the cousins of the Red Headed Hamburger all share the same bright red hair color. I envy every last red-hued one of them, watching as they exit the car, yawning and stretching. A little one carries a blanket, blinking in the morning sun, and his mother grabs his hand and the group enters the Red Headed Hamburger's house. I sit alone on my Big Wheel for a moment after they close the door, feeling bereft.

When I ask why I don't have cousins, my mother tells me that I do: I have six cousins.

"SIX cousins? Why don't we ever see them?"

"I don't want family sticking their nose in my business. That's why we live in Las Vegas, and they all live in California. I don't want any family around."

We are so very different from other families in this way. I have two grandmothers but I've only met each one once or twice, and didn't particularly care for either of them. They don't live nearby. They never invite me to visit their farms in the summertime. They don't bake cookies for me like the grandmothers in the books I read. There are two grandfathers married to the grandmothers, but they aren't real grandfathers, since the real ones died a long time ago. I don't understand much of this either. If someone isn't a 'real' grandfather, then what is he? Something that isn't real is fake or imaginary. Since I can't quite grasp the fact that my grandfathers are not real, I prefer that they stay away. Sounds like a dangerous business to me. My own parents didn't even know their real fathers, both having passed before they had much of a chance to say hello, let alone get acquainted.

My mother's father had been a firefighter who was killed while fighting the worst fire in the history of the Montana town where he'd moved after my grandmother left him. My father's father died at 33 when he abruptly slammed on the brakes of a truck he was driving and a can of paint flew from the back, striking him on the head and causing him to die screaming from the pain of a bleeding brain hemorrhage three days later. It didn't bode well to be a male in my family. While I reflected upon this, I took private comfort in the circles and creases that predicted my future womanhood. When the men in my family died, as they seemed to do quite frequently, the women just carried on with life as usual and replaced the men without a whole lot of fanfare. Apparently, this is our way.

Besides grandfathers, the characters in the books I read had families full of relations I couldn't understand. Brothers. Sisters. Cousins. Godparents. Aunts. Uncles. Grandparents. Cousins once removed. Second cousins. Third cousins. Half cousins. Great-grandparents. Great-aunts. The list of relations a person could have was a long and confusing list. Some babies were fortunate to burst forth from the comfort of the womb and land in plush familial layers of relations but I am not fortunate in this way: it's just me, my mother and my father. Since the three of us are rarely all together at the same time and in the same place, our sense of family dwindles from there.

I consider this elusive sense of family quite frequently, a legato backbeat of longing that punctuates my view of the world.

Even though there's an entire deck of family members ... we have only three face cards.

Chapter Two

Underlay: A bad bet; an event that has more money bet on its happening than can be justified by the probability of it happening.

When my mother announces that one of my cousins will be visiting in the afternoon, I pepper her with a bevy of questions all day. I imagine a towheaded boy about my age who plays with Barbies and dollhouses and watches Underdog and Godzilla. Maybe he will bring along a Lite Brite by Hasbro since mine is broken and only half of the bulbs light up anymore. It will be even better if he brings the cool monster maker toy where you pour in the green goop and the machine cooks it into a little gelatinous monster. One of my neighbors down the street has this toy and I covet it to the point of trying to think of ways to sneak it home when he's not looking.

"I don't know much about your cousin except that his name is Robert and he's older than you," my mom replies to my question, looking up to me from where she's kneeling on the floor to scrub the inside of the oven.

"I don't know. I think he has brown hair," she calls down to me from where she stands on a ladder dusting cobwebs from the lamp that hangs in the entryway.

"He's probably in ninth grade," she says as she stacks freshly washed towels in the guest closet.

"Yes, he has a sister and her name is Marcie, but she's not coming today," she explains as we pull on opposite corners of the sheets to make the guest bed.

"What? I can't hear you," she yells over the sound of the vacuum.

When I exhaust my supply of cousin questions, I go outside. Squatting in the dirt on the side of our house, I concentrate on the business of catching red ants for my ant farm. Troy, my best friend from down the street, is with me. Troy and I spend so much time together we could have been brother and sister, but I'm often painfully reminded that we're not. He has a little sister of his own and we're often forced to include her in what we do even though she is only two years old and gets in the way of everything. In the living room of Troy's house there's an oil portrait of Troy and another of Tiffany. When I ask why there isn't a portrait of me in their living room Troy's mom gives me an odd look. Our mothers are best friends, but aren't related. People who are related to each other have beautiful oil portraits hanging in their living rooms, but if you aren't related your portrait will not hang in their living room. It should be hung in your own living room. So when I ask my mom why I don't have an oil portrait of me hung in our living room, my mom gives me an odd look. This proof of my existence is important to me, however my mother doesn't seem to want to understand this and although I continually ask for an oil portrait of me to be hung in our living room, this doesn't happen. My oil painting joins the Things That Won't Happen pile, along with the racehorse, unicorn and twin sister.

Our mothers often take Troy and I bike riding in plastic seats that attach to the backs of their bicycles. When they ride over the bumpy asphalt streets of our neighborhood, Troy and I sing loud, flat, long notes until one of our mothers says, "Shush now!" Troy and I tell our parents we're going to marry up when we are older, and in every picture we take together, it appears we may do just that. On Christmases and Easters and birthdays, Troy and I pose, he in his rust-colored wide-lapeled suit next to me in my white lace dress, his arm awkwardly positioned around my waist. Sometimes

Overlay – A Tale of One Girl's Life in 1970s Las Vegas

Tiffany joins us in our photographs, her fine-haired pony tail sticking up straight from the top of her head like a beacon to God.

I'm holding my fingers pincher-style above a big ant when I hear the exciting sound of a car pulling into our front driveway. Troy and the ants instantly forgotten, I race to the front door and yell inside, "They're here! They're here!" then trail my mother down the driveway to greet my aunt and my cousin. Peeking out from behind my mother's strong, suntanned legs, I watch the dazzlingly beautiful Aunt Ana glance in her rearview mirror, give her hair a fluff or two, and step out from behind the wheel of her shiny new car. Her white-blonde hair is a halo in the afternoon sun that crowns a flawlessly beautiful face. "Why, Sandy!" she calls out to my mother with the voice of an angel, lifting her sunglasses from her eyes and gracefully positioning them on top of her head. "Oh, let me see her!" she coos, moving forward toward me. She kneels down at my feet, carefully adjusting her strapless floral print dress as she lowers herself. "I'm your Aunt Ana! Come hug me, darling girl!"

I hug my delicate Aunt – my family – and close my eyes momentarily against the anticipation of meeting my cousin. Aunt Ana is surprisingly soft and warm. With a child's intuition I sense her fragility enclosed within my arms. I'm afraid if I squeeze her she could crack like the thin shell of a refrigerated egg. Aunt Ana pulls away and gently cups my shoulders with her jeweled hands, "You lovely, lovely little thing!" Her breath smells of the summer. Her voice fades into a strong smile, revealing perfectly shining white teeth. She stands, gently pats down her dress and introduces my cousin Robert.

There must be some mistake, I am thinking.

Robert is no cousin at all – at least not the cousin I had imagined. He looks like a fat man; nothing like the cousins of my neighbors. This is no blonde-haired boy cousin, but a large man-child with huge hair and a bulging stomach. He brushes past me carrying a suitcase, trailing the rank odor of teenage sweat and hormones in his wake. I turn my head to watch him enter our house, absently sticking a finger in my open mouth to chew on a fingernail. Troy waves goodbye from where he'd joined us, and heads down the street to his house. I stand alone in my driveway watching Troy walk away, not sure what to do next. The urge to run after Troy and sit in his darkened living room amidst the oil paintings builds inside me. I doubt Robert brought either the Lite Bright or the monster goo making machine.

At dinner that evening I watch Robert as he hunches over his plate, moving forkfuls of roast pork and potatoes into his mouth. He smacks his puffy lips on the soda pop bottle, swallowing with so much noise I can hear the liquid gurgling down his throat. He doesn't close his mouth when he chews until my aunt places one of her manicured hands on his arm and quietly says, "Robert. Dear. Please. Close your mouth. When you chew."

"Want some seafood?" he ignores her and says to me.

Surprised and a little excited by his attention I answer, "Sure," and grimace as he opens his mouth wide to reveal pork and potatoes and corn and peas in various stages of mid-chew.

"See? FOOD!" he laughs, and pork and potatoes and peas fall from the maw of his mouth and bounce down to his plate and then onto the tablecloth.

"Robert! Mind your manners, young man!"

12

"It's just a joke, Ma, relax."

"If John were here...." Aunt Ana says absently to no one in particular, her voice trailing off and replaced by the tinny sound of forks striking plates.

Apart from the seafood joke, Robert appears not to be the least bit interested in me. I don't much mind the lack of attention since he didn't bring anything of interest for me to do. I give him a wide berth that evening and instead dance in Ana's steps, breathing in the sense of peace and beauty she emits like a fragrance.

Ana had been a promising movie starlet and had acted in several Hollywood films. "That was before I met your Uncle John, darling, and I left Hollywood and that crazy life behind me. That world was no place for a lady." She sips her glass of wine and smiles at my mother before addressing me again. "Your father was in a movie, darling, did you know that? He played a bodybuilder in a movie called 'Athena.'"

"I didn't know that! Did you, Mommy?"

My mother is sitting so erect in the easy chair next to the couch that she looks anything but easy. A moment later I realize it's because ordinarily when she's at home in the evenings she holds a paperback book before her face, slowly lowering it now and then to look at me in answer to one of my questions. "I didn't know, Ana, but you know Buddy, he rarely talks about his past. Getting information from him is like pulling scales from a snake."

My Aunt takes another delicate sip from her wineglass. "My brother didn't have an easy time. Neither of us did, really. Now, beautiful darling girl," she interrupts herself and beams her shiny smile on me, "tell me about your favorite things. I want to know everything about my only niece!"

The next morning Troy arrives with his mom and while the women gather in the kitchen, Troy and I play checkers in my room. My mother pops her head in the doorway and says, "We're going to the store. Robert's going to stay here and watch you."

I immediately stand up. "Can't we go with you?"

"No, we won't be gone long. Just mind Robert, and we'll be back soon."

I whisper so as not to offend Aunt Ana, should she be nearby in the hallway. "Please, Mom. Don't leave us here with him." My lips stretch across my teeth to accentuate each whispered word.

My mother turns away, absently calling out behind her, "You'll be fine. We'll be right back."

The front door slams and I look into Troy's large, round, brown eyes and he looks right back at me. It's apparent from the look passing between us that neither of us know exactly why we each feel a sense of alarm crawling up our spines. His eyes stare unwaveringly into mine for several moments, and then my bedroom door opens just as if it is exactly what we've been waiting for. The large fluff of Robert's hair appears in the doorway, followed by his face, then his beefy physique. "We're playing hide-and-seek," he announces in one long exhale. His words run together like oatmeal.

"We don't want to. We're already playing checkers," I say.

Overlay – A Tale of One Girl's Life in 1970s Las Vegas

"Checkers are for stupid babies. Besides, you don't have a choice, you big dummy. You have to do what I say. You heard Aunt Sandy."

Biting my bottom lip, I realize Robert is probably not going to go away, so I agree. Robert wants to play hide-and-seek but his version is not the same version I know. Rather than let Troy hide, he says, "Go in the closet and don't come out. We'll find you."

Troy stands uncertainly and looks up at Robert, twisting one corner of his shorts with his fingertips, "But I'll be scared in the closet."

"Yeah, plus we'll already know where he is-" I begin.

Robert reaches out and shoves Troy in the chest with his open palm so hard he sends him backward into the closet. He closes the door with a snap. "You come out of there and you're dead meat, pansy-boy." His hand grips mine. "We're going to hide in the bedroom."

This doesn't feel right. Even though I am only four, I know that certain things are wrong. Robert's hands are so moist that my palms sweat as he leads me back to my parent's bedroom. "Lay down on the bed," he grunts, launching his considerable girth onto my father's side of the bed. I picture my dad lying on his side of the bed as I sometimes see him in the mornings, his black hair spread out across the white of the pillow. I close my eyes and will him onto his bed, his presence into this room, his protection around me, but he doesn't arrive.

Robert pulls off his red shorts. "Come here."

"No."

"You have to do everything I say."

"No. I don't."

Come into my parlour, said the Spider to the Fly...

"You really are the poor country cousin, aren't you? You don't even know anything. We're rich and you're not. You have to do what I say." Robert grows bigger like my bedroom corner monsters as he lumbers on his knees across the bed toward me. My eyes are drawn to the thatch of hair that grows where I didn't know hair grew. He makes a quick, jerky grab for my hand, and when I yank it backwards and out of his wet grasp, he makes an awkward grab for my long hair.

He dragged her up his winding stair, into his dismal den...

I swing my hair back and away from his hand and bolt from my parent's bedroom and down the long hallway. I reach my room and am just opening the closet door where Troy is crouched in a corner when I feel Robert's moist hands wrap around my neck. He pulls me backwards, swings my body sideways and throws me back down against the ground. My head strikes the carpeted floor with a whump. Troy screams.

Within his little parlour -- but she ne'er came out again!

I raise my feet as Robert approaches. He is crouched low; a fat cougar with a fluffy afro. When he's close enough, I kick out as hard as I can kick and feel the satisfying contact of my bare foot

14

against his meaty shin.

"You little bitch!" he yells, grabbing his leg. As he bends over me, I know I am dead meat until I hear the snappy sound of car doors opening and closing. Robert looks up, and then races down the hallway toward the darkness of my parent's bedroom. Troy runs from the closet and into the living room, hitching and hiccoughing. He wraps his skinny arms around his mom's legs when she walks in.

I don't run to my mother. We stand apart from each other, our eyes meeting across the expanse of the living room. She holds a brown bag of groceries in front of her like a shield. Her bright blue eyes are round and searching. A vacancy spreads across her face as Troy's sobs fill our living room. Aunt Ana looks so desperate and unsurprised that I decide on the spot not to say anything that might hurt her feelings. I remain silent.

Robert saunters into the living room, the red shorts replaced. "What a couple of babies these two are. I tried to play hide and seek with them and they did nothing but whine, whine, whine…"

Robert underestimated me. He placed an underlay and lost.

No one but me seems to notice that his shorts are on backwards.

Chapter Three

Deal: To give out the cards during a hand.

My parents weren't always estranged. The story goes that they met in a bar two years before I was born on a night when neither of them happened to be working the night shift. My mother sat straight-backed on her bar stool, sipping a mixture of wine and seltzer while her black poodle, Mustachio, rested comfortably on her lap.

"Nice poodle," my father said and the romance began. They married two weeks later in quick courthouse fashion, the way second marriages often happened. It was probably the only day off they had together, so they had to act quickly. Though a key player in jump-starting the romance between my mother and father, Mustachio the black poodle was not guaranteed a revered place in our household. He made the unfortunate decision to run away from me when I was a year old. Crawling furiously after the beleaguered poodle, I reached out one chubby arm and pulled his tail to bring him back to me. When he turned and snapped a warning snap at the air near my face, he earned himself a quick ticket to the Desert. My father loaded him into the car, drove away and returned without him. In Las Vegas when you were no longer wanted, you were taken to the Desert and never heard from again. It was the way things were.

My mother was a former beauty queen. Boarding a Greyhound bus in her small hometown of Morenci, Arizona at the age of 17, she traveled all the way to Hollywood to enter her first beauty contest. She won first place, beating out all those taller, lovely ladies. Even more surprising was that when all the contestants took an impromptu trip to Palm Springs to compete in another beauty contest why there by the side of the hotel swimming pool, sat Frank Sinatra in a lounge chair wearing a smoking jacket and well, smoking.

"Who is Frank Sinatra?"

"Frank Sinatra is the greatest singer in America," my mom answers, opening the lid of our big console turntable. She carefully places the needle on the outside edge of an album. The familiar scritch-scratch of the needle reaches my ears first, and then it's as if Frank just walked right in from Flamingo Road to softly serenade my mother and me. My mother smiles as the deep voice of Frank Sinatra fills our living room. As the sound pours forth from the turntable in the corner, I watch my mother's face. I open my mouth to speak, but my mother places her index finger against her lips, closes her eyes, and turns her head from side to side, swaying as if she were dancing with Frank himself.

"I met him," she says to me as the song ends. "The director of the beauty contest told us girls to say hello to Frank. 'Go cheer him up, girls. Lana Turner has just broken his heart,' he said to us. So we walked over in the ballroom gowns we'd worn for the contest and said, 'Hello Frank!'"

"What did he say?"

"First he said, 'Well hello, girls!' right back to us and after all the other girls had walked away, Frank called me back and said, 'Say beautiful....whaddya think about meeting me for a drink later?'"

"Did you meet him later?"

Overlay – A Tale of One Girl's Life in 1970s Las Vegas

"No, I didn't. I told him I had a boyfriend."

"Was it my dad?"

"No, it was someone else ... someone whose name I no longer remember. Then, Frank Sinatra asked me for a date again when I was married to your dad and pregnant with you!"

"Did you go out with him then?"

"I was married, silly. No, I didn't go out with him!" she laughs then, high and happy. My mother had been asked out on a date with Frank Sinatra and she had said no because she was Married. She was In Love. She was Pregnant. Surely these were the greatest things in the world one could Be. If the simple memory of these three statuses was enough to make my mom smile and to cause her to laugh out loud, then they must be truly wonderful things.

My parents aren't together often unless we're on vacation. In the days before The Other Things, there are many vacations. Unplanned and unexpected, they smell of Coppertone suntan oil and fresh oranges and salted sea air cloaked in the essence of adventure and excitement and new landscapes and fresh chances.

The most delicious part of our vacations is that I never know where I will wake up. My parent's inability to plan anything in advance allows me to reap the benefits of their glorious spontaneity, a habit I will forever practice. From my makeshift bed on the backseat of our car, I delay opening my eyes in the mornings until I can stand it no more, my consciousness rising like a tiny bubble from the ocean floor that passes through layers and layers of space and sensation. Conscious of the road rushing beneath our car and the warm morning sun on my face, I lay still for as long as I can, savoring the thought that I might see the mountains of Utah, the deserts of Arizona, the lakes of Colorado, or even the Pacific Ocean when I open my eyes.

My father cruises slowly along the desert highways, his left elbow perched on the open window. His Kool Menthol cigarette burns down with predictable regularity between the fingers of his left hand. If I lean my head out the back window, in the rear view mirror I can see the big USMC bulldog tattooed across his left bicep. The bulldog face ripples whenever he moves his hand to bring the cigarette up to his mouth.

The hours tick by as we travel the highways, our lone 1967 Chevy Impala making its sure and steady way toward the water like a family of lemmings in search of a new home. The wind rushing through the open windows whips my long hair into knots and tangles that will invariably take a week to comb through. I play with my collection of tiny plastic dinosaurs, and draw pages of mountains and rivers and setting suns. My suns still have happy faces during these days, with large smiles that stretch from ear to ear. I read the books my mom has packed for me, amongst the blankets, pillows, coloring books, crayons, pencils, blank paper and stuffed animals. I hop around my domain in the back seat, bounce on my knees, and stare out the back window to count the painted broken lines that pass beneath our car.

"Dame una cerveza, por favor," my father calls, and I reach into the iced interior of the Styrofoam cooler next to me and pull out a Budweiser beer. I pull back the tab, enjoying the cool hiss of the escaping carbonation. I don't understand why my parents drink beer. I think it tastes like rotten orange juice but it's an important part of their lives, and there is no denying this fact. I'd inherited this part of life just as I'd inherited blue eyes and freckles.

Overlay – A Tale of One Girl's Life in 1970s Las Vegas

"Muchas gracias, Chiquita." The smell of exhaled alcohol grows thick inside our car despite the wind and the open windows.

One inconvenient thing about beer is that it makes you pee – a lot. My father pulls over often along the sides of the highways to pee. He stands just barely off the road. I have to follow my mother to find more privacy behind whichever scrub brushes and tumbleweeds have the unfortunate luck to be growing there. Back in the car comes the long and uncomfortable afternoons, punctuated by pee-breaks. The hours pass and my father drives slowly, weaving across the highway lines until he eventually pulls over to the side of the road, conceding that he is too drunk to drive. He and my mother fall asleep, snoring softly in concert through open mouths, their heads propped up against opposite windows.

I on the other hand, am always wide awake. Though the back windows are open, the car quickly builds heat. My legs slide around, sweating against the unforgiving leather seats. Cars and trucks roar past, shaking the car and blowing my papers about the car like little white ghosts. I read and draw and color and hum and open the ice chest and suck pieces of ice, melting them across my sweating forehead and along my arms and legs.

When my parents awake, we set out on our way again, but the magic of the first part of the day is irrevocably broken by the nap. I stick my head out of the window as our car picks up speed so the air can dry my sweating face.

"Dame una cerveza," my father calls and we head off into the early evening, windows rolled down, our white Chevy weaving across the lines.

Sometimes we land in a hotel on the beach in California or Mexico. If I am lucky our hotel will have an Olympic-sized swimming pool and I will swim underwater from end to end while my parents drink beer beside the pool. Sometimes we rent a cabin on a lake in Utah or Colorado and I am free to skip around the edge of the water, tossing in rocks until one of my parents admonishes me for scaring away the fish. If I am unlucky, we end up in one of those motels you rent when you're not quite where you want to be yet. These are the sad halfway-there-motels...the ones with faded linens that offer nothing to do other than sleep off road fatigue. Yet it is the half-way-there motels I have to thank for the beginning of my writing career. With hours and hours to spend and nothing to spend it on, I pour my stories onto the blank pages I bring along for my art. I craft horror stories, what-if stories, sad stories, happy stories, silly stories. My characters are both real and make-believe. If any real life characters don't act in ways I would have chosen, I re-craft them into characters I can trust. Writing becomes my saving grace.

When I'm not writing, I meet many new friends on our vacations. One afternoon we stop at the guard's booth at the border crossing into Mexico. The guard leans down and peeks briefly into our car and says, "One moment," in flat punctuated English before going away. He returns with a dusty barefooted boy as if he is a border guard magician and has just voila! pulled this boy out of his border guard hat. The boy wears only a pair of dirty shorts that surely once had color but can't seem to remember what it might have been.

"Can you take him back to his village?" the guard asks my dad. "It's on the way to where you're headed." My father is given a vague set of directions to a blue shuttered building in a village several hours down the highway. The little boy is placed in the back seat next to me. We drive away and I don't want to be Rude (an unpardonable offense in my family) and Stare, so instead I take small darting peeks at this stranger in our car. The boy is silent and keeps his head straight forward, his chin tilted down. When he inserts a small finger into his mouth to pick at one of his teeth, I see that his teeth are black. I've never seen black teeth, and crane my neck sideways in curiosity to catch another glimpse. The boy turns to look at me with an expression of pride and disdain, a misplaced adult expression on the face of a child.

My mother offers the boy a peanut butter and jelly sandwich, which he accepts and after a surprised grimace, swallows in three bites. Next she hands him chips and fruit and when she turns back around, I watch as his tiny brown hands furiously tuck the fruit into the pockets of his baggy shorts. During the long drive, each time my mother offers food, the boy accepts it without a word and adds it to the growing stash in his discolored shorts.

The boy and I exchange glances each time he squirrels away a parcel of food. I don't want for anything in my life at this time outside of family and can't understand how he is so far from home, alone and unprotected, wearing nothing but a pair of dirty shorts. Sneaking peeks at his bony knees and ankles, I think it's a fairly safe bet to assume our lives are in stark contrast to each other. I'm reasonably sure he was lucky enough to have a big family…with siblings and aunts and uncles and cousins and grandparents, while I was lucky enough to have food. I hand him a piece of paper, a coloring book, and some crayons, and he holds the crayons in his dirt-wrinkled hand and stares at them, uncomprehending. His little nails are black and dirt is crusted into the little creases of his hands.

"See?" I instruct, holding a crayon and drawing circles on a piece of paper. I show him my completed drawings of animals, and people, and houses, and families, and mountains, and rivers and a smiling sun. I smile at him tentatively, a little white girl with white skin and white hair and white teeth.

He doesn't smile back and turns his bottom lip at me instead. He looks down at the crayon while he moves it a little, slowly drawing a long line. Then he abruptly hands the crayon back to me. He returns his little fisted hands to guard his two stuffed pockets and turns his head away from me to stare out the window. I try to talk to him and at first he bestows his strange, sad adult look on me, and then just ignores me completely. When we arrive at his little village several hours later, he comes to life, yelling, "Aqui! Aqui!" until my father slows our car to a stop. Before the wheels have stopped turning, he opens the door and bolts from the car.

My mother yells, "Momento!" in cupped hands to his retreating back. He stops and turns. Coming around to my side of the back of the car, she opens the door and the boy warily walks back toward us. When he is close enough to outstretch his tiny arms, my mother hands him my things. I watch my crayons, paper, coloring books and snacks pile high in the cradling arms of the boy.

"Mommy!"

"Shush!" she says in the voice that means I better not say another word.

His arms now full, the boy runs crookedly away across the sand. The backs of his skinny legs flash in the sun. I watch as he heads toward a small trail leading up and over a hill. I watch until I can no longer see him or my things. My mother returns to the car, and we continue our drive through Mexico. She admonishes me for my selfishness, explaining that I couldn't possibly understand what it's like to go without, to be hungry, to have a need, to want something I don't have. Surprised by the severity of her speech, I look down at the floor and spy the crumpled paper the boy had drawn one hesitant line upon. I am saddled with the wonder that I'm supposed to understand want. Even more perplexing is why she wants me to understand such a thing.

I haven't been dealt want.

This is good, right?

Chapter Four

Shut Out: What happens to a bettor who gets on the betting line too late and is still waiting in line when the window closes.

As the summers pass, things change and we transition from givers to receivers. Late one afternoon on a desert road in Mexico, my father pulls over to a tiny building off to the side. "We'll stop at this restaurant," he announces, his voice slow and muffled. As we exit our car the puzzled faces of an elderly Mexican couple appear at the front window. The old man opens a side door and gingerly descends the few steps to meet us outside. In Spanish, he asks my parents what they need. The woman appears at his side, and I watch a large wrinkle develop between her eyebrows as my parents ask in Spanish to eat at their restaurant. She whispers something to the man and we are at once invited inside, the man's arm spreading expansively in a welcoming gesture.

When the woman shuffles into her miniature kitchen, I follow to watch her drop forkfuls of shredded beef into corn tortillas. She rolls and places the tubes into a cast iron skillet now bubbling with hot oil. She fries them quickly, picks them out with a pair of tongs and places them onto a towel-covered plate. When she's accumulated a plate piled high with the steaming taquitos, she motions for us to sit at their humble little table with the salt and pepper shakers before the window, the window my parents thought advertised their home as a restaurant.

As she places the food before me, I say, "Muchas gracias, Senora," in my best accented Spanish. I think I will impress her, but instead of smiling at me as I anticipate, she leans down and hugs me fiercely with a surprisingly strong arm. "Pobrecita!" she whispers against the skin of my cheek, her breath sweet and moist in the way I think the breath of all grandmothers would be.

Poor little thing? Why did she say that? Is there something wrong with me? Her unexpected pity hangs over my head at the little table where I eat the taquitos with my parents, a cocoon from which I don't know how to escape. Back on the road after dinner, the fear hits me like a punch to the chest. As our car travels the hills of the desert highway, I am inexplicably gripped with the worry that if I can't see the road in the distance in front of us then the road doesn't exist. "Please slow down!" I entreat, leaning over the front seat to place my face between my parents. "You can't drive so fast if you're not sure the road continues!"

My father's explanation that the engineers would not design a road that ends in the middle of nowhere does nothing to appease me. Who knows what an engineer does or why? My mother shows me the roadmap, indicating where we are and trailing her finger along the little blue line of the road that continues on for some time. She shows me the mileage scale and how many more miles the road continues. But it doesn't matter what they say or how many times they explain it to me. I know I am no longer safe in a car piloted down the empty roads and highways and am now convinced the road can arbitrarily end without any notice at all. My chest grows tight, rendering breathing difficult. Sweat gathers between my shoulder blades and along the nape of my neck. The kindly Mexican grandmother's pitying hug passed along the information that I am something to be pitied, that I am in danger. Just because it didn't make sense for an engineer to design a road that abruptly stops without warning doesn't mean it isn't possible.

With the realization that a broken road is possible, arrives the realization that every thing I can imagine is possible. Any thing is possible. I am not thinking about the self-help and power coaching belief that Anything Is Possible, either. I Am thinking of the You Better Watch Yourself Carefully

Overlay – A Tale of One Girl's Life in 1970s Las Vegas

Because Anything Is Possible kind of possible. Our vacations lose their magic for me then, for as the only sober member of our car, I know if I don't maintain a strict vigilance about where our car is headed we might very well never reach our destination. We can fly off the edge of a cliff and crumple into a twisted, smoking conglomeration of metal and body parts on the desert floor below.

My new task on vacations is to sit in the back seat and watch the road ahead, crayons, books and stuffed animals forgotten. Travel then takes on a whole new rhythm of its own. And regardless of how long it takes for us to arrive at our destination, one thing is certain: we will meet new friends the first day we arrive and I will get to spend that evening, and most likely others, with them while my parents go out. I never know where I will be sleeping, or who I might meet. There is a Canadian family who speak in unfamiliar accents who teach me to play Mille Bornes. There is the mother from Iowa with a bespectacled 8 year old boy with allergies. There is a freckle-faced girl my age from New York whose mother promises my parents she will be home during the night, but leaves shortly after my parents drop me off and doesn't come back. The girl and I jump on the bed until we tire and eventually fall asleep watching a Halloween special. I don't know her name but I know she snores. There are workers from the hotels with tassels of children of their own who are paid to watch me. I probably have more friends than any other kid in the world.

On a hot day on the beach in Acapulco, my father wanders off and doesn't return. A few hours after his departure, my mother takes action on the pronounced line growing between her eyebrows and decides to look for him. Taking my hand, she leads me to a Mexican mother sitting with two children near us on the beach. After introducing herself and negotiating with the woman, my mom turns to me and says, "Just play with the kids until I get back. I'm going to find your father." Her voice is squeezing out from the tightness around her lips, her anger and embarrassment barely disguised. Adjusting the patterned wrap around her bikini bottoms, she pushes her sunglasses against the bridge of her nose and marches down the beach, her head held high like always.

I look at the little boy and then the little girl. They look back at this little white girl whose mother has walked away from her. The little girl reaches a brown hand forward to stroke my long sun-bleached hair. "Rubia," she murmurs.

My numerous failed attempts to communicate make it clear they don't speak any English at all so I ask, "Dame una cerveza?"

The mother looks at me as if I have just sprouted a cerveza from the middle of my forehead and the children giggle in unison. The mother hands me a Mexican orange. "Naranjo. No cerveza, pobrecita."

That word again!

After a time, my mother returns without my father but it's too late for me - I've already eaten more Mexican oranges than I should have. I spend the evening moaning on the cold blue-tiled bathroom floor of our hotel room. Thankful my parents don't take me to a new friend's room when they go out for the evening, I listen patiently when my mother instructs me through the bathroom door that they are going to the bar downstairs for a little while. "Don't answer the door for anyone."

As if I could get up. Santa Claus himself could be at the door and I wouldn't be able to open it for him. I roll around on the cooling tile, gripping my stomach to assuage the pain. The next morning I'm no better. Waves of cramps rip from one end of my body to the other. Unfortunately, it doesn't stop my parents from continuing with their plans to hire a guide for deep-sea fishing. It is briefly discussed whether I should be left in the room or brought along on the boat. Too ill to contribute to the conversation, it is decided over my head that I will have to come along, as it won't do to leave me alone in such a state.

We walk down to the beach to meet our guide, a wrinkly dark-skinned Acapulcan inexplicably called Peachy. He smiles a lot during the fishing negotiations, revealing big horse teeth. With negotiations completed, we board Peachy's boat and he slowly rocks us against the waves as he takes us out of the marina. When he cranks the little boat's engine into high gear, I place my head between my knees and spatter my toes, feet and ankles with vomit. We don't turn around, but head further out to sea. I wear no life jacket or bathing suit top and the bright early morning sun bakes my already feverish body. I shake with waves of stomach pains.

It's Peachy who responds to my distress, motioning for my father to take over the wheel of the boat. Peachy strips off my bathing suit bottoms, picks me up under my armpits and holds me over the edge of the speeding boat. I'm simply too sick to be terrified at being dangled over the edge of the speeding boat, and hang limply as Peachy dunks my body in and out of the water to clean me. He wraps a towel around my shaking shoulders, placing me on one of the hard benches. Lying flat only intensifies the rocking motion of the boat, and I vomit out whatever little fluid is left in my system.

"Es no good, Senora Sandy," Peachy yells to my mother over the noise of the motor, shaking his head. "Es no good. La guerita is sick."

"She'll be fine, she's just a little seasick," my mother answers. She's next to me on the bench, placing her hand against my forehead and the smell of her Coppertone suntan oil is overwhelming. Coconut. "What would happen if she were to fall in?"

"Es no problem. She falls in, she comes up. Once, maybe twice. I jump in when she comes up the first time. In this way, is okay."

The thought of falling into those dark depths in my weakened state is so much worse than my fear that the roads could end at a cliff. Driving off a cliff likely meant instantaneous death. Joining the myriads of creatures in the ocean likely meant to be eaten alive, torn to pieces by sharp biting teeth.

Turning to my side on the hard bench to vomit with greater ease, I retch all over the wet floor of the little boat, the smell of fish and blood in my nose.

Somebody please shut me out.

Chapter Five

Odds: Ratio of Probabilities.

September brings a temporary end to the vacations and I anticipate starting kindergarten with all the trepidation imaginable. Holding the starchy material to my face, I close my eyes and breath in that new clothes smell of my school clothes. Laying out different combinations of outfits, I combine and recombine the dresses and stockings and shiny black patent leather shoes with the new ruffled socks in several different shades of pink.

I hold my mother's hand as we walk the few blocks to school, my movements as stiff as my new ruffled dress. My stomach churns and rumbles. The smell of my new clothing makes me feel nauseous. "I don't want to go," I murmur. I try to tell her how I'm feeling and that my stomach's upset, that I'm worried about meeting new kids and worried they won't like me but she isn't listening. At the playground, she chats with the other mothers, her smile turned on. In the yard outside the kindergarten classroom, I hold my mother's hand so tight my fingers hurt. She laughs and talks with the other mothers, while I look around at the other children in a state of anxiety. Even though I know I'm disappointing her I can't let go of her hand. When the bell rings, she leans down to kiss me goodbye, and says she will meet me in the front of the school at the end of the school day.

"Can't you come in with me?"

She says no and gives me a little shove forward, a bird pushing her chick out of the nest.

I push back against her hand but kids are staring at me from the doorway. I go inside to escape the eyes and sit primly in a seat on the front row. My teacher's name is Mrs. Farris and she writes her name in big block letters across the chalkboard. Her hair is piled on the top of her head in a beehive hairstyle and she wears cat's eye glass frames with silver rhinestones around the rim. I can't stop looking at the rhinestones as the overhead fluorescent lights flash in them when Mrs. Farris turns her head to and fro. She writes the alphabet on the board and asks us to copy it onto the piece of paper she hands to us. She reads a book about a mouse starting his first day at school. We color pictures of our home and family. At lunchtime, we retrieve our lunch boxes from where we'd placed them earlier outside our classroom. The Las Vegas sun has had sufficient time to do its magic and opening my lunchbox, I wrinkle my nose at the pungent whiff. At the look on my face, the girl behind me in line laughs out loud. "Hot bananas!"

"Fried baloney!" I correct her, and she laughs even harder.

Her laugh whistles out from the space where her two front teeth would have been. She tells me her name is Leah Goldberg as she grabs my hand with an unprecedented ease, chatting happily as she swings our paired hands back and forth. At the lunch table she tells me stories about a ghost named Elijah who eats dinner with them during special holidays. Elijah's name whistles from between her teeth, just as her laugh did. Since she is the youngest child in her family it's her job to set a place for Elijah at the table, including a folded napkin for him to place in his lap. While I marvel at the new information of roles and jobs within a family structure that includes siblings, I ask, "Do ghosts use napkins?"

"I don't know but it's a good idea for him to have one in case he spills," she says between bites of her sandwich.

"Does he come in when you open the door?"

"Well, you can't see him, because he's a ghost and that means he's see-through. Sometimes I think the wine in his glass goes down just a little bit after we open the door. My mother says you have to have faith that Elijah is there. That you don't have to see him, but just know that he's there. That's the important part."

"Elijah drinks wine?"

"Of course!"

"My parents drink beer but Santa Claus drinks milk." I explain how Santa Claus climbs down our chimney every year on Christmas Eve, leaves presents, drinks the milk and even eats the cookies we bake for him. We don't see him either, but I know he's been there because when I wake up in the morning, half the milk and most of the cookies are gone.

Leah thinks Santa Claus sounds groovy because Elijah doesn't bring gifts when he visits. "He's like my Aunt Eileen. She comes from New York and never brings any gifts. Not even a lousy box of Devil Dogs."

The months at school tick by and I experience bizarre attacks of vomiting that gradually increase in frequency. The pediatrician recommends I visit the local hospital for testing where I drink a thick, pink syrupy liquid, and have many x-rays taken of my insides. While I'm waiting for the results, I watch 'Dark Shadows' on the small black and white television set in the waiting room. I have a secret crush on Barnabas, the handsome vampire.

The doctor arrives, sits down and places his elbows on his knees, joining his fingers in a way that makes me think he's going to ask me to look at the church, look at the steeple, open the door and see all the people! Instead he says to my mother, "Frankly, I'm perplexed. The tests indicate there is nothing physically wrong with her. No ulcers. No tumors. The only thing I can suggest is that she has a nervous stomach. This is generally a sign of anxiety. She appears to be unusually sensitive to her environment. Is there something going on at home that would cause her distress of any kind?"

My mom answers negatively, shaking her head from side to side. I think about the distress of missing days of school at a time because I'm on the couch vomiting into a bucket. I try to get up and make it to the bathroom and when I don't make it in time I vomit on the hallway carpeting instead. Later I hear my mother scrubbing the carpeting: squash, squash, squash. Leah is annoyed that I miss so much school. "I wanted to tell you all about Passover, but you weren't even here that week," she complains after I return from one vomiting bout. "I mean, there is just nothing to do when you're gone except chase Stanley around the blacktop. Plus you missed our performance of Jeremiah Was a Bullfrog! We sang in front of the fifth graders and cute Troy Fisher was looking straight at me!"

I pass my fifth Christmas Eve watching Christmas specials on television with my mother while my father works. She reads a paperback book for most of the evening, but she says I can open one present. She hands me a red-wrapped box from under the tree that contains a black jewelry box. When I open the lid, a tiny ballerina pops up and twirls around to the 4 notes of the Love Story tune. The miniature pink crinoline tutu is scratchy on my finger as I watch her twirl and my head fills with the sound of the television and thoughts of Leah and her family sitting together at the table together waiting for Elijah. I imagine Leah's family laughing and talking with each other, all as outgoing and happy as she is. Leah has a few older brothers, and of this I am fiercely jealous. Older brothers mean protection. From what, I'm not yet sure. I just know it's a good thing to have older brothers. Looking at my mom, I purse my lips together and stare at her as she replaces the paperback book in front of her face.

"Guess what?" she asks without looking at me.

"What?"

"That's what." She smiles and continues reading.

That was Christmas Eve. The next day is Christmas, and my mother works while my father stays home. He smokes while I open the rest of my gifts. I don't much like being around him when he's drinking, which is all the time he's home, because his reactions become increasingly slow, making it nearly impossible to hold a conversation with him. Perhaps this is distress? Whenever I ask a question he turns his head, gazing at me through the blue haze of cigarette smoke.

"What… Penut?"

"I asked why you call me Penut."

He pauses for a long time as if the answer to my question could only be found deep within. I think he isn't going to answer me at all when he finally says, "When you were born, you looked like a shriveled little peanut…."

"Then why do you call me Runt?"

Moments pass. "A runt is the smallest animal in the litter. You're the smallest so that makes you the runt."

"Why don't you have more kids then? I wouldn't be the runt anymore."

My father exhales a lungful of smoke and doesn't say anything for a long time. "More kids?" He laughs, a strange sort of laugh-chuckle-cough. "You weren't even supposed to be here…."

To this, I have no response. How in the world could you be here when you weren't supposed to be here? I leave the living room and its Christmas tree smell and run down the dark hallway into my parent's bedroom. Tucked against one edge of the dresser mirror are two faded sepia photographs of two dark-haired children that have been there for as long as I can remember. The edges not tucked under the mirror curl up sideways as if they are reaching for freedom from the mirror's grasp. The boy is my brother and the girl is my sister and they live with their father in California.

I take the pictures down and examine them carefully as I sometimes do. These two children don't look anything like me. My brother has dark hair and big ears that stick out from the side of his head like two happy beacons. I stare back at his joyful, crooked smile and imagine it is just for me. I switch my eyes from his smile to look at my sister's elfin face. Her short black hair falls unevenly above her dark, troubled eyes. So envious of the similarity in their dark features that bonds them together, makes them a team, marks them as family, I look unhappily into the mirror at my own solitary blonde hair. I hold their pictures in my hands, side by side, gazing at their dark, secret looks.

Perhaps they aren't supposed to be here either. Perhaps that's why they aren't here with us today. What does this mean for me?

What are the odds that I will remain here?

Chapter Six

Upcard: In the blackjack dealer's hand, the card that is face-up for all the players to see before they play their hands.

One evening the Winnebago Brave arrives. My father says the motorhome is named after a Sioux Indian tribe that the French referred to as the Stinkards. Our motorhome is the Brave, which is the smallest one, but I don't care. Regardless of its size compared to the others, the Winnebago is the most wondrous thing to happen to our family ever. It's a magical place, full of possibilities and new worlds. The tiny bathroom becomes a shower that flows right over the toilet. There is a bed above the Captain's chairs in front with a tiny rectangular window that looks out over the passing yellow lines beneath. The kitchen table transforms into a bed. The hallway is a perfect lane for my Barbie motorhome. The windows have curtains that pull tight against the sun. There is a tiny refrigerator that is already stocked with vacation snacks like white powdered donuts and chocolate covered peanuts. My mother prepares a bed for me in the back bedroom. I pass the white Styrofoam ice chests as I make my way to the back of the motorhome. I drift to sleep amongst rows of every stuffed animal I own, thoughtfully lined by my mother. The best part is that from my bed in the back I can no longer see if we are about to parade off a cliff when the roads runs out in the middle of the night. Whew.

The next morning I sit at the tiny kitchen table and watch my milk slosh side to side in the paper cup. I keep myself busy writing and drawing during the drive, looking up every time a gust of wind hitches the motor home to one side or the other. My parents find it hilarious when the motor home creeps across the highway. "Well, I'll be…" my dad exclaims as he corrects the steer and brings us back to our lane. Strike one against the Winnebago: as the day wears on, I can't ignore the changes that come about when my father drinks beer as he drives the Winnebago. We travel at a slower speed than in our car. The drive takes longer, and my father has the unfortunate opportunity to drink more beer. When he announces he needs to sleep, he slows the motor home and maneuvers it off to the side of the road, killing the engine. He has parked unevenly, and it feels like we're tipping dangerously to one side. "We're going to fall over," I say as he stumbles past me on his way back to the rear bed. He doesn't answer, and continues his weave along the narrow hallway. I'm still looking down the hallway after him when the sounds of his snores reach my ears. My mother joins him.

I creep to the front of the motor home and crawl onto the Captain's chair and delicately pull the side window curtains against the sun. The motor home rocks each time a vehicle passes. I refuse to move, convinced that if I add my weight to the passenger side of the motor home, we'll tip sideways and fall into the scorching desert. There is a peculiar lonely silence that ensues when my parents Pass Out and I find myself alone. Moments and hours can pass unnoticed in the solitude of my bedroom when surrounded by my own familiar items, yet time slows when I am the Guardian of our Vacation Safety. I bring my legs to my chest and listen, and feel.

I hadn't noticed before that I can sense my parents in the back of the Winnebago. While I can't hear their breathing over the heavy cocooned silence of the desert, I can feel their two dulled pulses. As the moments pass a more particular awareness grows within me. While I can sense all around me I know that my parents are not the same as me. Their 'presence' is shallow….expanding not too far from their own physical bodies, while mine is larger, searching.

A gripping loneliness settles over me.

31

Overlay – A Tale of One Girl's Life in 1970s Las Vegas

I am alone in just about every way a person can be.

Even the Mexican boy probably had a big family. My parents are isolated from me and from each other. My brother and sister live in two curling sepia photographs on my mother's dresser mirror. My cousin is, well ... I stop there.

My parents awake and our trek begins anew. I go to the back bed and place my chin on my knuckles, staring out the window at the straight asphalt line cutting through the desert.

"A hitchhiker," my mother says some time later. "In this heat?"

Unfamiliar with this word, I go to the front and see in the distance a tall, skinny man standing on the side of the road. His thumb juts hopefully toward the passing cars, a hopeful digit seeking respite from the wind and heat of the desert. Clad in bell-bottomed jeans and sneakers, his long hair blows back with each passing car. As my father slows the motor home to a stop, my mother unlocks the door. I move behind my mother and peek out from behind her legs as the door swings open. The hitchhiker runs toward us, a huge grin on his ruddy face that contrasts with the stark white of his chest. "Thank you!" he breaths with relief, at once a greeting, a proclamation and an exhalation of thanks. A dirty red, white and blue headband wraps around his forehead, right above his blue eyes. At least I think he has blue eyes, since I really just can't look away for too long from the four circle-shaped scars on his white stomach.

My father says, "We can take you as far as San Diego, brother."

"Right on," the hitchhiker raises the victorious digit up again into the air, this time in a gesture of victory.

The hitchhiker's name is Don. He extends a rough hand to me and says, "Ain't you a pretty princess?" A faint downy mustache grows on his sweaty upper lip and curves upward like a second smile. "I got me three little sisters back home and I'd sure hate to choose which of you four would be the prettiest."

I blush.

Don is not shy, which is probably why we discovered him alone on the side of a highway in the middle of the desert. For example, at one point during the drive he opens his mouth and just begins to sing...without the radio. I'm almost startled by the unexpected power of Don's voice belting out from that skinny body. It's so unlike anything that happens in my family, where there is no singing, no dancing, no hugging. There is some laughing, but not much. A person who can just open their mouth and sing from pure joy is just about as confounding as a unicorn.

When he finishes the verse, I ask, "Don?"

"Yes, princess?"

"What happened to your stomach?"

"I was shot in 'Nam.'"

"'Nam?"

"I was in the Marines like your daddy, and was sent to another country called Viet Nam. I was having a good old time with my buddies in camp, just a-laughing and carrying on when someone just shot me right down and fired at my buddies. I didn't wake until I was in the hospital. Thought for sure I was gonna die, but God was watching out for me that day, Princess. He knew my little sisters just couldn't carry on without their big brother."

Don's scars shift and pucker as he speaks, since he uses many hand gestures; an Indian making smoke signals to call forth the demons from his past.

"What happened to your friends?"

"They mostly died, Princess. I guess maybe they didn't have little sisters at home."

"'Mostly died'? Like they became vampires or something?"

"Nah, baby, not like that. Sometimes you can be hurt so bad you're better off bein' dead, 'cept you ain't. That's what I call mostly dead. There's lots of different ways to be dead in this world, and for some people, losing parts of your body is a death."

"Can I touch one of your scars?" I ask when I'd finally collected enough courage.

"Sure," Don turns toward me, and I reach out a finger toward his skinny ribcage and trace around the edges of one of the scars.

"It's shiny, and soft-like."

"There ain't nothing soft about getting bullets in your belly, Princess." He turns to show me four more circular scars on his white, bony back. "Those holes are where the bullets came out the other side."

"I didn't know you could live after being shot."

"You can live after a whole lotta bad things."

I didn't know this either.

My father drives Don all the way to Mexico and says it's the least he can do for a fellow Marine. Not too long after dinner we reach the little town on the beach in Mexico where Don will be staying with friends from 'Nam. As he gathers his belongings I bounce up and down on the bed, watching him reorganize his back pack. I am high on Don's energy. He is humorous and alive and warm. He pulls out a little gray plastic statue of a mostly shapeless shrugging man with outstretched arms and places it ceremoniously in my hands. "What do you think of them apples?"

I turn the little statue around in my hands. Across the bottom, it reads 'POOP ON EVERYTHING.' I laugh out loud, a short guffaw of unexpected delight.

"When things are bad Princess, just pick up this little guy and say to yourself, 'I won't let that bother me: Poop on Everything!'"

I smile down at the cherubic-faced statue until I hear the final zip of Don's backpack and remember he's leaving us. The smile slides from my face.

Overlay – A Tale of One Girl's Life in 1970s Las Vegas

Outside the Winnebago, my mother hands some folded bills to Don, which he tries to push away. "Take it," she insists, shoving the bills into one of his front jean pockets. "You never know when you'll need it."

Don looks down at his pocket with a humble face. "Thank you Sandy and Buddy, for everything." Squatting down, he faces me. "As for you Princess, just remember 'Poop on Everything' and that Princess is only a few letters away from Priceless and you are both."

I wrap my arms around his neck, inhaling his man-smell of sweat and stale aftershave. I'm surprised at how skinny and narrow he feels in my arms. I expected him to feel bigger; not bony and all delicate-like.

Back in the motor home, I position myself so I can look through the back window. My father pulls onto the highway and I watch as Don grows smaller and smaller until I can't see him anymore. I'm lost in a world where I am Don's little sister. I run around barefooted with the other sisters on the farm with the pigs and the chickens and the cows, while we wait for our big brother to come home from the war. Suddenly I want a big brother more than I've ever wanted anything else in my life; more than a horse or a unicorn or the black box that provides the answers to any question you could ever think of asking. That empty feeling returns and spreads throughout my body, as if someone pulls a plug and all the happiness drains through the soles of my feet.

As the motor home travels slowly through the dark Mexican night, I feel the uncertain blackness of the world pressing in from all sides.

Uncertainty has become the upcard.

Chapter Seven

Two Pair: In poker, a hand consisting of two sets of pairs and a singleton.

One afternoon after school I find my mother and father home at the same time. Even more unusual is the somehow vaguely familiar dark-haired teenage girl sitting straight-backed on the couch in our living room. An uncomfortable looking teenage boy sits by her side. I set my back pack down next to the front door.

"This is your sister, Linda," my mother announces in a formal voice that's looking for something to say, " and this is her boyfriend, Chris."

Linda and I look at each other for the first time and I think that I would perhaps not have recognized her from her sad little sepia picture in my parent's bedroom. Her big, dark eyes are now rimmed in thick black eyeliner, and she wears her long, shiny black hair parted in the middle. Her hair is so dark I wonder how we can be related at all. Standing before her in my white-haired, blue-eyed, freckled-nose glory, I think she is simply the most exotic and beautiful thing I have ever seen. We smile our mother's smile at each other. I ask how old she is because she looks like an adult.

"Sixteen. How old are you?" Her pink lips spread into an easy, perfect smile.

"Seven."

Despite the movie-star smile she has undoubtedly inherited from our mother, her discomfort is belied in the nervous way she keeps tucking her hair behind her ears. My mother - our mother – offers food and drink to Linda and her boyfriend long after it's clear they are definitely not hungry. My sister glances shyly at my father, and I marvel that we are related but not related at the same time. He is my dad and not hers, yet we have the same mother. We come from the same place, yet we've never spent a night under the same roof. She doesn't feel like I imagine family would feel, yet somehow she is.

My mother asks Linda a series of questions such as, "So what grade are you in now?" and "What is your favorite subject?" and "Do you like school?" and "Do you have many friends?"

My sister answers each question in the polite kind of voice one uses to speak to an elderly neighbor across the hedge in the front yard: "Eleventh grade, thank you. Home economics. Yes, sometimes. Yes, a lot."

"Where do you live?" I ask her. She is my sister, yet we don't live together.

"California."

"With who?" She is my sister yet I know nothing about her.

"My dad and my brother."

"Oh." I don't know them either.

From the corner of my eye, I see my mother primly uncross and recross her legs. My mother quietly clears her throat. Linda looks up and around at the ceiling. Her boyfriend studies the weave of the fibers of his jeans. My mother clears her throat again. I wonder if my mom used to wash my sister's hair on Sunday nights when my sister was seven, as she does for me. Then I wonder if my sister even lived with my mom when she was seven. The clock hanging over our fireplace unabashedly ticks off the seconds, one after another. Linda's boyfriend claps his hands quietly together and smiles when I look at him. My father breaths a lungful of Kool Menthol into our collective air.

Linda and her boyfriend don't stay at our house very much longer. She stands and says, "It's a pleasure to meet you," to my father. When she and her boyfriend prepare to walk outside, we all shake hands at the front door as if we are strangers saying goodbye on a street corner in New York City. I've never been to New York City, but I imagine they shake hands there as we did that day, quickly and without any emotional investment.

Two pairs taking leave of two pairs.

I want to hug her, but she is whisked away from me as quickly as she'd arrived.

Chapter Eight

Nut: Either the overhead costs of running a casino, or the fixed amount that a gambler decides to win in a day.

When my mother isn't sleeping or cleaning up the desert dust from our house she is busy with a variety of artistic pursuits. In her painting phase, she paints every room in our house, including the bright yellow walls and matching yellow shelving in my bedroom. I work alongside her with my own 1" paintbrush, and pull out any stray hairs or bugs that are accidentally painted onto the walls. There is something incredibly satisfying about being the detailed eye to a project, rather than the one that has to create the big picture. I crawl along the floor with my eye to the wet walls, pull out the aberrations and repaint the tiny spot. Since I'm only a couple of feet tall, I imagine all kinds of hairs and spiders and ants above my head, but their presence doesn't seem to bother my mother if they are indeed there. When she finishes painting the interior, she stands on a ladder and paints the entire outside of our home while I play with black bugs in the dirt and run back and forth to fetch glasses of ice water and cans of Fresca. When she finishes painting the exterior walls, she paints the trim underneath the roof. I play with black bugs and do a lot of running that season.

When the entire house has been painted, she enters her planting phase. We plant a row of oleander bushes along one side of our property that borders our neighbors' yard. They own a pesky German shepherd dog named Ruby who likes to poop in our front yard. My mother tells me that oleanders are extremely poisonous and I should never, ever put a leaf in my mouth. I wonder at the idea of placing something so dangerous in your immediate vicinity. This makes absolutely no sense to me at all. We could have just as easily planted oak trees or Christmas trees or peach trees. When I bring this point up to my mother, she says nothing. Perhaps in deference to my line of questioning, our next project is a vegetable garden behind our house, which requires enough tending to keep my mother busy for a time. As our garden produces, she cooks artichokes we cull from our garden. We eat alone together and delight in the creation of meals we grew. The corn isn't much of a success, so we replace it with eggplant and eat much eggplant parmesan. We pull baby carrots from the ground and my mother sautés them in butter. The herbs are sprinkled over everything, and all of our meals take on a greenish tint. When we've planted enough food we turn to flowers, planting six packs of multicolored flowers along our front walkway, and rosebushes underneath the bedroom windows. "We'll be able to smell them when we wake up," my mother says. Flowers fill all the corners of our home, and our tables and our nightstands. They breathe beauty into the air.

The vegetables and herbs are eaten. The flowers die. My mother enters her Buddha phase. Different sized unpainted ceramic Buddha statues are set on our dining room table where they are painted shiny hues of greens and blues. She paints their skin different shades of brown and ceramic white. Our house fills with Buddhas that replace the flowers. The larger Buddhas take up residence beside our front door, along the sides of our couches, and along the fireplace. Smaller Buddhas find homes on tabletops, nightstands and shelving, beaming their innocuous smiles upon us as we eat, read and sleep. My mother tells me to rub their tummies for good luck, and I do whenever I remember, and feel guilty and worried when I forget. What if I accidentally spurn good luck by forgetting to stroke the cool ceramic Buddha belly?

The Buddha phase completed, we move into the decoupage phase. I accompany my mother to the Second Hand Shop where we sort through crates of old, dusty books. We part the pages of the purchased books in the middle, then decoupage the pages down hard. Next we spray-paint glimmering golds and browns and antique reds across the open frozen pages. Last, we apply photos and pictures we cut from magazines to the two open pages, then decoupage them as well. We place the golden, hardened open books on standing frames and give them away as gifts.

Exhausted by her efforts to satiate her frantic desires through creation, my mother falls asleep on our living room couch in the afternoons. Our house is large, so I confine myself to the living room when she sleeps. In the afternoon silence of our house, the smiling, happy Buddhas take on a decidedly sinister air, as if in understanding that a sleeping guardian means I am unprotected. I'm suspicious of their squinting, half-lidded, reptilian eyes. Afraid they might open their eyes wide and morph into towering, hulking evil Buddha giants, I often sit on the floor right next to the couch where my mother sleeps.

It isn't just the smiling Buddhas that frighten me. I have recurring nightmares about a blowing, howling, sand-throwing tornado monster who manifests at the end of the long hallway that leads to the bedrooms in our house. An angry, swirling mass of gray and black, his yellow eyes glare at me from the place where his face should be. I know if I get too close to him he'll suck me into his mass, and I will cease to exist inside his angry vortex. In the initial dreams, the monster remains at the end of the hallway, blowing and spinning in suppressed rage. Since my bedroom door is the furthest door from him, in these nightmares I'm able to run into my room and hide under my bed. In the more recent dreams the monster whirls down the hallway and toward the living room where my mother sleeps on her side, one hand dangling off the edge of the couch. In the dreams, as the monster spins toward me I pull on my mother's hand frantically, begging her to wake up and save me. She never wakes up in my dreams, but when I do I am sweaty and shaking.

One afternoon during the quiet hours when she sleeps, I hear the wind blowing underneath our front door, and know the house is going to fill with sand and suffocate us. Frightened that the monster might be real after all, I sit next to the couch, listening to the soft snores of my mother for a long time, wringing my hands and debating what to do until I can stand it no more. I grab her outstretched hand and shake it furiously, begging her to wake up.

I assume she won't wake up since she never does in my dreams but I'm wrong. She jolts upward and scares me backwards. I try to explain about the tornado monster and she becomes angry with me. It's the first time I've seen her angry. She yells at me to go to my room and when I start to cry, she says she'll give me something to cry about.

A few weeks later in the predawn darkness of my bedroom, I'm awakened by the sounds of muffled tussling from the hallway outside my bedroom door. Convinced the tornado monster has come to life this time, I throw back the covers and jump from the bed. Throwing open my bedroom door, I expect to face the tornado monster, who will be blowing and throwing sand as he does in my dreams. Instead I see my father's hands wrapped around my mother's neck. She wildly flails her fists about, pounding furiously on his forearms.

"Shut UP!" he snarls at her. His lips are twisted into a grimace I couldn't have imagined on his ordinarily placid face.

I jump up and grab his closest forearm in a futile attempt to pry his hands from my mother's neck. Yelling and kicking, I dangle from his huge forearm underneath the rippling USMC bulldog tattoo. The three of us twist and turn in the hallway until my father looks down at me and a dull realization crawls across his face. As his eyes meet mine, a deep sadness washes across his hazel eyes like a receding whiskey-colored wave. He drops his hands to his sides and lowers me back down to the ground, hesitates for a drunken moment and shuffles away down the darkness of the hallway. The bedroom door opens and closes.

My mother leans forward and coughs hoarsely, placing her hands upon her knees. She looks up as if she's just noticed me standing before her in my gossamer butterfly print pajamas and orders me back to bed. As I lay in the dark I listen to make sure my mother remains safe from this man I had only known as gentle and drunk. I grow sleepy and fight to keep my eyes open, trying to reconcile this violence with the slow, gentle man that I know.

When the sun rises in the morning, I open my eyes and feel a fleeting peace before the remnants of last night's events trickle into my consciousness. Had I dreamt the entire event? The line between what's real and what's imaginary is becoming hazy at best. The nut - the overhead emotional cost of keeping our household together - is growing.

Chapter Nine

Low Poker: Also called lowball, is poker in which the pot is awarded to the hand with the lowest poker value.

There's an undeniably distinct correlation between my parent's failing marriage and the increasingly spontaneous vacations. My once reasonably safe and solid existence shakes a little more each time I feel the hand of my mother shaking me awake in the predawn darkness. We drive without my father to La Jolla, California, and she takes me with her to a bar when we hit the seaside town. The bar is loud and smoky, echoing with the cheap bass from the jukebox.

My mother laughs loud and often as she speaks with the different men at the bar. I've never seen her in this environment before and it's like viewing her twin sister. I watch uncomfortably from my seat at a red leather booth as she turns her smile up as loud as Mac Davis' voice on the jukebox. She orders Shirley Temples for me and hands me quarters to feed the jukebox. I play Wayne Newton and Gilbert O'Sullivan and Jimi Hendrix - more than a few times each. Several hours later, after I've exhausted the quarters, heard every song on the jukebox at least once and drank more Shirley Temples than I would have bet a dollar I could drink, I'm taken to the home of a woman my mother met at the bar. I think this portly woman may have been the bar's janitor since her house reeks of Pine-Sol.

I'm vomiting by the second day of my stay. My mother retrieves me on the third day. I vomit in the car during the five hour drive back to Las Vegas. This time I don't care that she has to clean it up.

A month later, I'm awoken again by my mother in the early morning, and this time I sleepily argue that I don't want to go with her this time. I don't want to miss school, regardless of how many new friends I'll meet on our trip. I just want to stay with Leah Goldberg. She whispers to me that we will have great fun, so I begrudgingly follow her to the car, barefoot, carrying my blanket and pillow.

Initially, she keeps her word. During the drive, I see yet another side of my mother I hadn't seen before. She turns the music up loud, and laughs even louder. Her mania is contagious and I hop up and down on the front seat like a crazy pet, screaming for her to drive 100 miles per hour and she does and we fly up and over the hills across Nevada and California. We wear no seat belts and we follow no rules. We speed up and down the highways with the windows rolled down, reveling in the force of the fierce, whipping desert winds. Caught up in the glorious peak of my mother's mania, I forget to worry about when the road is going to run out from underneath us. Unlike my father, my mother has no dietary rules and when I ask to stop at a 7-11 and get a large Slurpee, we do, and even better, I'm allowed to drink it while hopping up and down on the front seat. My mother says yes to everything on the drive, no matter what I ask. The backseat is a glorious littered pile of wrappers from Ding Dongs and Jolly Pops and Apple Pies and Moon Bars.

"We're free! No one can catch us!"

"Free!" my mother echoes and bestows one of her glorious dimpled smiles upon me. She wears her giant, bug-eyed sunglasses, her hair tucked under a pink scarf with roses. Her lipstick matches the pink roses and this is no accident.

Later, after we've slowed and are drinking twin Frescas through straws she asks, "It's nice to be free, isn't it?"

"Oh, yes!"

"No one should be trapped in a situation they don't like, should they?"

"Of course not."

"I'm glad you feel that way. Because I feel trapped right now. I need to be free."

I am fully conscious of the fact that I've missed what she's really saying because I'm only seven years old. Free of what, I wonder? Me? My dad? Life? So I change the subject. "What were you like as a girl?"

"I was small, like you."

"Were you happy?"

She seems surprised by the question. "Happy? No, not really. My mother was very mean."

"Nana was mean?"

"She had three kids, and eventually five husbands. That made her mean, I guess. She was often gone, and my sister and brother and I had to fend for ourselves."

"What does that mean?"

"If we wanted something we worked for it. She didn't give us a thing. So we babysat the kids in the neighborhood. We cleaned houses. We picked tomatoes at the tomato farm. We bought all of our own things, even clothes and food."

"What about your dad?"

"I never knew him. When I was a baby, my mom came home to find me lying on the bed next to my dad as he watched a scorpion crawling across the sheet toward me."

"What did your mom do?"

"She packed a suitcase, grabbed my two year old sister and me and we walked along the railroad tracks until we came to a main road. She was pregnant with my brother so we had to walk slowly and it took a long time. We sat down on the side of the road until a couple drove up in a car and invited us inside. Cars weren't very big in 1932, so my mother put my sister and me in the jump seat while she rode on the running board outside of the car from New Mexico to California with her head poking in through the open window."

I've only met my grandmother a few times and feel no particular attachment to her. I only know when she's coming to visit because my mother buys packaged coffee cake and makes coffee. Nana and her husband Wally arrive and sit on the couch and drink the coffee and eat the coffee cake. They ask me one or two questions that a real grandmother should already know the answers to. When I ask Nana something important like why she has black teeth, she claims it was the iron level in the desert water she drank while growing up. I suspect it's really from the long years smoking cigarettes and drinking alcohol and coffee. She smells like sweaty polyester. She's so old and plump and unfriendly that even though I don't know her very well I can imagine her perched on the running board of some old car. "She didn't sound mean, Mom, she sounded smart."

"Why do you say that?"

"She knew to leave that bad Dad, and save you from the scorpion."

My mom purses her pink lips. "I was young then. Many things happened afterwards."

"Like what?"

"That was a long time ago, Marlayna, and it doesn't matter anymore." She turns up the radio again and begins singing. Story time is over.

A few hours later we pull into the cluttered driveway of a track house in California. I get out of our car and approach the front door with a growing sense of suspicion. My mother introduces me to Ruth, a large woman standing in the doorway of what must be the messiest house I've ever seen. "We've known each other since we were children. She has five kids, and you'll be fine here," my mother says to me as if she expects to guarantee my good manners by dropping the I'm-leaving-you-here bomb in front of a stranger.

"You tricked me! I told you I didn't want to stay with anyone else! I want to go with you."

"I have some things to take care of here. You can't come with me."

"Then why did you bring me? Now I'm missing school for no reason at all!"

"Children should be seen and not heard, young lady." She tries to be stern and fails to pull it off. I see the worried look on her face as she gets into her car and backs down the driveway.

Ruth makes the mistake of grabbing my shoulder and I twist so violently out of her grasp that I knock her off balance. I run down the driveway and piston-stamp my foot so hard I hope I crack the cement. "I wish that scorpion would have stung you!" I yell at the back of her car. I don't think she can hear me though, and the angry tears fill my eyes even as I tell myself I Will Not Cry. I stand in the driveway and swallow my emotions with my arms angrily crossed over my heart until her car vanishes from my field of vision. I walk into Ruth's cluttered house because I have nowhere else to go. From her spot on the couch Ruth introduces me to Roberta, her daughter that appears to be close to my age. I dislike her on sight. She's as skinny and scraggly as a feral animal. Her messy blonde hair falls uncombed over the eyes of a starving rat, beady and watchful. She suggests we go to the store, and for lack of anything else to do I follow her outside to the beat-up station wagon parked in their driveway.

"We're walking."

"Alone?" Roberta doesn't even have shoes on her feet.

"Of course, alone. What are you, scared or somethin'?"

"No, but don't you need to ask your mom first?"

43

"Nah, she doesn't care what we do."

We walk several blocks to the store while Roberta chatters on about nothing at all. I'm still so angry that she could have been talking about how to win a million dollars and I wouldn't have listened. We each buy a candy bar with the dollar I have in my jacket pocket. On the walk home I peel back the wrapping of my candy bar and from out of the corner of my eye I see Roberta pull out a pack of jawbreakers, three more candy bars, and several packs of gum from the pockets of her dirty yellow jacket.

"You didn't pay for those!"

"Aren't you the smartest girl in the world!"

"You can't just steal."

"Says who? What are you gonna do? Go back in and tell on me?"

"No. I'm just saying it's wrong. You shouldn't steal."

"Who cares?"

"I do."

"So what?"

"I don't want to go to jail, that's what."

"You try being the youngest in a house full of hungry people. You'd steal too." She unwraps one of the jawbreakers and pops it into her mouth. I smell a sickening combination of sugar and unbrushed teeth every time she opens her mouth to roll the jawbreaker around. Back at the house an older boy I assume is one of her older brothers meets us at the end of the driveway and asks Roberta what she has. He doesn't ask what she bought.

"None of your business, turd," Roberta turns her shoulder in an attempt to rush past him.

He's faster than his little sister and when he grabs her by the fake fur hood of her jacket, her little body jerks backward and hits the ground with a whump that I feel in my belly. He straddles her while he searches her pockets and pulls out all of her candy as she screams 'muthafuckersumbitchasshole!' at him and pummels his chest ineffectively with her dirty little fists. When he takes all the stolen candy from her, he laughs. He unwraps one of the candy bars and takes a bite. He tosses a purple jawbreaker at her which hits her in the stomach, bounces once and rolls to the cement, down the driveway and into the street.

"You think you can hurt me?"

"You stupid mother fucker!" she screams and runs into the house, slamming the door so hard I wonder if the impact won't knock out a few windows. Her brother shuffles off down the street. He is barefoot, too I see. I stand alone, and look up at the sky. My mom is driving to be with people she prefers over me and they are probably men. Men she doesn't even know, yet she'd rather be with them than her own daughter. Was this what she did to my sister and my brother? I wonder about my dad, and what he is doing. Does he miss us? Did he even notice that we're gone? Does he know that

I am stuck at a house of mean, dirty people?

I refuse to talk to my mother when she retrieves me several days later. During the drive home, even when she looks sideways at me and pushes the gas pedal down to make us fly 100 miles per hour over the hills I had just screamed and laughed about three days earlier, I refuse to say a word. I won't accept the Slurpee she offers when we pull into a 7-11 along the way. I turn down the Ding Dong. I sit sullenly in the back seat.

Unwilling to abdicate the power to me, she refuses to ask me what's wrong. Unwilling to abdicate the power to her, I refuse to offer my feelings to her on a silver platter.

After that trip, I'm no longer invited on any future trips with my mother and that's more than okay with me.

I don't want to win this low-poker hand.

Chapter Ten

Don't Pass: This is the opposite of the Pass Line bet. This bet is placed against the shooter and wins if craps (2 or 3) is thrown on the come-out roll and loses if 7 or 11 are thrown.

"Wake up, we're going to Hawaii."

With great effort, I pull my eyelids open. Pitch black darkness. There is no way I am going to spend another vacation parked at the house of one of my mother's 'friends'.

"No."

"We're all going. Let's go! Our plane leaves in two hours."

"No. I'm not going."

It doesn't matter what I say this time. I'm going. During the drive to the airport, I hear that my father has been given a week's vacation by the casino to 'sober up.' My parents decide to spend that week 'sobering up' in Hawaii. My parents are both 'happily plastered' as they call it these days. They giggle and laugh as my father weaves the car all over the road. 'The Age of Aquarius' is turned up so loud on our AM radio that it nearly eclipses the sound of my parent's drunken laughter. I'm wide awake and perched in the center of the back seat of course, afraid that if I lose my vigilance for a millisecond, we will end up wrapped around a telephone pole. As a result of my focused concentration we make it to the airport and board our plane.

"How long is the flight?" I ask the flight attendant as I buckle myself into my seat.

She answers that it's five hours. If they sleep, my parents could conceivably be sober by the time we land on Oahu. Then I hear my father ask in his slow voice, "When will you be serving cocktails?"

Honolulu is crowded and dirty, and the air smells of fried tortillas. After we check into our hotel, I follow my parents to the beach, heading down side streets lined with vendors hawking calendars, pencils, post cards, leis and grass skirts. We cut through a public park and I fall behind to watch a man dig through an overflowing garbage can. He is methodical and careful in his search, pulling apart paper bags and crumpled tin foil. When I ask my mother what he's looking for, she tells me he's probably hungry. She answers in a clipped voice, distracted by all around us.

I don't believe her. I can't believe her. As we pass him I hold onto my mother's cool hand, but turn back to see him one last time. His face is wrinkled; his stringy gray beard dingy and dirty. I suggest we buy him something to eat but my mother says no, this is the life he's chosen. I can't stand the thought of a grown man being hungry while all the people pass by him in this beautiful Hawaiian park. I think of the little Mexican boy we fed during our trip to Mexico, not so long ago. "It's not fair, Mommy, can't we feed him?"

"We can't feed everybody."

We used to be more generous. What has changed?

Though we spend the day at the beach in Honolulu, I don't enjoy it. On the second day of our

47

trip, my mother leaves her wallet in a public phone booth during a walk home from a beach bar. When she discovers her wallet is missing, we hurry back to the phone booth to search for it. We search the booth, the nearby bushes and trashcans, but it's long gone, and with it have gone all the cash and credit cards. Will we have to dig through the trash now, too? Since we can't change our plane reservation, we have to spend another week in Hawaii whether we have money or not. My parents spend much time on the public phone during the next few hours, taking turns calling our relatives collect. Both my father's sister, my lovely Aunt Ana, and his mother refuse to wire us money so we can finish our vacation. I squat on the ground at my father's feet, listening to him asking his closest friends for a favor.

My mother finally reaches Nana, who says she will borrow money from her neighbors down the street and wire it to us. When the wire arrives, I understand it isn't very much money, which forces us to pack our suitcases and move from our luxury hotel to a motel. Lugging our bags up the stairs to our new motel room, I feel that familiar nausea building. Someone has peed in the stairwell and the stench is thick and cloying, hanging in the moist island air of the stuffy stairwell. I try my best to hold my breath until we reach our floor but I can't do it, and I have to take in one last huge, gulping breath before reaching the relative safety of our motel room.

When we set down our bags, my parents want to change clothing and head to the beach bar. I hope they will leave me alone in the room but they insist I accompany them. We trudge back down the pee pee stairs, and stop at an open air market for my parents to order tacos. They won't listen to me when I say I'm not hungry and when I bring the one forced bite of a taco to my mouth I catch a whiff of old grease and refried meat and immediately vomit all over the floor. Weakened, I drop the taco to the floor, place my shaking hands on my knees, and with my next lurch splash vomit all over the tops of my hands, knees and thighs.

"Just great," my father says. He stands with his muscled arms perched firmly on his hips. He looks as if he's trying to hold his own body together while I vomit out the inside of mine.

Crying and spattered now with vomit, I beg to go back to the motel room, promising to lock the door and not let anyone inside. My parents refuse, promising to clean me in the ocean so I can rest in the sun. Our day at the beach bar is long and stretches into the warm, wet darkness of the Hawaiian evening. I spend most of my time lying on a lounge chair on the beach, covered by a floral-print beach towel and vomiting into an ice bucket placed next to me in the sand.

I drift in and out of sleep, trying to pretend I'm lying in my own bed on Flamingo Road and that the beach bar's island music is just a sound from our living room's television set. The days of our borrowed vacation pass and I spend them in the motel room. My parents leave me alone but I'm too delirious to care. I have a few stuffed animals with me so I arrange them in a half circle on the bed next to me for company while I sleep.

When the day at last arrives for us to fly back home I am too sick and dehydrated to walk. The thick smells of the airport are overwhelming, and I slump against the stall door in the airport bathroom while my mother tries to get me to stand.

"You just have to make it to the plane. It's about to take off!" she pleads. There's a deeper crease between her blue eyes I dully realize I've not noticed before. I hear her talking but can't focus on what she is saying. Finally she gives up and carries me onto the airplane.

The flight attendant regularly hands me new barf bags, quickly taking away the ones already used. The good news is that I get a row of three seats to myself. It seems no one wants to sit next to me.

Don't pass.

PART TWO

(1972 – 1975)

Overlay – A Tale of One Girl's Life in 1970s Las Vegas

Chapter Eleven

Burn Card: In card games, the card temporarily removed from play. After a shuffle and cut, one card is placed on the bottom of the deck or in the discard tray, which is called burning the card.

The world is a strange place. I teeter on the precipice of accepting that I never know what might happen next and trying not to think that the world is truly such a random place. A month after the Hawaiian disaster, I run home from school on a warm September day and open the front door. Leah Goldberg has invited my family to her house to celebrate Passover! I can't wait to experience the Ghost Elijah, and see him use a napkin. A ghost using a napkin! I'm smiling still and I shut the door behind me and see the packed cardboard boxes neatly stacked in our entryway. Elijah hasn't yet crept from my mind when my mother utters the obviously inevitable as she enters the hallway carrying another box.

"I'm divorcing your father and we're moving today."

My head balloons with the weight of progressive thought, each one growing and crowding out the one before. My Partridge Family lunchbox is still clasped absently in one hand. My hand is sweating. I can smell the uneaten banana in my lunchbox, and wonder inanely why I hadn't eaten it, and then wonder why I'm thinking about bananas at a time like this. My mother turns her back to tape the box she'd just brought, so I walk to my room and see that she packed everything while I was at school with Leah Goldberg chasing Stanley Atkins around the blacktop. While we talked about Passover at lunch, my toys and stuffed animals were being crowded into brown boxes. While I read a story in front of my class, my books were moved from my yellow shelf to brown boxes. My room is now empty except for a naked mattress, the sheets stripped away and likely packed in one of the many boxes. Only a couple of wire hangers dangle in the empty closet. I can see One Hour Martinizing! printed on the paper of the hanger closest to me, a small niggling detail of this process called Divorce and Move.

My mother hums when she walks back and forth from our front door to the car while I wander around, not sure what to do with myself. When she fills the trunk and the backseat of our car with boxes, she shuts the trunk and gives it an uncharacteristic satisfied slap. We drive in our car full of boxes across town and pull onto a tiny street behind the MGM Grand Hotel. I watch from the window as we roll past a series of stark-white apartment buildings with peeling apple-green trim. Pulling up in front of one of the cinderblock structures, my mother points to the upper right corner and announces, "That one is ours."

The entire apartment building could have fit into our house. A single spindly-branched tree not much taller than me stands alone in front as if guarding the integrity of the faded cinderblock building. I follow my mother past the little tree and up the cement stairs and into the interior of the apartment. Standing on my tiptoes on the orange shag carpeting, I peek out the bare bedroom window that's now mine and see the parking lot below shrouded overhead with a canopy of thick black power lines. Just slightly past the parking lot, looms the back of the MGM Grand Hotel. Our apartment rests in the shadow of the giant hotel and casino.

"I need you to help carry boxes," my mother calls from the living room – a mere four feet away.

I pick up one of the lighter boxes and work at balancing it as I climb the cement stairs. After we've carried all the boxes inside, my mother shuts and locks the front door. "We have to be very careful to lock the doors here. Particularly when you're alone."

"I'm going to be alone?"

"I'm going to be working days, so you'll be alone after school now."

"We never locked our doors before."

"This is different."

"I don't like it here. When do we go back home?"

"This is home now." She presses the back of her hand against her forehead, careful not to smudge her makeup.

We sleep in separate sleeping bags on the orange shag carpeting, she in her room and me in mine. I can't sleep for a long time and stare out the naked window from my place on the floor. Although I hadn't packed them, I see the monsters have come with us and have positioned themselves in the four corners of my new bedroom. I bury my head in the sleeping bag.

The next day we go furniture shopping. Flashing a credit card, my mother buys a new white canopy bed for me, a king sized bed for herself, and a red velvet couch and matching love seat for the tiny living room. She also buys a brooding black iron coffee table with two matching end tables, a velvet painting of a Castilian soldier, and a stereo with an eight track player and a collection of eight track tapes.

The strange thing was that while I wander around completely lost in my own head, my mother is maniacally happy. She busies herself like always with cleaning and organizing and placing everything in its proper place. My bedroom remains unorganized, as if psychologically my refusal to root into the tiny apartment will ensure a move back to our house. I wonder how I will get to the homes of my school friends now that we live so far away.

"You won't. You'll be going to a different school now," my mother replies when I ask her.

"What about my desk, and all of my things? What about my friends, Mom?" I think of the Halloween project I'd been working on, the orange pumpkins I so carefully cut and pasted onto black construction paper. I'd been so diligent about adding the outline of the stem to each pumpkin. On each one I'd cut out the outline of the different letters spelling out H-A-P-P-Y-H-A-L-L-O-W-E-E-N-! What about Leah Goldberg? What about Passover? What about my opportunity to see Elijah?

"You'll get a new desk and new crayons and new friends."

"I don't want new friends! I want my old ones!"

"You'll make new ones. It always feels this way at first. Soon you won't even remember your old friends."

"That's not true! And what about my dad?"

"We won't be seeing much of him anymore."

Overlay – A Tale of One Girl's Life in 1970s Las Vegas

I didn't get a chance to say goodbye to him, or Leah Goldberg, or Troy Wood. Who was going to chase Stanley Atkins around the playground now that I'm gone?

Our furniture is delivered a few days later and it's as if the apartment attempts to seem a little cheerier with the ill-fitting pieces. My mother's attempts to buy furniture to placate me or the apartment fails. She demonstrates how to make the canopy bed, which requires a lot more work than my old bedding did. The frilly comforter has to be folded neatly down in the evenings, first in halves, then into quarters and finally into eighths. It isn't to be used for warmth, but only for show. The pillows with shams aren't to be used for sleeping, but instead stacked at the end of the bed on top of the comforter. It seems kind of ridiculous to have a bed full of bedding that I'm not supposed to use.

My mother wants to celebrate, so she drives us to a restaurant bar near our apartment, commenting that it's close enough to walk if we need to. Inside, we slide into a big red vinyl booth near the bar. My mother orders steamed clams, a Shirley Temple, and a glass of Rose. During the meal, she gets up to talk to men at the nearby bar while I sit alone in the bar booth. I finish the clams and drain the Shirley Temple. After a suitable amount of time, I approach and pull on her arm. "Mommy, can we go home now?"

She looks down at me mid-laugh. "In a minute."

I return to the table after being handed another Shirley Temple which I try to drink slowly to make it last. I take small sips. When the liquid is gone, I chew on the pieces of ice, one by one. I suck on the maraschino cherry for as long as I can before chewing, and by then I've sucked all the flavor out and the sad little cherry is as tasteless as Silly Putty. I finish the second Shirley Temple, and stare for a time at the third when it arrives at the table. I don't even eat the cherry.

It's very late when my mother wakes me from my slumber in the red booth to go home. The jukebox is silent and the restaurant bar is empty. As we walk to our car I hear my mother say, "Ten minutes." Following the direction of her eyes, I see a man following us who then ducks quickly behind a car to avoid my gaze. As I drift back to sleep in our apartment a few minutes later, I hear the man enter our front door followed by soft murmurs of conversation behind my mother's bedroom door. I'm too tired to fold down the comforter or stack the shammed pillows, and instead place the pillows over my head and pull the comforter up for warmth. And silence.

My mother walks me into the school office of Paradise Elementary the next morning wearing tight turquoise blue shorts and Legg's suntan-colored nylons. Everyone looks at us. She fills out the necessary paperwork to enroll me at the new school, making small talk with the school secretary while my stomach churns and rolls. I switch my weight from one foot and back to the other. Looking down at my feet, I see I've worn two different colored socks. Paperwork is concluded, and my mother walks with me to the classroom, opens the door, nudges me in ahead of her with the heel of her hand, and announces to the teacher, "This is Marlayna."

The elderly teacher moves forward with a smile, and the entire class turns toward me. Twenty-three pairs of eyes burn my face red, and I push back against my mother's hand, whispering 'I don't want to go!' through clenched teeth.

"You'll be just fine," she says and pushes me forward and shuts the door. The sound of her high-heeled shoes click-clacking on the cement outside the door gradually fades.

Overlay – A Tale of One Girl's Life in 1970s Las Vegas

I take a seat in the chair the teacher indicates to me, conscious of the fact that I'm followed by the eyes of every kid in the classroom. Once I sit down, the teacher smiles and asks where I'm from.

"Las Vegas."

The kids laugh and I turn even redder. Next to me is a boy with hair perfectly combed and greased to the side. He's clad in a stiffly starched gold button-down shirt and matching shorts with perfectly ironed creases. "I'm Arthur," he announces formally at recess. "I have a girlfriend named Suzy."

"Hi."

"We had sex in my fort."

"What's sex?"

"Boy, are you dumb. It's when a boy sticks his thing in a girl's thing."

"Oh."

"You haven't had sex?"

"No. I don't think so."

"Well, Suzy and I have sex every day after school." He pulls at the crease of his golden shorts, and then pulls smartly on his collar, straightening it imperceptibly. I think of Stanley Atkins and wish I was back at my other school chasing him around the blacktop. When I don't say anything else, Arthur asks, "Would you like to have sex sometime?"

I shake my head from side to side, my long hair brushing against my cheeks as if waving goodbye. To what? To Arthur? To my old life? To my dad? To normalcy? Arthur gets up stiffly and saunters off to the playground. I sit on the bench until recess ends, watching the other kids playing foursquare and tag.

We watch Electric Company in the afternoons at this new school and then we cover the addition and subtraction rules I learned the year before. I am so bored I make up stories in my head that I will write down when I get home. The teacher reads from 'A Wrinkle in Time' to our class, and after school I check the book out from the school library and devour it that very evening. I fall asleep thinking there probably isn't anything I wouldn't do to find a tesseract like Meg Murray did. I would do anything to escape into another dimension, another world, another existence. Another life.

In the coming days my mother learns that I won't be accompanying her out in the evenings to the bar. Apart from dragging me out while I kick and scream, there isn't a whole lot she can do about my firm decision. "You can't just stay here alone," she attempts to reason with me from where she stands in my bedroom doorway. A new silver purse dangles from one forearm, complimenting the low cut of her new red polka-dotted mini dress that was recently bought from an expensive clothing store.

I can see the tops of her boobies, and quickly focus my eyes back down on her purse. "Oh, yes, I can. I'm seven years old."

Overlay – A Tale of One Girl's Life in 1970s Las Vegas

"Okay, well I guess I'll lock the door. Make sure you don't open it for anybody. I have my key."

Staying alone is not as easy as I thought it would be. Even with the little black and white television in my room turned up for company, it's difficult to sleep when my mom isn't home. Every sound in the apartment is amplified, from the slight creek of the settling roof to the click of the refrigerator cooler. I regularly jump up to turn down the television set and listen closely for sounds that someone might be trying to get into the apartment. I don't sleep well until I hear the sound of my mother coming home in the early mornings, tripping and falling up the cement stairs leading to our apartment. Next I hear the laughing, the fumbling with the key in the door, the whispering to the company who has followed her home. Only then do I sleep soundly. Or try to.

Since our vacations have ended and I no longer have to worry about whether the highway is going to run out from beneath us, I develop a new concern. I'm convinced my mother is going to die while she's out at night. During the long hours when I'm alone I just know that every police siren is the mournful notification that my mother has died in a car accident. I stand at the window in our tiny living room and watch the silent black street below.

I wait for the police to arrive and tell me that my mother is dead, her guts and body parts spread across the street in a pulpy bloody mess. I wait nightly for news of her death and during the days I adjust rather groggily to my new life at the cinderblock apartments. In the mornings my mother drops me off at school on her way to her bar tending job at King Arthur's Bar. I'm given a ride home by our downstairs neighbor, Mrs. Stabler. Mrs. Stabler drives an old '57 Chevy colored black, white and gray in all different places like a colorblind clown car. It sputters and stops and starts when she drives and the back seat is so spacious that her daughter Michelle and I laugh and tumble all around the seat whenever Mrs. Stabler turns a corner. When she pulls into the back parking lot of the cinderblock apartments, I always say thank you. When I'm not invited inside I use the house key that hangs from a piece of yarn around my neck and return to my empty apartment. Usually I raid our collection of antique dimes and wait for the music announcing the arrival of the Ice Cream Man on our street. Each afternoon I hand over the antique dimes to the smiling ice cream man and receive Fudgebombs and American Bombs and ice cream sandwiches in return. Then I watch television. Sometimes I run around outside with the neighborhood apartment kids playing 'red light green light,' 'tag' or 'hide-n-seek.' Usually my mother returns to the apartment in the early evenings and fixes a quick dinner of hot dogs or macaroni in our tiny kitchen before changing clothes to go out for the night. Sometimes she doesn't return after work before going out, so she has showed me how to cook TV dinners and pot pies in our little oven for those nights that the dinner hour passes and she doesn't arrive.

My mother and I never talk about the men that now come home with her, and since I never see them in the mornings it's easy enough to pretend they don't exist at all. It's as if we simply stepped from one life and directly into another with no overlap whatsoever, and now use a completely different set of rules. Our previous life simply ceases to exist. We don't talk about anything or anyone from before, like our entire previous life disappeared in a cloud behind us when we drove from Flamingo Road.

Often I wake up not knowing where I am. In the moments before I open my eyes I feel as if I might have dreamed the existence of the cinderblock apartments. At least that's what I hope. Mornings become decidedly unpleasant as I repeatedly face the reality of my circumstances.

Morning after morning I recall the burn cards of my young life.

Overlay – A Tale of One Girl's Life in 1970s Las Vegas

Overlay – A Tale of One Girl's Life in 1970s Las Vegas

Chapter Twelve

Fish: A player who loses money.

There is so much to learn in this new life. People have strange nicknames at the cinderblock apartments. No one I meet is called by their given name, which seems tied hand in hand with the fact that people move in and out of the apartments with predictable uncertainty. The short names are synonymous with short term relationships. Why bother getting to know George when it will be easy to forget about 'Woody' when he moves away? Since we all live in the shadow of the Las Vegas Strip, many parents move in to take menial jobs at a hotel and often move back to wherever it was they came from when it doesn't work out for them. The kids I play with might only be around for a month or less, and it isn't uncommon to come home from school to find a moving truck or station wagon being loaded with the belongings of my friends.

There is Leann, or 'Lee-Lee' as she's called by her single mother, who wears nylons to school and moves away on the night we'd planned to watch "The Wizard of Oz" on television. There is Adam, or 'A-man,' as he's called by the kids, who I often sit next to outside on the patio as he struggles over the Hebrew letters he's learning for Hebrew school. I am particularly disappointed when he moves. One day he and his family are simply gone, their apartment door unlocked and the living room empty. I don't get to finish learning the rest of the Hebrew alphabet, and had hoped for an invitation to Passover. We call Chris 'Bump' because of the knot he earns on the front of his forehead when he falls out of the one tree in our neighborhood that's big enough to climb. I never learn the real name of 'Sassy,' but the day she joins us for tag with a pixie hair cut, I decide I want my long hair gone too. When 'Buckeye' mashes a wad of gum in my hair and my mom is so mad she demands that I lead her to his apartment, I tell her I have no idea where he lives. He moves away soon after the bubblegum incident anyway, right after I get my pixie hair cut when it proves impossible to remove the gum. I'm known as Runt, of course, because I prefer to keep the nickname Penut that my father used to use most often to myself.

Even the adults have nicknames in our new life. One evening my mother arrives home from her night out quite a bit earlier than usual. I'm still awake in my room watching Night Gallery on my little black and white television, keeping company with a big bag of Cheetos. Still licking the orange crumbs from my fingertips, I see her throw her new silver purse down in a hurry on the coffee table. "Go back in your room!" she whispers, her blue eyes wide and frightened.

Before I have time to move, loud footsteps on the stairs cause us both to turn toward the front door that my mother hadn't locked behind her in her haste. A red-haired man throws the door open and shuts it behind his back, locking it as he trains his gaze on my mother and I.

"Go home, Bullfrog!" my mother says in a high and stringy voice.

"I ain't going anywhere," he pants. He pauses before turning his glittery eyes on me. "A daughter? Why, you never mentioned a daughter before. Where's she at while you're out at the bars, Sandy?"

I wonder if Bullfrog knows my mother's real name is Avis, and she is only called Sandy because of her sandy-colored hair. I wonder why he's called Bullfrog when he is red and not green like a real bullfrog.

Overlay – A Tale of One Girl's Life in 1970s Las Vegas

"She's none of your business!"

"I'm making her my business. Maybe I oughtta just take her head and shove it straight through the refrigerator door. Maybe that would get your attention, Sandy."

Bullfrog is quick to grab my forearm when I try to run. I can't wiggle out of his grasp. He drags me toward the kitchen. I dig my heels into the orange shag carpeting and yank my arm back and forth. White spittle gathers at the corners of his dried lips as he yells over my head at my mother. Dogs with rabies foam at the mouth and this means they're crazy and you should run away fast if you see such a thing. However, this foaming Bullfrog has my arm and as hard as I try to twist away from him I'm unable to break his grip on my arm.

My mother grabs his arm that's holding mine and shakes it. My forearm is wrenched back and forth in the struggle between the two of them. Bullfrog pushes my mother backwards with his free arm. She hits the wall behind her at the same time that we all hear the snap of my arm. I scream and Bullfrog drops my arm. He looks at my mother with an expression on his face like he wants to ask something. Then he stumbles to the front door, unlocks it and races down the stairs. My mother gently touches my arm. Sweat is beaded on her forehead and on the fine blonde hair of her upper lip. "It's nursemaid's elbow. It will be better in the morning," she says to me. She walks me to my room and tucks the covers around me like she used to when we lived in our big house. "Don't tell anyone about what happened here tonight. People won't understand."

"Please don't leave again. He might come back," I call out to the closing door, not trusting her return answer that she won't leave. I reopen my bedroom door so I can monitor who comes and goes in the night. I stay awake as long as I can, but even with the pain in my arm sleep causes my eyes to fall shut.

When I return to school the following day and my teacher asks me if something had happened the night before. She listens patiently to my story about staying up too late to watch a movie. Even as I talk I can see past her glasses and into the dark middle of her kindly blue eyes and know she doesn't believe a single thing I say.

I've become a fish.

Chapter Thirteen

Cold: A player on a losing streak, or a slot machine that isn't paying out.

I'm sitting alone on my canopy bed eating a pot pie that I realize with disgust I haven't baked long enough to warm the center when "Invasion of the Body Snatchers" comes on television. The black and white shadows of the television set flicker against the walls of my darkened room as I watch, absently chewing cold chicken chunks because I'm too hungry to reheat the darn thing. The seed pods break open on television and perfect alien copies of their human counterparts emerge from the broken pods.

It hits me - at last - the answer! Aliens have come and replaced my mother with the one that lives in this apartment with me. It's the only reasonable explanation for the decisions the alien mother is making - I've been kidnapped. My real mother must still live at our old house on Flamingo Road with my father. The alien mother must have told my father that I'd died so they didn't even know to look for me in the white cinderblock apartment complex in this bad part of town. My theory explains the sudden change in my mother's personality and why my father never visits. I chew the cold chicken chunks with renewed vigor, suddenly hopeful that this cinderblock apartment nightmare will soon come to an end. I just need to find my way back to my father.

Over the next few weeks I watch my mother carefully for evidence of alien ways. When she asks if I've brushed my teeth before school I lie and say yes. She never checks. When she drops me off at school she doesn't notice that I no longer kiss her goodbye. Many days I lie and say I'm sick and don't go to school at all. I don't leave my room when she comes home in the evenings. I keep my door closed and pretend I'm already asleep. I avoid all physical contact with her just in case it's dangerous to touch an alien. I stop calling her Mommy, and only call out 'Mom' if I absolutely need to get her attention. My real mother would have noticed something was wrong. This alien mother doesn't know how things used to be and therefore doesn't know to question the changes I've initiated. Months pass in this way, during which time my experiments only continually prove to me that I am no longer living with my real mother.

This alien mother doesn't seem to like her new form very much. Sometimes she talks to me about how she's going to die very soon. "You'll wake up in the middle of the night and feel a cold breeze in your room. That's when you'll know my spirit is here visiting you," she explains hours after I should have been asleep. "I'll sit on the end of your bed and you'll feel the bed dip down and the room grow cold." Even though I am achingly tired because she's woken me up in the middle of the night, a waking sense of alarm now crawls up my spine. An alien mother is better than no mother at all, so I plead with her not to die.

"I'm forgetting things, so I went to the doctor and had a brain scan. A shadow appeared on the scan, and the doctor thinks I might have a brain tumor."

"What's a brain tumor?" We hadn't yet learned this in second grade.

"It's a growth on your brain, like a lemon or an orange. It starts off small but then grows and grows until it covers your entire brain. Then you die."

"Maybe you're just drinking too much?"

Overlay – A Tale of One Girl's Life in 1970s Las Vegas

"Who told you I drink too much?"

I've said something wrong. My head fills with the buzzing noise of a beehive, and my heart beats so fast I think she might hear it. I don't want to upset the alien mother as I haven't yet learned what she's capable of doing. I'm afraid of her. In the silence of my bedroom I hear the crackle as her lips slide into a dry smile. I look to where I should have been able to see her teeth if her smile is a happy one.

"Just don't die, Mommy, please."

She doesn't even notice that I call her Mommy. "I just may. I guess we'll have to wait and see. You never know what will happen with a brain tumor." She slams the door behind her when she leaves.

My rooms grows cold with her exit.

Chapter Fourteen

Blind Bet: A bet that certain poker players are required to make because of their betting positions.

Second grade ends and summer arrives with days that are scorching hot and long. I try to sleep as late as I can to burn the minutes of the day, but then I only stay up later at night, long past the time the television programs end. This isn't a good thing, because it only gives me more hours to be awake at night while I wait for the police sirens to announce the death of my alien mother. Jealously, I watch the kids in the apartments leave for city-sponsored camps during the day, and hear from my mother for the first time that we don't have enough money for me to go. I didn't know there was an end to money, and with this realization sink further into the pit I'd been trying to climb from. I play outside if I can find any friends. Since I'm not allowed to swim alone, I don't get to use the pool unless I'm lucky enough to find another mother already there with her own children. I turn eight years old and spend my birthday alone outside.

One searing afternoon several weeks after my birthday, I answer a knock at the door and find my father standing outside in the July Las Vegas sun. "Hello, Penut. Happy birthday."

I hug him and he smells good and clean, like cologne and soap and vitamins just like I remember from the old days. I ask where he's been.

"I was in the hospital, honey." He pokes his head inside the apartment. "So this is where you live?"

"Yes."

"Let's go get something to eat. I didn't buy you a present because I didn't know what you'd want. We could go to the store and you could pick something out."

"I'm not allowed to leave the apartment without my mother's permission."

"So you sit here in this apartment all day, then? I knew your mother was crazy and she's getting crazier and crazier…."

"She's not crazy. She's an alien. The body snatchers made this mother up. Don't you have my real mother at home with you?"

"What in the world are you talking about?"

I can tell by the look on his face that the body snatchers have taken my real mother completely away. Forever. This mother I now know is the only one left. I suddenly feel so sick I back into the apartment and sit down hard on the red velvet couch.

Oblivious to my distress, my father says, "Let's go to lunch. Hey, Penut, are you even showering or brushing your teeth, anymore?"

"Not really."

"Go brush your teeth, then. I'll be waiting downstairs in the car." He refuses to come into the

Overlay – A Tale of One Girl's Life in 1970s Las Vegas

apartment like a vampire who has to be invited inside to cross the threshold. Though I don't think my father has become a vampire, I look briefly at his retreating back and wonder. It is daytime, and everyone knows vampires can't come out during the day because they will burn up in the sunlight. What if he is a particular kind of vampire that can survive in the sun? If my mother is an alien, surely my father can be a vampire? I'm still sitting on the couch trying to decide if it's safe for me to go with him when he honks his horn impatiently. Since I'm hungry and tired of Hungry Man TV dinners, I decide to take a chance.

During the drive to the restaurant I reflect that my mother isn't the only parent I'm having trouble reconciling appearances with. During my long days at home, I'd dug through the closet and found a box of photographs. Amidst the photos of my parents during the early years of their marriage and dog-eared photos of me as an unsmiling toddler, are images of my father taken when he was a competitive body builder. He was the subject of several magazine articles, and I pulled them out of the box and slowly turned the mildewed, yellowing pages, marveling at my dad's younger face on such a muscular body. The magazine article read:

We met John Glynn shortly after he was discharged from the U.S. Marine Corps, and we photographed him at that time. He was 21 years old, weighed 165 pounds, and was 5'8" tall. He has managed several of the gyms in Southern California.

A featurette of ten 4x5 double weight matte prints is offered on John Glynn. The price is $2.50 Prepaid. Airmail 15c extra.

The man in the photographs is a younger, handsome version of the man driving the car. His suntanned skin was greased and shined to accentuate his chiseled muscular definition. He was naked in some of the photos, with a turned leg or strategically placed hand covering up evidence of his masculinity. In several photos, he was wearing a G-string. Someone had colored in the white sides of his hips with a blue ink pen to make it look like he was wearing a pair of blue swimming trunks. Of course, against the blacks, whites and grays of the photos, the blue ink pen only stood out as a prudish and failed attempt to hide something that only made it that much more remarkable.

I ask my dad about the magazines. He explains that when he was 21 he was working at a quarry where his job was to move rocks. His car broke down and the mechanic wanted $25 for repairs, which he didn't have. Without the car he couldn't get to work, and needed to find a way to quickly make some money. Someone mentioned this particular photographer to my dad while he was working out at the gym, so my dad gave the photographer a call. That afternoon he posed for the images and was paid $25 for his time, a good amount of money for just a few hours of work. The car was repaired, and he resumed his work at the quarry.

I associate the smell of Brewer's Yeast and vitamins with my father. When I was younger he seemed enormously tall to me. I would stand next to him in the kitchen with the top of my head still below the countertop, and ask to taste the Brewer's Yeast. "You little Runt," he would laugh and place a tiny bit of the yeast in my mouth. At lunch I wonder if he still takes his vitamins or makes carrot juice in his juicer. The vitamin days were the good days, in direct opposition to the bad days when he was drunk for days, weeks and months at a time.

After our lunch date he arrives several weeks later to pick me up for a sleepover at his house. Not wanting to go alone, I ask if I can bring my friend Michelle along. Parents are asked, bags are packed and Michelle and I join my dad in his white Chevy to head back to my old house.

Overlay – A Tale of One Girl's Life in 1970s Las Vegas

Walking back into my house feels like walking into a chapter book I read long ago. Our furniture is the same, but none of our personal effects remain – as if my mother and I have been erased from the house's memory. My room still contains the naked mattress I left behind. My closet is dark and empty. The two guest rooms are unlit and empty so I don't show these rooms to Michelle. My parent's room is skeletal; stripped of my mother's clothing, jewelry and personal items. The pictures of my brother and sister no longer hug the mirror over the dresser and I wonder why they didn't earn a place in the new apartment. I'm a stranger wandering through the house where I'd spent the first seven years of my life.

We watch television until it grows dark. I'm embarrassed since there are no toys or books at the house and we run out of things to keep ourselves occupied. My dad sits in his black leather recliner smoking Kools and drinking VO whiskey. I'm disappointed to see that he's drinking again – a fact which would have kept me from bringing Michelle if I'd known. He makes a few attempts to have conversation with us but as the night wears on his words slur together like whatchawatchinpenut and whydjaturnthetvup. Michelle has such a normal family: her mom is a waitress and her dad is a high school coach. I wonder what she must be thinking. I'm feeling a growing sense of discomfort, and although our living room is large the smell of smoke and whiskey is choking me. "My dad is sick," I whisper to Michelle. "I think he has the flu, and it's making him talk weird."

Her big blue eyes are two saucers in her round face.

I can't be sure if she believes me or not. It's then that I get the brilliant idea that we should go out to dinner. After a bit of cajoling, I talk my dad into driving us to the Sizzler. Surely his slurring words and goofy smile won't be so obvious in a restaurant and I can practically guarantee that Michelle will be distracted enough by the dessert buffet that she won't notice my dad's unfocused eyes.

"Okaypenut," he finally mumbles, draining his glass of VO. He stands uncertainly and bends over to set his glass down on the coffee table with slow, exaggerated care.

Michelle and I run outside and climb into the front seat of the car. I sit in the middle so Michelle won't have to smell my father's sour aroma. We wait. Just as I worry that he might have passed out, he finally exits the house and crookedly makes his way to the car. He fumbles repeatedly while trying to put the key into the ignition. I'm overpowered by the smell of stale sweat and cigarette smoke, and say a small prayer that Michelle can't smell him. After repeated attempts, he finally starts the car and backs down the long driveway and into the street.

When we reach the first major intersection near the house, I don't panic until I see he isn't going to stop the car for the red light directly ahead of us. My scream is too late or not loud enough and we head straight into the intersection without slowing. The first car hits my dad's side and slams us into a utility pole across the street, smashing in Michelle's side of the car. The sullen silence after the impact is dull and heavy until the next car slams into us from behind. I'm thrown forward and strike the bridge of my nose and my right eye on the dashboard. Then our car is still and a man's face appears at my dad's side asking him in a loud voice if anyone is injured.

Blood is running down from my nose and across my lips and Michelle is crying from far away but I can't remember why or what happened and my dad answers that yes, we are just fine even though I am not. After a bit of slurred negotiation my dad tries to turn our smashed up Chevy around but the man says, "Whoa Buddy, you're not going anywhere," and I wonder how he knows my dad's name is Buddy. He must be a friend. If so, my dad is not very polite to him when he tells the man in no uncertain terms that if he knows what's best for him he will back off and let us be on our way. Only his words are so slurred I'm just certain the man can't understand a single thing my dad has said. The man thrusts one of his arms into the car and tries to wrestle the keys from the ignition, but my dad beats on the man's arm until he removes it. The man yells There Are Kids Inside Buddy, but my dad somehow starts the car and moves it forward and back a few times until he dislodges it from the telephone pole. He drives the car over several curbs and we head back home instead of going to the Sizzler restaurant. The extra noise of a tire rubbing against metal on his side doesn't seem to daunt him. Michelle and I sit quietly, stiffly, not moving or talking. The taste of blood is in my mouth, and I wipe the inside of my wrist across the bottom of my nose and it comes away wet and red.

Michelle asks politely to call her parents when we return to my father's house. While she's on the phone, I look in the bathroom mirror and see that the bridge of my nose is so swollen that even the white parts of my eyes are red with blood. I look as if I could cry blood tears. I rinse my face with a stiff, moldy washcloth lying near the sink, taking a long time to delicately remove all the blood from my face without touching my nose too much. Then I spend even more time rinsing and rinsing and rinsing the now-pink washcloth to erase any evidence of my injuries. When I walk back into the living room my dad is holding the phone and attempting to give directions to whoever Michelle called for help. The reasonable hour comes and goes as Michelle and I watch television until the programming ends and the colored bars line the television. My dad reclines in his chair and continues to drink and smoke. My head hurts and my face feels like someone crammed a giant red clown nose smack in the middle. It's late even for me when Michelle's parents finally arrive and Michelle jumps up and runs to the door when she hears the car pull into the driveway.

Pent up sobs break forth from her as she opens the front door.

"You gave me the wrong address!" Mr. Stabler says through clenched teeth to my dad as he walks in. His hair is sticking up from his head in a way that means he's run his hands through it so many times that it finally decided to just stick up straight and save his hands the trouble of pushing it up anymore. Mrs. Stabler's face is blotchy and puffy and her mascara is smeared underneath her eyes. Michelle runs to her mom and her parents check her head and ask her many questions. I stand near Michelle, wringing my hands and waiting for her parents to acknowledge me. When my dad approaches us in a sideways lurch from his leather recliner, the bottom lip of Michelle's father curls down in disgust.

"You drove my daughter in this condition?"

I back up slowly from the proximity I'd been keeping with Mr. Stabler.

My dad snickers, "S'alright..."

"No," Mr. Stabler begins, moving forward in the cautious way a cat might circle an unsuspecting bird he's about to devour. "It's most certainly NOT all right!"

"Ken, please," Michelle's mother grabs her husband's muscled forearm. "Let's not make a bad situation even worse. Let's take Michelle to the hospital and get on home."

Since no one is moving I ask if I can go home with them too, and Mr. Stabler turns his curled lip down and looks at me for a moment before he says, "Hell. No." Since the Stablers are devout Mormons, I'm more shocked to hear him say hell than I am to realize they aren't interested in saving me.

After Michelle leaves I go to the bedroom that's no longer mine. I find one dusty sheet in the hall closet, but there's no pillow, so I curl into a little ball. I think of the accusatory way Michelle's father looked at me, as if I was the one responsible for the accident. He didn't say anything about my bloody eyes or my clown nose and he didn't ask me if I was okay after he checked if his own daughter was injured. I fall asleep with the realization that people not only hated drunks, but also the children of drunks.

After the accident, I don't see my father again for a long time. I ask my mother where he is and she responds that he's in the hospital. When I ask if we can visit him, she explains that he's not staying in that kind of hospital. It's the kind where you 'dry out." People that are drying out can't have any visitors.

I'm forced to make a blind bet, and hug my pillow in hope that he will stop drinking.

Chapter Fifteen

Singleton: In poker, a card that is the only one of its rank.

When my mom needs to go to the hospital, I'm put on a plane and flown to visit my Nana in Northern California. She picks me up from the airport in a truck with a camper top that smells of old smoke and stale sunflower seeds. During the drive to the double wide trailer she shares with her fifth husband she asks me a few questions about myself but doesn't seem much interested in the answers. At the trailer she makes us 'cocktails': a screwdriver for Wally, a whiskey straight up for her and a Shirley Temple for me. I don't want to hurt her feelings and tell her I hate Shirley Temples now, so to be polite I force myself to drink and don't touch the cherry.

During the days I spend with her I color pictures and write get-well letters to my mom. I draw rivers and mountains and valleys and the sun and the moon. The days are long, and I fill a sketchpad with my art. When Wally arrives home each evening from his electrician's job, Nana meets him at the door with a Screwdriver. We sit around the coffee table with our drinks in the afternoons, watching the news and talking about nothing important. It is all very civilized. When I finally gather the courage from the apparent safety of my grandparent's home to talk to them about what's going on in my home, Nana tells me not to say a cross word about my mother or she will give me something to cry about.

"Your mother knows exactly what she's doing," she says, wagging her wrinkled finger at my surprised face. "You're nothing but a child and it's not for you to question her."

I sip my Shirley Temple in stunned silence, looking down mostly because I don't know where to point my eyes. It's probably not a good time to break the news to Nana that my mother is really an alien so I remain silent. I'm put to bed at 7:00 that night, and though I try to explain that I don't have a bedtime at home and can't possibly go to sleep so early, my words are ignored. There isn't even anything to read in that trailer, so I toss and turn for hours. I sing loud enough to annoy the two strangers called my grandparents in the hope that they'll invite me back to the living room to watch television with them. Apparently, they have nerves of steel and they don't and instead turn the television up louder to drown me out.

The days pass in such an agonizingly slow manner that I'm certain someone turned time back and I'm really in that trailer for over a month. Every day is the same monotonous passing of time....breakfast, television, draw, lunch, draw, television, walk to the mailbox, cocktails, dinner, bath, bed. Repeat again the next day. As much as I try to get to know Nana and Wally, I just can't connect to either one of them. They aren't much interested in anything I have to say either, so finally I just quit talking.

At the end of my 5 day stay, I'm so ready to get back home that I will forgive my alien mother for just about anything to be back in my own apartment and follow my own rules. My grandparents walk me to the gate to board the plane where I say goodbye politely and hide how excited I really am. A bag of peanuts later we land in Las Vegas and I excitedly grab my little pink carryon suitcase and breeze by the flight attendant who stands at the plane's door and say, "Thank you for flying TWA," to each passenger as they walk by.

I say, "You're welcome," and hurry past her to see if I can catch a glimpse of my mother waiting for me at the gate. When I don't see her, I scan the crowd for my father. He isn't there either. I stand near the gate, shifting my weight from one foot to the other as the passengers stream past me mumbling things like, "'Scuse me," and "Watch it," and "Hmmmmph." People run into the arms of their friends and family members and hug and kiss and shake hands and smile. Slowly the crowd at the gate thins until no one is standing there but me. The pilot and the flight attendants exit the plane, and one flight attendant remains behind to close the door to the plane. I think perhaps she might notice me, but after she shuts the airplane door she picks up her suitcase and says to the pilot. "Same time?" and he turns and smiles once at her. And then they are gone too.

I'm not sure what to do next. Surely my grandmother told my mom I was coming home today? What if she sent me home early and forgot to tell my mom about the change in plans? Trying to quell the fear rising in my stomach, I shift my carryon suitcase from hand to hand for several moments. Thinking that perhaps my mom has decided to meet me at the luggage carousel, I look overhead and follow the signs until I reach the carousels. I thread my way in and out of the crowd surrounding each carousel, searching for my mother. She isn't there.

Thinking to check at the gate again, I carry my pink suitcase back up the escalators toward the gates. The Las Vegas airport hums and rings with the sounds of slot machines and the blurry, indistinct murmurs of talking people. Lights flash and an occasional bell rings when someone wins money. Once I reach the gate area I realize I can't remember which gate I'd come through and now they all look the same. So I walk up and down the hallways from gate to gate, dragging my pink suitcase behind me.

After an hour of searching the gates and the carousels, I take the escalator to ticketing and wait in a long line. When it's finally my turn at the counter, I tell the smiling woman looming above me that no one came to pick me up. She stops smiling and picks up the telephone. A security guard arrives and escorts me down a long hallway with doors opening to dark offices. He carries my pink suitcase for me. Through the back office windows I see the sun has now set and it's getting dark outside. The security guard asks for my home phone number, and I sit still and quiet on the edge of one of the desks as he listens to the number ring unanswered. Next he asks for my father's number, after I explain that they are Divorced and he lives somewhere else and I sit still and silent as he listens to his phone ring unanswered too.

"Is there anyone else we can call?" he asks me as he replaces the handset on the receiver. "Grandparents? Aunts? Uncles? Neighbors?"

"No, my mom said we live in Las Vegas so no family members can stick their noses in our business."

Suppressing a smile, the guard shifts his weight a bit before he says, "Well, we need to think of somebody we can call. Otherwise you're going to have to sleep in the airport, little lady."

"Try the King Arthur bar. Ask for Sandy."

The guard pulls open a desk drawer and removes the yellow pages. He thumbs through until he finds the listing for my mother's employer and hums to himself as he dials the number. He smiles at me when our eyes meet. "Yes, may I speak to Sandy, please? Security at McCarran Airport. Yes, Ma'am, she's here. No, Ma'am, he didn't. Two hours ago. Yes. Address please? Surely. Will do." He hangs up the phone and looks at me. "I'm to put you in a cab and send you to King Arthur's. Your mom is still working, but should be finished by the time you get there."

Overlay – A Tale of One Girl's Life in 1970s Las Vegas

"Why didn't she pick me up?"

"Says your dad was supposed to pick you up since she's working, and it seems she can't rely on that good-for-nothin' for nothin.'"

When I walk into King Arthur's, my mom is standing behind the bar with a white towel draped over one shoulder. Her face visibly relaxes at the sight of me and for a moment I forget that she is an alien and really isn't my mother. The men on the barstools turn to look at me and begin to clap and cheer. One stands and says, "I'll get the cab," and ambles past me to pay the cabdriver. I take a seat on one of the barstools and sip the inevitable Shirley Temple my mom places in front of me because I am really thirsty now.

"I'll be finished in a couple of minutes," she says off handedly, but her mouth is stitched up tight and angry. I don't find out why my dad forgot to pick me up that day. He never calls to explain, and eventually I forget to ask.

As much as I hoped things might change, my mother continues to go out in the evenings and occasionally calls in a babysitter to stay with me. If I leave my room to get a glass of water or to use the bathroom, I never know who I might find asleep on our red velvet couches. One of the sitters wakes me up when my mother leaves for the night and asks me to sit with her in the living room. She pats the cushion next to her. She says she doesn't want to be alone and asks if she can brush my hair. She looks so much like my sister with her long, dark hair and exotic black-rimmed eyes that I instantly trust her. It's been so long since anyone has touched me, and her offer is sweet like sugar. I sit delicately next to her on the red velvet couch, and we silently watch "The Twilight Zone" as she brushes my hair, repeatedly. It feels good to be the object of her attention and I revel in feeling the long strokes of the brush against my skull and the occasional grab of my forearm to steady me from leaning into the stroke. Occasionally, she asks about school or my friends and listens like she's really interested, even when I tell her about Arthur and his stilted way of dressing and sex with Suzy in the fort. Mostly we sit quietly together. After Twilight Zone, we watch Night Gallery and she says she is so glad I'm awake with her because she would have been scared to be alone and watch such a scary show. I really want to hug her but agonize so long over initiating the touch that I must fall asleep, because the next thing I know it's morning and my mother is shaking me awake for school.

My mother is unpredictably furious when I tell her the sitter brushed my hair after she left. I think she will be happy that this lady took an interest in my personal appearance, but instead she threatens to call the agency and complain about the sitter disturbing my sleep. Only my frantic begging keeps her from picking up the phone. I'm stunned by my mother's anger. All the sitter did was pay some attention to me and I can't understand how this could ever be a bad thing.

My mother tries a new tactic the next time she wants to visit a friend which is to wake me up and take me with her. This is so much worse than letting the sitter stay home with me and brush my hair. My mom's friend lives in a trailer park far away, and we arrive late at night when not so many cars are even on the road, which is saying something for 24-hour Las Vegas. Walking into his darkened home, I see the end tables on either side of his couch are big lighted tanks full of darting, fluttery fish. The coffee table is made of glass on all six sides and houses a gigantic snake who coils in one corner of the glass enclosure. I move backwards until my back is against the wall furthest from the snake.

"We're going to spend the night here tonight," my mother says while the man stands quietly in his bedroom doorway. I assume I'm supposed to sleep on the couch. In the gloom of the trailer's living room I eye the bedroom door and then the couch, trying to gauge the distance in case I need saving from that huge, lurking snake.

"I'm going to sleep in the bedroom and you just curl up on the couch," my mother confirms my fears, then addresses the man, "Do you have a blanket and a pillow?"

The man hesitates, and I watch his dark form move into his room and return with a blanket and a throw pillow that he tosses onto the couch. My mother adjusts the blanket and pillow and pats it to indicate I should lie down. I debate how to handle this latest turn of affairs. My mother and the man stare at me from the gloom while I weigh my options. Throwing a tantrum probably won't accomplish much of anything at all, isn't really my style and I'm already tired and have school the next day. Still…the thought of sleeping next to a snake's den in some stranger's house isn't exactly appealing either. I sigh dramatically and lay down on the couch. The blanket smells like french fries. Mission accomplished, my mother and the man go into his room and shut the door.

I promise myself that I won't sleep all night (or at least what's left of it) as I'm convinced that damn snake is going to escape, wrap his long black body around my neck and suffocate me while I sleep. Perhaps he will hyperextend his jaws like I saw on television and simply swallow me whole like a field mouse. I steel my resolve and prepare myself to remain awake until the sun rises.

Then my mother's hand is shaking me and I'm so tired the next day I can't stay awake in school. At the end of the day I wake up after my classmates have already left the room and see that I've fallen asleep on my math paper and drooled all over my multiplication tables. My teacher is looking at me with an expression I can't discern, but I don't think it's a good one.

The first of my mother's suicide attempts occurs the following week.

When I ask why she's been home for three nights in a row, she raises her bandaged wrists to me like a cry for mercy. The wounds must have healed on the fourth day. She doesn't come home after work, and I go to sleep alone in the apartment as I'd become accustomed to doing. More importantly, as I now prefer to do, being the singleton that I've become.

Chapter Sixteen

Shuffle: Before each hand the dealer mixes up the order of the cards.

The day my mother announces that she's going to dental hygienist school I almost feel like brushing my teeth in celebration. Explaining that she's learning how to clean teeth, she says that when she's finished school she will work alongside a dentist, assisting him in taking care of their patients. This glorious bit of news is a shining beacon of hope for our future, and I realize all at once that I had been embarrassed that my mother was a Bartender. When my mother brings home the first plaster molds of teeth she created in her class for home study, I run my fingers around each chalky tooth as a smile spreads across my face. My mother will have a career, a real career ... surely more meaningful than serving alcohol to drunk men in a bar. She will be a Dental Hygienist! I place one of the white plaster sets in the honored position on the top of my black and white television, right next to the POOP ON EVERYTHING statue. Never failing to give me a smile when my eyes drift upward from Speed Racer or Twilight Zone on the little television, the little plaster set of teeth is as bright as the sun itself.

My mother quits her job as a bartender and takes a part-time job as a receptionist at the Desert Hospital to make ends meet while she attends school. I'm so happy and optimistic about our future that I forget to worry about my mother's death. Instead I am so happy for her life. Since she doesn't work as often, she is sometimes at home in the afternoons when I return from school. No longer dallying around the apartment complex after school, I rush home to find her head bent over a book at our little dining room table, surrounded by a sea of white plaster teeth. Molded mouths multiply around our house. They are stacked on the coffee table, tucked into kitchen cabinets, piled neatly next to the red velvet couches, lined up in our medicine cabinets. Each set of white teeth is a chalky smile for a bright future.

Things change as things do and one morning I stumble out of my bedroom to find a man sitting next to my mother on the couch.

"Marlayna, this is Russell."

I mumble a hello and pull at my pajama gown to make sure my underwear isn't showing.

"We're getting married."

My eyes are still blurry from sleep, and I say a small prayer to God that it's the same case with my ears. I peer at Russell's black, greasy side-combed hair and thick rimmed glasses. He's wearing a flowered print short robe of my mother's and his kneecaps are hairy. Very hairy. With my eyes still stuck on his kneecaps, I whisper, "Married?"

"Yes, he'll be your new father," my mother says next in that tone of voice that means she is trying to slip something past me. I suddenly miss my old mom with an aching intensity that makes my knees shiver. What happened to the mom who was married to my dad, and painted my bedroom yellow and sat next to me on the couch reading books on the nights when she wasn't at work?

"His friends call him Mr. Nice," my mother continues in that empty space where no one else seems to want to speak.

I push both hands on my stomach to keep from vomiting. Soon my mother drives our car to Mr.

Nice's apartment to help him pack and load his belongings. Mr. Nice doesn't own a car but he sure has many plants. Creeping Charleys hang from the ceiling in beaded macramé hangers, and big pots of green and yellow Pothos dot the tiny apartment. Perhaps I can have one or two of the plants for my bedroom. Surely there has to be a bright spot in this unexpected turn of events. A man with houseplants can't be all bad. But when I ask if I can have one of his plants he says no without further explanation. Mr. Nice makes clocks out of dice he collects from the Vegas casinos, another strange fact to add to the growing collection. Since he has a big stack of dice-clocks I ask if I can have one for my room. He says no again. He also makes jewelry boxes out of the dice and sells them for $400.00 in some of the Casino gift shops. I can't have one of those, either.

Mr. Nice isn't so very nice after all.

I'm not invited to the wedding and don't know when it takes place. One day they aren't married and the next day they are, and shortly thereafter my mother signs the backs of my report cards 'Sandy Smith' instead of 'Sandy Glynn.' The S's are tall and loopy when she signs her name; more than double the size of the other letters. I stare at this little detail but can make no sense of it. How can her entire signature change? The name Smith takes on a whole new importance, a Slithery badge of honor that doesn't include me. A package arrives from the mother of Mr. Nice containing two short silk robes for wedding gifts. There is nothing in the package for me. Doesn't she know I exist? My mother and Mr. Nice often wear the short robes around the house. Secretly I think that they look stupid in the little silk robes, like overblown Geisha girls.

Mr. Nice teaches me a nice new song shortly after moving into our tiny apartment:

Drunk last night

Drunk the night before

Gonna get drunk tonight

Like I've never been drunk before

And when I'm drunk

I'm as happy as can be

'Cause then I'm a member of the SMITH family!

I thought being a drunk wasn't a good thing. Where's the humor in a song that celebrates drunkenness? My mom just laughs and laughs as Mr. Nice sings the song. I sit openmouthed pondering how the world of adults is endlessly confounding. I wish I could ask my dad to explain this turn of events but I think he's still in the hospital drying out.

I'm never alone once Mr. Nice moves in, and I hate it just a little bit more than I hated being alone previously. He's smoking and drinking in our apartment when I arrive home from school every day. I make my best efforts to get to know him. Initially, he may very well make what may be his best efforts to get to know me. Since my mother no longer goes out in the evenings, the three of us are sometimes together.

Mr. Nice shows me how to draw cats using only circles for their cheeks, eyes, bodies and paws. He shows me how to trace a pencil around your outside of your hand and then draw in feathers, eyes and beak to turn the drawing into a turkey. And there isn't a thing Mr. Nice can't cook. Soon TV dinners and frozen pot pies are blessed relics of the past, replaced by Linguini with Clams and Pasta with Marinara Sauce and Steak with Peppercorns. He prepares salad dressing from scratch with oil and vinegar and mustard and garlic and fresh spices, so our bottles of stale manufactured salad dressings gradually disappear from our refrigerator. Fresh fruits and vegetables fill the lower bins of our refrigerator to be chopped and diced and sautéed and sweetened and tucked into the various dishes prepared by Mr. Nice. I often ask to help him cook, and am rewarded with the jobs of washing the lettuce or chopping the onions. Eventually he learns to trust me enough to show me how to peel garlic, and tear lettuce for salads.

Mr. Nice has many friends who come over in the evenings to smoke cigarettes and drink wine in our tiny living room. If I don't remember to remove my homework from the living room coffee table I will inevitably find it the next morning underneath dirty ashtrays and tipped over wine glasses, covered in circular wine glass stains and dusted with cigarette ash. One night my mother appears at my bedroom door and asks me to bring out my collection of scholastic award certificates to show to the friends of Mr. Nice. I look up from where I am sketching horses in my bedroom and demur as politely as I can. My mother's voice has the irritated edge I've come to know is associated with drinking. Wishing to avoid further hassle, I take my stack of coveted paper certificates for 'Highest Math Grade!' and 'Ms. Conklin's Honor Roll!' and 'Certificate of Excellent Citizenship!' out to the group of people smoking and drinking on our red velvet couches. My jaw tenses as they pass around my awards, and I cringe when they pull their ugly faces back in strange grimaces to read the print.

"Oh, wow!"

"Aren't you smart!"

"Smart and pretty!"

"The boys at your school better watch out!"

When I ask for my awards back now I anger my mother with my insolence. I'm ordered to go straight to bed this instant and told that she will hold on to my awards until her friends are finished looking at them. "Say good night to these nice people before you leave," she adds. I want to ask who said they were nice, but think better of the idea. The next morning my certificates litter the coffee table, wet with wine. An unflattering red wine glass stain is nearly centered on my right ear in my 8 x 10 school picture. I glue all my awards and school pictures to my bedroom wall. That should solve the problem of having them ruined ever again.

Mr. Nice buys a bar called The Back Street. I overhear him talking with my mother and they think they are very clever for coming up with this name since the bar is on a back street behind the Las Vegas Strip. We visit the bar one afternoon and there's a soda gun with C for Coke and P for Pepsi and S for Seven-up. There are jars of Maraschino cherries and salty green olives with pimentos. There's a jukebox that plays "Smoke on the Water" and "Macarthur Park." It's dark and smoky, filled with the damp smell of spilled alcohol. I can't wait to go back home to the chalky dental sets.

My mother begins working days at the bar, and since Mr. Nice works nights, my mother spends most of her nights at the bar as well. I thoroughly enjoy having the apartment to myself in the evenings again and am gloriously thankful for the end of the smoke and noise of the all-night parties in our living room. When I ask about dental hygienist school my mother explains that Las Vegas is a Service-Oriented City, and she can make more money Tending Bar that she can Cleaning Teeth. I don't know what she means by 'Service-Oriented' except that I return to a life as the daughter of a Bartender. I leave the set of chalky white teeth on top of the television set in my bedroom for good luck. The rest of the plaster teeth in our home gradually disappear, never to be seen again.

As hard as I try to like Mr. Nice, I just don't. I don't like having him around, and wish he spent days with my mother at the bar since she's kind enough to spend most evenings at the bar with him. It's uncomfortable to live with another person, especially one I'm now related to, and have no interaction with him when we are alone. When my mother isn't home, Mr. Nice completely ignores me. He's content to work on his dice clocks and smoke cigarettes, and except for an occasional mumbled 'hello' when I walk in from school he doesn't speak to me. I can't understand why Mr. Nice doesn't like me or why he doesn't make an effort to get to know me.

Though I feel like an intruder in my own home, I soon find an unexpected opportunity to be thankful for my cloak of invisibility.

God is shuffling above.

Chapter Seventeen

Between the Sheets: Two cards are drawn. You can wager on whether the third card drawn would rank between the first two cards. The tighter the spread between the first two cards the higher the payout if the third card drawn ranks between the first two cards. It's easy to play!

Christine is one of the rare children in our neighborhood who doesn't have a nickname. Though only a year older than me, Christine knows so very many more things than I do that I find her both intimidating and intriguing. At her apartment she grabs my hand and leads me to the bathroom. "Look," she says, pulling back the red-checkered shower curtain to display a giant suction cup attached to the shower nozzle.

"What is it?" I ask, reaching a hand forward to squeeze the squishy plastic disc.

"You put it on your boobies and it sucks them to make them grow bigger."

Quickly yanking my hand back, I check Christine's dark eyes for sign of a joke and don't find it.

"It's my mom's."

"Does it work?"

"Yes, her boobies are getting bigger."

"You can tell?"

"Sure."

"Ewwww. You look?"

"Sure. I want to see if it works. Then I can use it sometime. Boys like big boobies."

"Gross." I couldn't care less about attracting boys. Yet another thing Christine has over me.

Christine has a lot of chores to do after school every day, even though her apartment is always extraordinarily clean. If I want to play with her I help her clean so she can come outside before the sun sets. So we spray the tables with wood cleaner and dust them with a velvety rag. We vacuum the carpeting. We scrub the hall toilet and the toilet in her parent's bathroom. We clean the kitchen, wash the dishes and mop the kitchen floor. With the amount of work that has to be done every day, I wonder if her parents do any cleaning at all.

One evening after Christine and I have cleaned her apartment thoroughly, I ask my mother if Christine can spend the night at our apartment. Generally I don't invite anyone to my apartment because I'm too embarrassed about everything in and about my place of living. My mother agrees and makes a bed for Christine out of blankets and pillows on my bedroom floor. I crawl into my bed and Christine and I giggle and laugh in the dark as we trade scary stories. She tells the one about the couple that finds the prosthetic arm hanging from the car door. I tell the one about the witch from Albuquerque who travels the world in a flying mortar and pestle in search of souls to steal. She counters with the legend of Bloody Mary that you can call forth by saying 'Bloody Mary' three times into a mirror in the dark. I make up a story about aliens who steal your parent's bodies except I don't really make it up.

Christine is really scared by my alien story and I want to tell her it's real and that it happened to me but I don't. I don't want to scare her any more. I must have fallen asleep, because when I smell the cigarette smoke I think Christine is smoking in my room. In the moonlight streaming through my bare window overlooking the parking lot, I can see Mr. Nice at my bedroom door, gazing down at Christine as he sucks on his cigarette. His thin, hairy legs extend from beneath the short robe he wears, two white beanstalks in the moonlight. Faint murmurs from the television in my mother's bedroom indicate that my mother is asleep. I'm still and pretend that I'm asleep. I hope Mr. Nice can't see my open eyes in the darkness, so I lay there in the dark and squint my eyes to watch him.

When Mr. Nice leaves I breathe, but he returns a moment later without the cigarette. Crossing the threshold to my bedroom, he lies down on the floor next to Christine. Over the pounding of my own heart, I can hear him whispering to her until she wakes up. I hear her quiet giggle. He tells her to 'touch this' and she giggles. He asks to touch her and she giggles. I'm having a hard time recalling the magic when Christine and I had been laughing about scary stories a few hours before and yet now I think Christine knows something I don't because she's in fourth grade and I'm still in third and I can't think of a single thing on Mr. Nice I would want to touch that would make me giggle. Then I remember my classmate Arthur and his description of sex. The movements of Christine and Mr. Nice make me careful not to make a sound or they'll know I'm awake. But when Mr. Nice moves his face down between Christine's legs, I nearly give myself away when I try to suppress the gasp crawling up my throat.

Imprisoned by the sounds and actions of Christine and Mr. Nice, my mind races about what to do, what to say, where to go. I fake a sleepy half turn so that I can turn my head away. I hope he will leave. They're silent for a moment and then the strange noises and murmurings resume.

The next morning Christine and I are in the living room, giggling behind our cupped hands. She's telling me about having sex with Mr. Nice. He's still asleep, and my mother enters the living room from the tiny kitchen where she's making pancakes for us. She asks what's so funny, a curious smile on her bright face.

"Mr. Nice and Christine had sex last night," I giggle.

Christine reaches down and pinches the outside of my thigh. Hard.

My mother holds a spatula loosely in her outstretched hand. Her smile falls off her face in a hurry, and I instantly regret what I've just said. "What," she asks, but her word is flat: a sentence rather than a question. Her face sags down toward her neck, mimicking the energy of her word.

I repeat the story that Christine has told me, even though her little fingers are pinching me. The smell of burning pancakes drifts in from the little kitchen and sulphur smoke fills the living room. My mother sits down delicately on the coffee table in front of us, a former beauty queen who has not forgotten how to pose. She says that isn't what happened. Her dimples disappear into the slack of her face. For the first time, I think my mother looks old. Fleetingly I wonder if alien mothers age quickly and what my real mother would have looked like now, and how she might have handled the Mr. Nice-having-sex-with-Christine thing. I focus my gaze on the pancake batter stain near the neckline of my mother's robe as I can't look her in the eye. Her humiliation is too much for me to bear. "But I saw the whole thing," I stare at the hardening lump of batter.

"You saw nothing. You were dreaming."

"No, I-"

"This is very serious. You can't just go around saying things like this. You could get people in trouble. You could get Russell in trouble. You could get me in trouble. You saw nothing because nothing happened."

"Shouldn't Russell get in trouble?"

"No. Russell was next to me the entire night. I would have known if he left the room. So there is no trouble for him to get into."

"But he did, I saw him, I-"

"You saw NOTHING because there was NOTHING to see!" She slams the spatula down so hard on the coffee table that hardened pieces of batter flee like rats from a sinking ship.

Christine is sent home immediately.

I go into my room and watch the Soul Train dancers. And then everything else that comes on television that day. It is a beautiful Saturday, yet I do not want to go outside. The world feels uncertain and unsafe, ridiculous, nonsensical. Trees could melt. Fires could turn to ice. The day could be black and the night blue. The sun could never set or never rise. In this new world, nothing follows the rules.

On a sunny spring afternoon a few days later, I play downstairs at Michelle's apartment. I am still allowed to go to her house, but she has not been allowed to go to mine since the auto accident. We're dancing to 45 records in her Partridge Family/Sean Cassidy/Donny Osmond poster-covered room when we hear a thunderous pounding at her front door. In the living room, Michelle's mother has her back to the door and her legs splayed forward as if she's the only thing keeping the door from being pushed in.

"Let her out!" a man screams from the other side. "Let her out so I can do to her what Russell did to my daughter!"

Me? Is he talking about me? Is he after me? With a catapult of horror, I realize that if he decides to break the window, Michelle's mother can't and most likely won't protect me. I'll surely be sacrificed so she can protect her own daughter. This is what parents do for their children. I'm alone. Trapped. Adrenaline floods my body as I frantically try to plot where I will run and how I can get outside and where I can find safety from Christine's father. There is no back door. If I run out the front door, I have to pass him and he can grab me. If I do manage to pass him, he's so much bigger than me he can easily chase me down. If I escape from a back window, I can run to....where? Where is there safety for me? The Back Street bar is far, far away. He pounds and thunders and yells and roars and rages and in between his noises I can still hear the sweet voice of Tony DiFranco singing, "Heartbeat is a Lovebeat" from the record player in Michelle's bedroom.

Michelle's mother hisses, "YOU! You are no good. You brought this upon our HOUSE, upon US, by your very presence here!" Her body jerks forward with each pound on the cheap door by Christine's father. "You are NO GOOD! Just like your lousy parents!"

Overlay – A Tale of One Girl's Life in 1970s Las Vegas

The dill pickle I'd just eaten rolls around in my stomach, sizzling in the influx of acid. Adrenaline is dumping into my system. I will not throw up. I will not throw up.

"I ought to send you outside to deal with him," Mrs. Stabler screams, baring her teeth at me. Her body shakes with each pound of the fist against the flimsy apartment door.

The world makes no sense at all. If offers no protection. No safety. All that I thought I understood I now realize I don't understand at all. Adults don't protect children, or at least they don't protect me. I know that I am not safe at all at any time, anywhere, anymore. All the good grades, high achievement, 100s on spelling tests, prayers and good thoughts are not a guarantee of safety. I've been dragged into the inexplicable world of my mother and Mr. Nice. I'm held responsible for their actions, no matter how heinous or wrong and regardless whether or not I had anything to do with them.

Christine's father tires himself out after some time and leaves and I watch from the window of Michelle's apartment for a long time before I scurry upstairs to my own apartment like a cockroach running from the light. I protected my ears during the talk time Michelle's mother had been talking on the phone in the kitchen about the 'white trash that lives upstairs' but her words pricked my skin like a horde of tiny, biting, hurtful insects. I realized she'd been speaking out loud to someone just to hurt me, and while I'd rather she didn't I felt a strange sense of compassion for her because she felt the need to hurt an innocent eight year old girl.

I'm never welcomed at Christine's or Michelle's apartments again. It's an unspoken understanding that Michelle's mother will no longer give me a ride home from school and I never again slide around laughing in the back seat of her battered 57 Chevy. I walk home alone across a busy highway and through the desert to get to my apartment. I walk whether it rains or is too cold or too hot. When the apartment kids play outside after school in the afternoons I don't join in, not wanting to take the chance of meeting Michelle's or Christine's parents when I have no one to protect me from them. My world shrinks to the television set, books, ice cream and my sketchpad.

Oh how I want to disappear from my life and transport myself somewhere else. I want to be innocent, free from the knowledge of what adults do to children between the sheets. I want to be in a book or a movie with a different family. I want a family where the mother stays home during the day, painting rooms, cooking meals, hosting parties, playing tennis and drinking tea with her friends. I want a father who doesn't need to dry out, and who wears a suit and tie to work, carries a briefcase and mows the lawn on Saturday mornings. I want siblings who play together. I want family vacations to cabins on lakefronts. I want a new life.

The winds pick up and blow.

And blow.

Desert dust surrounds us all.

Chapter Eighteen

Button: In poker, a button is a small plastic disc used as a marker that's moved from player to player after each hand to designate the dealer position.

Mr. Nice buys a house and we move to another part of town. The house on Heflin is small but brand new and I happily run from one room to the next to pick the room with the best view of the unplanted desert yard full of fantastic giant tumbleweeds. Mr. Nice picks one room and says it's mine and that's final. He immediately vetoes my request for pink shag carpeting. God, I hate him.

The first evening in our new home I undress to take a shower. After running the water for some time, I realize the water isn't getting hotter so I wrap a towel around my body and walk into the living room. "The water is cold."

Mr. Nice looks up, and his eyes drop down the length of my body. "I'll see about it," he says to my mother, who's watching television.

I am cocooned in my little white towel in the center of the bathroom while Mr. Nice sits on the bathtub's edge and runs the water. "Try it now."

I delicately slip past where he remains perched on the bathtub's edge and reach my hand out toward the water. "It's still not hot."

"It will be. Just climb in and wait."

"You have to leave."

"I have to make sure the water is hot."

I never noticed that Mr. Nice has blue eyes. I thought they were brown. I stare at that blue color, and he stares right back.

"Looks like it will be a cold shower tonight," my mother says from behind me. I hadn't heard her approach, and jump at the sound of her voice. "I'll call the gas company tomorrow and get it switched on." Mr. Nice slides out of the bathroom and my mother follows. I lock the door and wash my hair with cold water that evening. I lock my bedroom door as well.

Moving to the new house means changing schools again, and once again in the middle of the school year. We're not quite within walking distance of my new school, so my mother drives me the first morning and takes me to the office to register. After the necessary paperwork is completed and my mom departs, I enter my new classroom and immediately vomit all over the desk top.

The classroom erupts with shouts of "Ewwwwwwwww!" Books hit the floor and papers flutter as kids scramble to move away from me. I can't get up as long as I'm vomiting, imprisoned by the streams of fluid shooting from my mouth. It splashes on my books and papers and drips onto the carpeting around my desk. I stand in horror and clamped my hand over my mouth when I can but with the next retch vomit squirts out from between my fingers. I run out of the room and down the circular halls of the school. As I search for a restroom, I vomit on the new clean carpeting of my new clean school. When I finally find the bathroom, I huddle on the toilet in the bathroom, crying miserably.

Overlay – A Tale of One Girl's Life in 1970s Las Vegas

The next morning, I don't want to go to school. "You're in fourth grade, you can't just quit school now," my mother says, exasperated. When she's through reasoning with me she makes me get out of bed and get dressed by using that voice I never dare to disobey. I've never found out what will happen if I disobey, but I'm afraid just the same.

The kids mostly avoid me after that. My life becomes a pattern that goes get up, go to school, come home alone, eat a Fudgesicle, watch cartoons, heat up a TV dinner, watch television, fall asleep. It's boring but drama-free. There are no parents trying to break down doors to have sex with me. There are no parents calling my family white trash. There is nobody at all. And that's more than okay with me. Sorta.

Then one fine day a new family called the Gordons moves into our neighborhood and they have two daughters my age. Katie and I immediately become best friends and I spend most of my time at their house. The Gordons have more food than I could have ever imagined and it's all gloriously full of sugar, preservatives and artfully packaged in plastic or aluminum foil. Besides having the best food in the world, Katie's family throws elaborate slumber parties and invites girls from all the different parts of the city where they previously lived. They buy a large trampoline and put in a swimming pool, we each bring our sleeping bags to the parties and sleep on the trampoline under the stars. We jump in and out of the swimming pool all night long until our sleeping bags are wet from the pool water but we don't care because it's a glorious food fest with cake and candy and chips and sodas all night long. If a bowl goes empty, Katie's mom just fills it right back up again. We're not told to slow down or stop eating or asked if it will be okay with our mothers if we eat all the icing from the cake and leave the baked part on the tray. Mrs. Gordon turns the music up loud on the record player and we dance around the edge of the swimming pool and scream with laughter whenever anyone falls in. Katie's mom smiles at us from where she watches from the kitchen window.

I wish she was my mother. Katie's mom is always home. She cooks. She sews. She quilts. When she gets pregnant I'm as excited as if the baby is my own sibling. But as the months pass I notice something very strange about the Gordons. On the occasional weekend when I sleep at my own house, I run across the back yards to Katie's house when I wake up. Sometimes they refuse to answer the door. I knew they're home because I can hear the television and see their little green car in the driveway. I knock until I'm a pest, then walk home dejected. I try again later in the afternoons and get the same result on those days. When her parents pick us up from school, sometimes when we run from our classrooms to pile into the back of the Gordon's car, one of the parents solemnly announces that the girls are in trouble. The tension in the car grows so thick my stomach churns and rumbles in response. It's never explained to me what Katie and Susie's transgressions are, but when the girls see they are yet again in trouble, I watch their bony knees shake during the silent drive home. When we pull into their driveway, I quickly scramble to get out of the car on those days.

The beatings always begin before I can get far enough away from the house not to hear the screaming.

I cry as I run. I don't understand the Gordon family. Most of the time it's all fun, fun, fun at the Gordons, so I can't make sense of what those two girls could possibly do to get into so much trouble. Katie and Susie are invariably absent from school for a few days following these incidents and I walk the several miles home through the desert by myself. When they show up at school a few days later their faces don't indicate that anything had happened. I ask Katie why they get in trouble so often. She replies that her stepfather has many needs, and closes her mouth with an audible snap.

She refuses to discuss the issue with me again.

After the birth of their baby daughter, Katie's parents adopt a new way of eating called The Natural Food Diet. They eliminate all sugar and processed foods from their family's diet and one glorious Saturday morning all the sugar and candy and pancake mixes and prepackaged foods are cleaned from the kitchen cabinets and donated to me. I run back and forth from their house to mine, carrying grocery store bags of food. Once I take the last bag to my house, it occurs to me that something very momentous has changed at the Gordon's house. I don't return that afternoon.

From then on, Katie and Susie's mouths are searched when we return from school each afternoon. If any evidence of candy, gum or cheeseburgers are found, I'm immediately sent home. As fast as I run, I'm never fast enough to escape the sound of the beatings that follow. Both of them are beaten, regardless of which one was suspected of breaking the rules. I stop going to the Gordon's house then and return to my solitary life of television, Fudgesicles and frozen dinners. I don't even accept a ride home from school anymore. Katie asks me to come over one last afternoon, and I'm roped into a disgusting dinner of canned organic tomato sauce and gluten free pasta. I throw up after eating it, and Katie apologizes to me as she holds my long hair out of the toilet. "It's disgusting, I know. I'm so sorry. You'll probably never want to come back here again."

I assure her differently, but I lie. I no longer want to visit the Gordon's house, but it doesn't have anything to do with the menu.

Something going on in that house just isn't right.

I'm learning that even buttons can have choices on where to position themselves.

Chapter Nineteen

Foul: In pai gow poker, a hand is fouled when the two-card low hand is set higher than the five-card high hand, or when the hands are set with the wrong number of cards. A fouled hand is a losing hand.

My mother's sister Micki arrives for a visit. She resembles my mother except her hair color is a dyed fiery red, as if she can't get enough attention with just a regular old hair color. Although she shares similar facial features with my mother she's altogether different in personality. I instantly dislike her in the way children sometimes do, even before she asks her first question.

"Has the girl been baptized, Avis?"

Oh no.

Even though I thought baptism is a big deal, my mother doesn't come with us that Sunday, saying, "No Holy Rollers for me, thank you." I hold the hand of my aunt and walk toward a doublewide trailer parked in the middle of a gravel lot. From what I'd heard from other kids, church seemed like a good place to find a sense of community.

Of all the things I expected, I hadn't realized that a building was one of them. This....is church? I'm not sure how she knew to find this place called a church. We walk into the big trailer, I can barely hear what's being said up front due to the roar of the air conditioning unit. We take seats in a couple of plastic chairs set up in a few uneven lines. My aunt raises her hand. "My niece here needs the word of God. Any chance of getting a baptism?"

A pimply faced teenager in the front row stands and turns, and makes his way back to where I'm sitting. His hand is sweaty when he presses it against my back to guide me to the front of the trailer. The preacher doesn't look anything like I'd imagined a preacher would look like. I'd expected a Santa Claus, but this preacher is thin, with lanky brown hair and thick glasses. He asks for my name but mispronounces it "Merlene" as he embeds it in a prayer of sorts. His thin, hairless hand holds my head down over a bird bath full of water. He scoops water in a plastic clam shell and runs it over the top of my head. We (The Congregation) eat stale white powdered donuts afterwards and the adults drink instant coffee from little Styrofoam cups. The end of the Baptism was about the only thing that went the way I'd imagined things, except I hadn't expected the donuts would taste so bad. On the drive home I tell my aunt that I don't feel any different.

"You should," she says, distracted. I turn to look at her profile, at once so similar to my mother's yet lacking all the soft lines of my mother's. The downturn of her lips grows when she says, "After all, you're saved now."

"From what?"

"From sin."

"Which religion am I, again?"

"Protestant."

Remembering Leah Goldberg and Adam, I say, "But I wanted to be Jewish."

Overlay – A Tale of One Girl's Life in 1970s Las Vegas

"Jewish? Why in the world would you want to be a dirty Jew?"

I start to tell her about Elijah and how he sneaks in the open door to drink wine on holidays but she interrupts me right away.

"Hog's breath! There is no such thing as an Elijah. There's only the Lord Jesus Christ, our Lord and Savior, and don't you ever forget that, young lady. No good Irish girl ever becomes a Dirty Jew. Why it's simply … unthinkable."

Leah Goldberg is certainly not dirty. With a peek at my thin, scabby knees, I think she's much cleaner than I am and have trouble understanding exactly what my aunt means by the term, 'dirty Jew.' I rest my head against the car window, recalling the story my mother told me about when her mother left her father. I try to imagine my mean-faced aunt as a little girl, riding next to my mother on the jump seat of the Model T Ford. Since she's older, maybe she remembers more than my mother does about their early life with their real father. Maybe their father really let a scorpion sting her when she was a baby. Maybe....worse.

A few nights later my Aunt Micki leaves our house in the middle of the night without so much as a see-you-later. I hear my mother on the phone saying that she walked into the Back Street to find my aunt having sex with Mr. Nice on a barstool. As for my mother and I, we don't talk about Aunt Micki's visit or my new status as a Protestant. We ignore both as if they'd never happened. Eventually I forget which religion I was baptized into and return to my previous heathen status. After this the relationship between my mother and Mr. Nice echoes the marriage between my mother and father. My mother works days, and Mr. Nice works nights at the Back Street. My mother no longer spends the evenings at the bar to keep Mr. Nice company. I'm alone with one or the other but never the two of them together.

My mother must be bored spending her evenings alone with me and makes a new friend who comes over for a late dinner every now and then. Walt is a friend from her days working at the King Arthur bar, and brings gifts for me when he comes to visit which I find totally charming because no one ever gives me anything. Although the dresses are several sizes too big, and the toys are not quite in my interest range, I'm secretly pleased by this attention even if it is from an old man with happy-faced wrinkles and long graying hair. One night Walt comes over for a late dinner and after saying thank you for his gift of a stuffed bear I go to my bedroom to read. My mother calls, "Good night," as she passes my bedroom door and I hear the click of her bedroom door locking. When I later pass through the living room on my way to the kitchen for a glass of water, Walt's striped suit jacket catches my eye from where it's still draped over one arm of our red velvet couch. Peeking out the front window, I see his old station wagon illuminated by a flickering street lamp.

I knock on my mother's door. "Is Walt still here?" I press my mouth to where the door meets the doorframe so I can be heard.

"No, he went home. Hours ago."

"The next time you see him, tell him he left his jacket and his car here." I run back to my room and giggle into my pillow. I'm not quite sure how I feel about Walt being in the bedroom with my mother. I don't like Mr. Nice, and know he had sex with my friend Christine on my bedroom floor and my angry aunt on the Back Street barstool, but my mother is married to him and even at nine I know it's not a good thing to invite another man into your bedroom when you're married.

Overlay – A Tale of One Girl's Life in 1970s Las Vegas

My mother appears at my door in the detested short silk robe. "Walt isn't in my room. Do you want to see for yourself?" She ties the sash a little tighter as if to seal the truth inside the silk robe.

I walk into her room, look at the rumpled covers and head straight to the master bathroom. My mother follows closely behind me. Walt stands awkwardly in the corner of the shower with his hands clasped over the front of his underwear. "Hi, Walt," I say, and since no one says anything else, I return to my bedroom. Walt leaves shortly thereafter and doesn't come to visit anymore. Afterwards, the subject of Walt joins the Vault of Unspoken Things, with Aunt Micki, Protestantism, Mr. Nice Having Sex With Christine and Cousin Robert.

The next week my mother makes a startling announcement: she is determined to adopt a collection of unfortunate children. In an unusual display of intimacy, she eagerly shares her plans with me. "Wouldn't it be wonderful to have a big family?"

"I thought you didn't like family?"

"I would like a family full of orphans."

"Why orphans?"

"Because they don't have anyone who loves them."

Despite recognizing that I don't feel anyone loves me, and that we already have two children who don't live with us, I am immediately swept away with the tide of excitement. These orphans are the community that could be the answer to every one of my prayers for family, companionship, friends, brothers, sisters. My heart thumps hard in my chest when I think of my future siblings for a good portion of each following day. I just know that once the siblings arrive, the roles will fall into an idealized place: an older brother to protect me, and a younger brother and sister I will help raise and nourish. We will be united; a force, a bond, a group, a community. Their arrival will create a family unit that will magically transform my mother and Mr. Nice into real parents.

In October, when my mother and Mr. Nice tell me that they've invited an entire orphanage over for Thanksgiving dinner, and will then choose several kids to officially adopt from amongst the visiting orphans, I can think of nothing else. Mr. Nice is going to prepare Turkey Basted in Garlic Sauce, Bacon Stuffing, Carrots Sautéed in White Wine Creme, Cranberry Relish made from Scratch and Angel Biscuits. For dessert, he's going to make Homemade Ice Cream and Pineapple Upside Down Cake. Knowing the menu has already been chosen gives me the permission I need to truly allow my hope to grow. How can this joyous event not happen if the menu has already been chosen?

October passes in a flurry of anticipation. As Thanksgiving Day draws near, my mother informs me that the orphanage has turned down her request to feed the orphans. "It would be cruel to allow the children access to a family home, and then take it away from them at the end of the evening," she reads from the orphanage Director's letter. Even though my mother calls and explains that she plans to adopt some of the children at the end of the evening, the Director remains firm in his denial of her request. I wonder if she noticed he didn't extend an invitation for her to visit the orphanage.

The air leaves the room and the walls inch in around my mother and I. The disappointment in my heart is so palpable I can see the faint beat of my heart through my tee shirt. Just like my mother's stint at dental hygienist school, the orphans and the hope they represented are plucked away from the possibilities in our future.

On Thanksgiving when Mr. Nice takes us to one of the casino restaurants for dinner and my mother asks, "Isn't this great?" more than once in an attempt to include me in the conversation, I remain silent. I don't want to be included in the conversation. My disappointment hangs over the three of us at the table like a foul, wet sponge.

Instead of speaking, I pick at my food and wonder what sort of food the orphans have for Thanksgiving Dinner in the orphanage. I wish I was eating dinner in the orphanage with them. I wish I lived in the orphanage with them. I finally mumble a "Yes," the next time I'm asked if I think dinner is great. At least this way I won't be asked again.

Overlay – A Tale of One Girl's Life in 1970s Las Vegas

Chapter Twenty

Flush: In poker, a hand consisting of five cards in one suit is a flush. This is a good hand.

My Aunt Ana and Uncle John invite me to spend the Christmas holidays with them in Palm Springs. At the airport my mother walks with me across the tarmac, carrying my little pink suitcase toward the small 4-seat Cessna airplane. I walk up the little metal stairs and board the plane. Since there is no copilot, my yellow teddy bear rides shotgun. I sit in the back for the 50-minute flight, the sole passenger, imagining that I am a princess. From the little windows I view the clouds that cover my kingdom below. I am rich. I am beautiful. My father is the King and my mother is the Queen and they are known as the best rulers in the entire world. With our riches we feed all the orphans and stray animals. All the orphans live in our castle and we run down the hallways screaming and playing hide and seek and driving the housekeepers crazy who are trying to tidy up the floors and floors of bedrooms.

I'm surprised to see that my aunt looks exactly the same as I remember, even though it's been nearly five years since I've seen her and I look so different. Since I already made sure that Robert had left for college and won't be home before I agreed to visit, I continue the glory of my princess fantasy and bask in the glorious thought of spending two weeks alone with my aunt and uncle. My aunt drives a brand new shiny white Cadillac, and buckles me into the front seat with her. Her driving is measured and calm as we thread our way down the two lane streets to their new condo that sits new and bright against the surrounding mountains of Palm Springs. The front doors are so tall it's as if a family of giants are expected to visit. The rooms are huge, full of bright light under soaring ceilings. Most of the furniture is white: white cushioned couches, white wicker couches, white carpeting, white shag throw rugs. The room where I will be staying has a wall of floor to ceiling windows that overlook an interior garden which my aunt calls a solarium. As I place my suitcase on one of the two single beds, Ana asks me to go take a shower and says she will fix me up when I get out.

My bathroom is stocked with Flex shampoo and conditioner and Neutrogena soap and Ana asks if I know how to properly wash my hair? I assure her I do, but she explains that she knows a special way to wash hair and would love to show me. So I acquiesce and face my embarrassment at being naked in front of another human being and let her wash my hair. Her technique is no different from mine, but she is much more detailed and attentive to scrubbing and rinsing. After my shower she wraps me in a thick towel and brushes my hair for a blissfully long time. She trims the ends, taking off nearly two inches of what she refers to as 'split ends'. She rubs facial cream on my face using her two ring fingers 'so not to stretch the skin,' explaining that this lotion is Queen Bee Cream which makes me smile inside. The fantasy continues! She applies mascara to my eyelashes. "Such a beauty," she announces and her face erupts into one of her movie-star smiles. "You remind me so much of my dear brother with your freckles and blue eyes. Do you know what dental floss is, darling girl?" she asks next, digging into one of her bathroom drawers and pulling out a small white plastic box. "Let me show you how to use it. People will judge you for the rest of your life on your teeth and your manners, you know."

An unusual, sweet feeling spreads across my face and even trickles down to my toes. Aunt Ana turns me to face the floor-to-ceiling mirrors and asks what I think. What do I think? I hardly recognize the little girl in the mirror. My blonde hair is clean and straight, cut evenly to my shoulders. My skin shines, my eyes look big and bright under my dark lashes. My teeth are clean and white. It's hard to believe this pretty little girl standing before me….is me.

Overlay – A Tale of One Girl's Life in 1970s Las Vegas

"Now, let's have some lunch and then we're going shopping. If ever anyone was in need of some new clothing it's you, darling girl."

I always thought heaven was above; separate and unattainable. Yet this curious feeling feels exactly how I imagine heaven would feel: safe. If heaven is above, I felt no lift to get there. Instead I feel more like I've closed my eyes and fell backward into the heavenly bliss of a family: into safety, security, reliability. I've fallen into a house that's quiet in the evenings and not roaring-full of drunks making exaggerated noises that make me gnash my teeth like the terrible monsters in Where the Wild Things Are. Safety feels like the routine we establish that borders on perfection: Aunt Ana, Uncle John and I eat breakfast together before John leaves for work in the mornings. Safety sounds like John's invitations for me to accompany him to work sometimes, an arrangement I intuitively figure out is probably predetermined and discussed with my Aunt when she needs time for herself. This arrangement is so foreign and respectful and delectable that I just eagerly go wherever I'm invited, knowing I'm wanted yet respectfully given the choice. At work with Uncle John, I follow him around as he inspects the operations of his motels and dry cleaning businesses. Safety feels like returning home for lunch where the three of us gather to eat tunafish sandwiches and chips in the solarium: an enclosed patio that overlooks a pristinely groomed golf course. Safety feels like meeting again for dinner in the evenings in the formal dining room where we 'dress for dinner' and use white or gold linen napkins. While Ana and John enjoy wine after dinner, I swim, jumping alternately in and out of the pool and Jacuzzi. Then we return to the den and watch comedy shows and Ana serves dessert on delicate china plates. The sound of John's deep and loud and rolling long like thunder laughter fills the den. My uncle John finds so much of life amusing. He is always laughing and smiling and telling jokes and I bask in the noise of his joy. Our days and nights roll into a routine both dependable and sure.

On Christmas morning I awake early to find my aunt and uncle, my cousins Robert and Marie, my grandmother Marge and her husband, John, are already in the living room with hands clasped around big coffee mugs. The Christmas tree is so crowded with presents underneath that the colorfully wrapped boxes overflow to the space around. My head still foggy from sleep, I stand at the doorway to the living room and look at all of these people – my family – and suddenly feel a crushing sense of shyness. My Aunt smiles when she sees me and calls, "Good morning, honey! Come see what Santa brought while you were sleeping!"

I approach the tree and sit on my heels and poke gingerly at the colorfully wrapped boxes. Most of them are addressed to me. There are games, Twister and Monopoly and Sorry, and unexpected things like Flex Shampoo and Conditioner, and thoughtful gifts like the Queen Bee face cream I like, mascara, colored hair bands and Neutrogena soap and so many, many clothes: Bell-bottomed jeans, and t shirts with macramé piping, high-heeled sneakers and socks and underwear. I've never spent a Christmas with anyone other than one or the other of my parents. That afternoon is so warm that we go swimming and make jokes that while the rest of the country is covered in snow, we are sunning in wonderful Southern California. I practice my jumps and dives while my uncle films me with the new movie camera Santa brought him for Christmas.

"Jump!"

"Now dive!"

"Backflip!"

The family calls out to me and they are smiling and the water is warm and the sun is hot and I never, ever want to go home.

The morning of my departure from the airport arrives and my aunt takes my face in her hands and looks into my eyes. "If you ever need any help, honey, anything at all, you call me right away. I don't care if it's in the middle of the night, you just call. Dial O, ask for the operator and tell her you want to make a collect call to this number." She presses a folded piece of paper into my hand.

Crying, trying to be stoic and failing miserably, my sobs reach the point where I hitch and hiccough with my attempts to hold them inside. I don't want to leave my aunt and uncle's white condominium and return to my dark isolated existence in Las Vegas. My stay with my aunt and uncle is the first time anyone had paid any attention to me in a very long time and now that I know what it feels like to be cared for, how can I possibly go back home again and survive? What will happen to me?

"Don't cry, darling. You'll come back for the summer," my aunt says, brushing away my tears with her delicate fingertips. "Remember to use the soaps and creams I gave you. They'll keep your skin lovely and beautiful when you're older." She hugs me tight, smiles one last time and stands up.

My uncle leans down next and gives me a quick and powerful hug. "Love you, darling."

I don't want to board that plane. I don't want to sit in the back. I don't care if my yellow teddy bear is sitting in the copilot's seat. I cry all the way home, my fall from heaven so real I hope the plane will just crash and end this pain. At the Las Vegas airport, I hope more than worry that my alien mother will forget to meet me again. As I walk down the steps of the Cessna at the Las Vegas airport, I see her standing alone at a distance. The pilot carries my bear and my luggage and hands them to my mother. She thanks him, says hello to me, and I follow her to her car. "I've left Russell," she announces to the windshield as we drive away, "and we've moved."

"Moved? Do I have to change schools again?"

"Yes, you start tomorrow at Ruby Thomas Elementary."

I don't say anything but I wonder inside what would have happened if the orphans had already been living with us. Would they have been as disappointed as I feel? Perhaps orphans were used to moving around and starting repeatedly over? Maybe they better weathered these constant upheavals than I do. Perhaps the orphans were still living in their home, safe and secure, while I drifted again into another home, another school, another environment.

All of our furniture, including the dining room table we never use, is perfectly repositioned in the new apartment. We live on the bottom floor this time, and the thought runs through my mind that I won't have to hear my mother stumbling and falling up the stairs anymore. The carpeting is a mashed-down green shag, which doesn't really compliment the cheap dark paneled walls. My canopy bed is set up in my room, my bed neatly made. I put down my bags and look around.

"Better get to bed," my mother suggests from the doorway. "We've got to get you to school early tomorrow to get you registered."

"Why did you leave Russell?"

My mother sits down on the edge of my bed, and I notice that her face is tired and a little bit sad in the shadows of the dim overhead light. "A friend of his came into the bar one day and said,

'Sandy, I won't be coming back to the bar any longer. I won't tell you exactly why, but you'll figure it out quickly. You seem like a nice lady and you should know the truth. If you want to find out why The Back Street isn't making as much money as it should, why don't you show up after closing time and see what you find.'

"What happened?" I ask, folding down the canopy bed comforter.

"I set my alarm for 2:00 in the morning, which was the time the bar closed. By the time I pulled into the parking lot, I could see there were only two cars left, Russell's and one other. I very quietly used my key to open the outer set of doors. I was opening the set of doors that led directly into the bar, Russell quickly opened the inner door himself, his face covered in red lipstick."

"What! Why was he wearing lipstick?"

"He wasn't wearing it, silly. Someone was smooching on him and smeared it all over his face. As he stood at the door, behind him appeared a blond gal who looked real nervous. She said to me, 'Lady, you've got the wrong impression here.' I just said to her, very quietly, 'You better scram before I give you a wrong impression on your face.'"

"Did she scram?"

"Oh sure, she scrammed! She took off so fast that the only thing Russell said was, "Looks like we won't be seeing her around here anymore.'"

"Then what happened?"

"I went home and went back to bed. The next day I found this apartment and moved us in. Then I did one last thing..."

"What did you do?"

"Russell's business partner couldn't figure out why the Back Street wasn't making any money. I knew what I was pulling in during the day, which was the slow time. Russell should have been making a lot more than I was. So I called the Business Partner and told him that I quit and that Russell was screwing around and giving away free drinks at night. He ended the partnership and closed the bar. Russell is officially unemployed now."

"What about you? Aren't you unemployed too, now?"

"No, Ma'am. I have my old job back at the King Arthur and they're happy to have me."

"What about dental hygienist school?" I ask, hoping against hope.

"That didn't work out, Marlayna." She kisses me on the forehead, flips off my light and closes my bedroom door. I lay in bed, thinking that life could be unexpectedly good.

Mr. Nice is gone.

Gone.

Gone.

Just like that, I don't get to stay in Palm Springs but I do get a new life without Mr. Nice.

I am hopeful that if I can score a flush, I can score a straight flush.

Surely, it's possible.

PART THREE

(1975 – 1976)

Chapter Twenty One

Bluff: In poker, players bluff when raising with a weak hand in hopes of driving out players with stronger hands.

The next morning my mother is waiting for me, dressed in a low cut white shirt, short black shorts and white go-go boots.

"You're wearing that?"

"Yes, what's wrong with it?"

"It's embarrassing, Mom. Your shorts are so….short."

"That's the style. They're called short shorts."

The difference between my Aunt Ana and my mother is that my aunt cares what I think and how I feel and my mother doesn't. What a curious feeling it is to consider that I don't care so much anymore that she doesn't care about me.

I don't throw up on my first day of fourth grade at the newest school, and for this I am thankful. I guess I'm getting used to change but I do quickly feel overwhelmed by the many things I don't know. Assigned a locker, I stand in front of it because I don't know how to open a combination lock. When I ask the boy near me for help, he looks at me like I am a complete idiot.

"Seriously? You don't know how to open a lock?"

"No."

"Turn it to the right a few times. Go to the number. Turn it left and pass the second number once and then hit it. Go to the right directly to the third number. It's simple."

After a few fruitless turns of the dial I ask another girl for help. She helps me with the lock and when she learns that I'm new she offers to show me around. She introduces herself as Julie, and I'm secretly overjoyed to land my first friend on my first day before my first class. Julie is Jewish and bears a striking resemblance to Anne Frank with her dark fall of hair and slightly sunken eyes. She lives in an apartment with just her mother like I do, and I feel a fleeting hope that maybe our mothers could be good friends, or that my father could marry her mother and Julie and I could be sisters. It doesn't seem odd to me that I consider these numerous potentialities within five minutes of meeting someone new. Unfortunately, Julie is diagnosed with Juvenile Diabetes shortly after I meet her and misses many days school. So I am really excited to be invited to spend the night at her house one Friday evening a few months later after her health has been somewhat stabilized. A few hours into my visit she becomes very ill.

"Call your mother to pick you up, please," Julie's mom directs me and my stomach sinks.

First I try our home number and listen as the phone rings and rings. At that point I ask Julie's mother for the yellow pages, and next call the King Arthur bar. The bartender tells me to check another bar where he thinks my mother might have gone after work. I look up the number of that bar and describe my mother to the man who answers the phone. I get lucky, and when I hear her

Overlay – A Tale of One Girl's Life in 1970s Las Vegas

voice on the phone I almost feel relieved until I hear she's been drinking quite a bit already. When she finally arrives to pick me up, Julie has been in bed for two hours while I waited in their tiny living room, flipping through magazines. Julie's mom didn't allow me to turn on the television because she didn't want Julie to be kept awake. I can tell by the way Julie's mother stands with her arms crossed that she is not going to be interested in being friends with my mom. I'm never invited to Julie's house again, and our friendship dies.

I walk to school in the mornings even though it's a long way on busy roads and across parking lots. Several other kids from my new apartment complex walk too and eventually we band together in loose groups of threes and fours. We always take care to avoid the school bully, Lisa. A big girl with a big, phlegmy voice, she picks on any of the younger and smaller kids who have the misfortune to be targeted by her, a group that seems to include nearly anyone and everyone at the school. She is known to demand lunch money from the kids and it isn't unusual for her to step on the backs of heels to give kids a flat tire, or reach down and pull the back of their underwear up hard to give them a wedgie. I'm infinitely glad she hasn't yet noticed me in my first few weeks of school, and do my very best to avoid her on the walks to and from school since she sometimes walks to school in the mornings with some of the other older kids. Part of our morning walk requires that we cross a large shopping mall parking lot. One morning we hear a scream and look ahead to see Lisa ... running. I can't begin to imagine what in the world could cause Lisa to run. Surely, it must be very bad.

"Earthquake!" one of my friends says and we giggle into our cupped hands, afraid even at this distance that she might hear us.

"Then it'll be the Poseidon Adventure when Lake Mead overflows!" another says, and we giggle even harder. As we near the car Lisa had run from and see the man sitting in the driver's seat, our laughs die on our lips.

The car door is open he calls out good-naturedly, "Girls! If you come over here, I'll give you a dollar." He sticks one hand up over the roof of his car and waves a dollar bill slowly back and forth in the air. Now a dollar is two days' worth of lunch money and I'm tempted to try to get close enough to grab the dollar from his hand before he can grab me. I'm reasonably sure this is possible and sure that I'm fast enough. As I edge closer I see that he's naked and has now placed the dollar on his erect penis. My friends scream and run and naturally I run along with them but all I'm thinking about as our feet slap the pavement is how to get that dollar.

Later in the day I found reason to really wish I'd been able to secure that dollar.

"Gimme your money."

There before me is Lisa, her muddy brown eyes bearing down on me. I've been waiting patiently in the ice cream line at school with my heart set on a Fudgesicle. I have fifty cents which is enough for either lunch or ice cream and I've decided on ice cream. Lisa is sucking air in and out in her labored way. Up close she smells wet and sweet, not unlike cotton candy. I hand her my fifty cents without a word and get out of line. My stomach growls in an uproar. Almost worse than handing over my money and realizing I will go without food all day is the nervous, shifting looks of the kids in line. I can see their relief that they weren't the chosen ones that day. Lisa takes my place in line and pushes her way to the front. The next day at lunch she approaches me again in the ice cream line. "Gimme your money," she demands. I hand her my fifty cents and get out of line again, this time sullenly watching as she pushes her way to the front and orders the very same chocolate

98

ice cream I want. At lunchtime on the third day, I wait in line. I see her lumber up, craning her head around as she looks for me. "Gimme your money," she says with an exhale when she sees me.

"No."

"Whah-" she wheezes. She doesn't finish the word as if she's forgotten what it was she wanted to say while pronouncing the word.

"No, I won't give you my money."

Lisa looks confused and by the look on her face it's clear this is the first time a kid has said no to her. Her eyes roll around in her head as she contemplates what to do next. She looks to the right and then to the left to check if anyone has heard our interaction. She leans down to me, making an intimidating effort to get in my face. "I'll kick your ass."

"Kick it then." My heart is pounding so hard I think I might faint. The kids around us watch, having fallen silent. In that silence grows the sound of subtle foot shuffling.

Clearly she isn't expecting this answer. We are so close I can see the sweat beading on the dark mustache on her upper lip. Looking around again to see who's watching, she whispers, "You better watch out. I'm gonna get you." I hear her make another wheezy demand for money, and turn around to see her standing over a tiny third grade girl near the end of the line.

"Save my place," I say to the boy behind me and walk to the end of the line, pulling my shoulders back and sucking in my stomach. The little girl near the end of the line is fishing in one pocket of her little jeans for coins, her little face crushed and drawn.

"You're not taking her money either."

Lisa rolls around and eyes me in surprise. I don't know how much luck I have left on this particular day, but I feel like pushing it. "In fact, you're not taking anyone else's money ever again. I'll make sure of it, even if I have to stand in this line every day." I'm not sure what my next move will be if Lisa chooses to challenge me, but I'm betting she won't. The little girl removes her hand from her little pocket and hope appears on her face. Lisa begins backing up and I see what I like to call a rat run across her face. Then the miraculous happens – she turns and walks away.

That is the end of Lisa's reign.

Since most of the children in my apartment complex come home to empty apartments after school we band together, unsupervised, unwatched, unnoticed. We venture away from the Cambridge Apartments in groups and explore other streets and complexes. Near our apartment complex is an unfinished twenty-building apartment development rising from the desert sand. It becomes a secret cinderblock city to us; gray, naked cinderblock structures full of kids and never adults.

I am quite tiny at ten years old, scrawny but not skinny, and already much smaller than most of my classmates but that doesn't stop me from leading our group of latchkey friends to roam the abandoned cinderblock buildings. We take care to avoid the pot-smoking teenagers who find it amusing to regale us with their stories about drug use. We clamor about the buildings, standing on each other's shoulders and finding handholds in the weathered cinderblock to climb to the second story and to the roof above. I love to just hang from the second story floor by my hands and let go, landing in the soft sand below. Sometimes I swing back and forth to gain momentum and then drop, a flying trapeze. Then I start jumping from the second story. Then leaping. Then flying. Then I climb to the roof of the third story and dangle from that great height too. It's liberating to be so unfettered at that height. I dangle freely for as long as I can, aware of the sound of the breeze rushing past my ears and the silence of my friends on the sand below. Letting go is glorious; free in the air, neither a part of the earth or the sky, but a brief part of a solitary movement.

It is when I realize I am fearless.

That is, until Diana moves to the neighborhood.

Diana is older than me, bigger than me and certainly much more frightening than I could ever be. Lean and scrappy with short ratty hair, she is different from all of us in more than appearance. We hear she moved to Las Vegas from the Bronx, which we hear is far away in New York. At the abandoned apartment buildings one afternoon, she walks directly up to me. "If I ever see you here again, I'll kick your ass," she says in a thick Bronx accent. Her brown eyes are so dark I can't see where her pupils begin or end. She wears a tight boy's plain white under shirt, from which she'd cut the sleeves. She is so skinny I can see the veins protruding from her muscular, skinny arms.

"Why?" I ask. From the corner of my eye I can see the other kids kicking at the dirt to the side of me, waiting, watching.

"Because I feel like it." She shoves me hard in the chest with her powerful little rock-hard fists.

The thing about being fearless is you have to know when to turn and walk away from the abandoned building and head back to your own apartment complex. I know without giving it a whole lot of thought that this is one of those times. Diana isn't like Lisa - she could explode into a sharp burst of fragments at any moment.

I have to be aware always since Lisa and Diana aren't the only threats in our neighborhood. One evening as I return to the apartment, three girls I've never seen before follow me to my front door. When I turn around and realize they've circled me and blocked any hope of escape, I fumble for the house key that I wear on a worn piece of blue yarn around my neck. The overhead light in the hallway outside our apartment has burned out and I can't see clearly enough to get the key in the lock before one of the girls slaps the back of my head so hard my forehead strikes the front door.

"White bitch."

I face them and the second girl punches me in the arm. The third, drawing courage from the first two, kicks me hard in the shin. I throw ineffective little punches and hope to reach some target but they're so much bigger and stronger than me and have the unquestionable advantage of being three. They rush forward and one of them pushes me backwards so hard the back of my head strikes the door. I shield my face with my forearms and blindly kick out as hard as I can until I feel a satisfying contact. A howl erupts and a fist lands on my stomach. An apartment door opens as I fall to my knees and a woman's voice yells, "You kids get out of here!" When the light streaming from her open apartment door hits us the girls turn and run, their beaded braids snapping behind them.

By the time my mother arrives home from work, my body is sore and my head is thumping. When she sees the purple knot on the front of my forehead, she sets her purse down on the kitchen table and asks what happened to me. Before I can finish the story she opens our front door and silently points, signaling me to walk out in front of her. Since she's just arrived home from her bar tending job she's still dressed in her short shorts, nylons and knee-high shiny white boots.

"It's okay, Mom, really-"

"You get out here and point those girls out to me immediately!"

There's no use in arguing with her so I walk outside and resign myself to the inevitable confrontation. I'm fairly certain the girls live on the other side of our complex since I haven't seen them before so we head in that direction. As my mother stomps her white-booted way down the sidewalk, I trail nervously behind. A motley group of kids begin to follow us chanting:

A fight

A fight

A nigger and a white

The white can't fight

So the nigger's all right!

My repeated requests for them to be quiet only incites them to increase the tempo and pitch of the growing chants. As my mother and I reach the area where I think the girls live, the ragtag group of kids parading along behind my mother resembles a miniature lynch mob.

"Please, Mom," I beg as I run along beside her. "Please don't go to their door. Please!"

"No nigger girls are gonna gang up on you. Take me to their house NOW." She pumps her arms back and forth with each determined stride.

I'm formulating a loose plan to fake that I don't know exactly where the girls live when one of the kids yells that he knows where they live. He leads us to the door of an apartment. My mother knocks firmly at the door until a tired-looking black woman in a faded orange and green housedress cracks open the door and peers out with one eye. She looks mildly surprised, and the thought crosses my mind that if I had one magic wish it would have been for my mother to leave this sad lady alone.

"Your daughters hit my daughter."

The sad woman sighs. She says she's sorry in a voice completely devoid of emotion.

"They need to apologize. I won't stand for this."

The woman turns and calls sharply into the darkness of the apartment. "Patrice! Shawna! Kenya!" The three girls appear around her in a cloud and train their angry, sullen looks together on my mother. I think of a bee's hive, these three stinging workers gathered around the queen.

"You don't hit my daughter ever again. Do you understand me?" My mother yells into their upturned faces and I'm embarrassed to see that she wags her finger at them like Nana did when I criticized my mother.

Overlay – A Tale of One Girl's Life in 1970s Las Vegas

The girls gaze back at my mother and their eyes are as empty of compassion as their mother's voice. "She started it," one says, and I'm sure she's the one that slammed my head into the apartment door.

"Apologize," the sad woman says to the girls without turning her head. In sullen response, they offer mumbled words of apology from behind her, a dull drone of a beehive.

"Why did you do that to me? I don't even know you," I ask.

One girl shrugs. Another rolls her eyes.

The third closes the door in our faces with a crisp snap.

Chapter Twenty Two

Board: In poker, the community cards dealt face-up in the center of the table are referred to as on the board.

My father occasionally picks me up during his bouts of sobriety and takes me to the Sizzler steakhouse. Our time together usually consists of him telling me how crazy my mother is, peppered with sarcastic remarks about how poorly I'm being raised. "Look at your teeth! Do you ever brush them?"

I shrug. I tire of all the talk. If he is so concerned about the state of my life, the state of my health, the state of my teeth, then why doesn't he do something about it? His constant complaining to me about my mother is getting old too. I become increasingly eager to escape him and his rantings for the safety of my bedroom and my books.

I read many books, everything I can get my hands on. When it's time to fill out book lists and book reports, my teacher does everything short of calling me a liar when she views my list. She says there's no way I could have read all those books and will only give me credit for half of them. Credit for even half of the books still puts me well above the top of the class, so I don't care a whole lot if she believes me or not. I'm losing faith in the world of adults anyway. The little I do care is part of a silent wish that I had someone to talk to. I don't discuss my situation with anyone. I know my mother's lifestyle isn't desirable and I make every effort possible to avoid the judgment of others.

Reading as much as I do gifts me with the understanding of and the ability to spell more words correctly than anyone in my class and I easily win every school spelling contest. While I understand the rules of words and spelling and grammar and punctuation, I find the emotions and behaviors of people perplexing. The characters in books make so much more sense to me than people in real life. They face issues just as people do in real life but they make the right choices and do the right things. There's a predictable rhythm to books that I find endlessly comforting. About three quarters through most books, the main character might make a bad choice or have an unfortunate accident, but the issue is always successfully resolved by the end of the story. Real life is nothing like this. There is no revelation. No guarantee of a successful conclusion. Things can just end badly with no hope of redemption or repair. Like Christine being raped by Mr. Nice. Where was the good in this act? What ultimate purpose did it serve? Mr. Nice never paid for his crime. There was no resolution. And Christine....what had happened to her?

So while real life is unfortunate and confusing, books and television are where I create my world view of right and wrong. Since my mother isn't home in the evenings, when I'm not reading one of my books, I watch Pa. Michael Landon plays Pa on 'Little House on the Prairie' and he is simply everything I think a Pa should be: handsome and kind, with a completely perfect and wonderful smile. More important than his looks is the way he involves himself in every aspect of his children's lives. Although I recognize that he isn't always on Laura's side, I envy the way he patiently explains right and wrong to her. He always takes the time to explain Why. Why what she did was wrong. Why she could have done something differently. Why it was wrong to steal, wrong to lie, wrong to deceive. Sometimes I cry to the television after 'Little House on the Prairie' ends. I want Pa for my own dad more than I want my own dad. Then I cry about the guilt I feel for my thoughts.

Even as frustrated as I am by my perceived inequity in the family department, I'm often reminded that I don't have it the worst in the Cambridge Apartments. All around me are kids struggling with poor circumstances. Some worse than my own.

A thin, shy, redhead girl named Noel lives in one of the smaller apartments with her mother. One night Noel joins a group of us as we prepare to go from apartment to apartment to perform our version of Neil Diamond's "Song Sung Blue." When we're satisfied we have our routine down, we leave to perform our show for whoever happens to be at our homes, if anyone. Cindy's mom and dad stand in the doorway of their apartment and watch respectfully as we sing in the hallway. They clap enthusiastically at the end, smiling at Cindy. Her mother waddles the short distance into the kitchen and returns with a piece of candy for each of us. Another mother invites us into her living room, where she sits on the couch, smoking and nodding her head to our a cappella beat. There's no one home at my apartment.

I hadn't seen Noel's mother before and am surprised she doesn't share Noel's startling red hair color. When we conclude our performance in her little living room, she claps artificially. It's obvious to me from the way her eyes travel around the room and keep landing on the television set she hadn't bothered to turn down that she isn't the least bit interested in our performance. Their apartment is very small; just one smoky room. I'm not sure where Noel and her mother sleep, but I suspect it's on the couch and on the floor. I have a feeling I know who sleeps on the floor.

The following Saturday morning word travels around the apartment-kid network that Noel is hurt. Real bad. We go in a group to Noel's door to find out what's happened to our friend. Noel's mother opens the door wearing a tattered, red silk robe. A cigarette burns lazily from one hand. She is wig-less. I'm horrified to see that her real hair is so short that patches of scalp are showing, while on other areas of her head, curly, errant red hairs protrude. I'm still staring at the curling red hairs when one of the kids asks if we can see Noel. Noel's mother takes a slow drag on her cigarette. She says that Noel is sick and won't be coming outside for a few days.

When she shuts the door, we turn around to find several mothers gathered in a loose group near Noel's apartment. Adults rarely involve themselves in our world, so their presence in itself is curious. Lingering nearby and hoping to be unnoticed, I overhear one of the mothers say Noel was beaten by her mother the night before and forced to sleep in the bathtub without a pillow or a blanket. We all mill about uneasily in rotating groups of threes and fours, whispering amongst ourselves. Though Diana shuffles around with the rest of us, except for a fierce glare or two she doesn't come near me. I ensure my safety by keeping close to the groups of parents, knowing she is too much of a coward to bother me while they're around. Whatever it is we're waiting for creates a growing, palpable tension that crackles through the air around us all, causing us to whisper like early morning shadow people.

When the first police cars arrive, I peek from behind one of the heavier mothers to see. I've never seen police officers up close before, and find myself admiring the intimidating power of their strong walks and the quickness of their sharp glances. They stride toward the apartment of Noel and her hairless mother, barely waiting for the door to be answered before being swallowed inside.

When Noel is gingerly escorted from the apartment by two of the bigger police officers, a collective gasp arises from the kids and the mothers. Black and red welts wrap around her bluish-white skinned legs. Her short red hair has been unevenly hacked and chopped, and as she passes us we see that it's matted and bloody in the back of her head where her pretty curls used to be. She leans against the arm of one of the police officers for support as she hobbles to the police car. Although she's a tall girl, she appears tiny and delicate next to the giant police officers. She doesn't look at us as she passes or turn around once she reaches the car. I know she doesn't ignore us on purpose, but seems to be so lost in whatever has happened to her that she just can't see us at all. My stomach lurches, and my breakfast waffles roll around inside with a familiar anxiety and fear.

Yells and scuffles from inside the tiny apartment filter through the open front door. The red robe changed for a short dress, Noel's mother is unceremoniously pulled outside. Unlike her daughter, she fights the police officers during her short escorted walk to the police car. I shuffle back and forth on my feet as I stare at her flailing body and limbs in the firm grasp of two of the police officers. If she breaks free, I'm prepared to get out of her way, but despite her desperate attempts she's unable to free herself. As she reaches the open door of the police cruiser, one of the police officers places his large hand on the top of her head and not too gently pushes her into the back seat. I can see her underwear as she kicks at the police officer. They are hot pink, just like her fingernails.

We never see Noel again.

Though I understand men can be unpredictable, and can become slaves to everything from their own temper to their physical desires, I can't make sense of the evil that mothers are capable of doing. Aren't our mothers supposed to protect us? Shield us from the dangers that exist in the world? Keep us safe? Why do some mothers flay their children and lay them on the board for all to see? What happens to the children whose mothers are their greatest threat?

Chapter Twenty Three

Caribbean Stud is a solo version of the most popular card game, poker. Caribbean Stud pits you against the dealer. You are paid out according to the rank of your poker hand. The better your hand, the bigger your payout. Caribbean Stud also offers a separate progressive jackpot bet for $1. If you play the progressive and your hand qualifies, you win big!

Before venturing to the abandoned apartment complex after school, first I always climb to the top of the cinderblock wall that separates our two properties. If I don't see Diana, I hop down into the dirt below and my friends follow. One hot Saturday just before school ends and summer vacation begins I hop over the wall. Some kids are already gathered there, lighting matches and throwing them to the ground. I bend down and light a piece of garbage on fire. I pick up the burning trash and try to put it out but it burns my hand. When I drop the paper it immediately ignites another dry piece of trash lying on the desert floor. Although several of us try to stomp it out, the fire quickly ignites all the other trash that's blown up against the cinderblock wall. It spreads to both the right and the left of where we stand. We watch as all of it catches fire. Then we run.

I run straight back to the empty silence of my apartment, my head and heart pounding fiercely. I prepare myself for the inevitable sound of fire engines, police cars and the clang of the jail cell door slamming shut. I imagine the same police officers that escorted Noel to safety arriving to take me to jail. I don't hear police sirens or a knock on my door. Towards evening I venture gingerly back outside and creep along the lengthening shadows toward the cinderblock wall. All is silent, so I clamber to the top of the wall and peer down. Blackened trash and half-burned tumbleweeds stretch both ways against the bottom of the other side of the wall. The fire had burned itself out. Thankfully, I hadn't caused any serious damage. What is curious is the way the fire solves a completely different problem in my life.

It's near dusk the next evening and I'm lying on the still-warm cement next to the swimming pool. My Barbie's lawn chair is set up on the cement next to the water, covered with her miniature pink towel. I move Barbie's limbs in the swimming pool water so she can take a late afternoon swim before she returns to her motor home to prepare for dinner with Ken. I'm alone, enjoying the solitude at the end of the day. My heels slowly rock back and forth behind me.

"I hear you started a fire."

Diana is standing several feet from me, just inside the gated pool area. I hadn't heard her open or close the gate behind her so I jump at the sound of her voice. With a mounting sense of alarm, I wonder what she's doing in my apartment complex. Alone. She's never ventured this far into my territory before.

"Did you hear me? I'm talking to you."

"I heard you." I sit up but don't stand in a conscious effort to appear unconcerned. I slowly pull my shoulders up and back with minuscule motions. I place Barbie slowly down on the cement behind me.

"Did you start that fire?"

At such a close distance I can see the scars that run along Diana's skinny arms. They're circular,

106

about the same size as the tip of a cigarette. There's a fresh bruise on one of her brown biceps, and both of her knees are scraped and raw.

I shrug in answer to her question, wanting to appear disinterested but inside my chest my heart is beating so fast I feel that familiar faintness coming. I can't faint. That would be entirely ridiculous. Don't faint. Don't faint. Don't faint.

"You little punk," she says under her breath. Her words squeeze so slowly through her clenched jaws I can almost feel their texture.

Without thinking, I whisper, "Why do you hate me so much, Diana?" In the gathering gloom, the furrow of her eyebrows is just barely perceptible. Perhaps she is contemplating the inanity of her rage against me. Perhaps I've given her too much credit.

"Shut up!"

Suddenly I have had more than enough of Diana. I've had more than enough having to hide and skulk away whenever she has the luxury of appearing. My rage isn't something that's been slowly building over a time, but rather an instant incarnation of total and complete intolerance. I see Diana for exactly who she is, just another scared bully tormenting others to assuage her own pain and fear. I have no pity for her. I narrow my eyes and theatrically whisper, "Yeah Diana, I did light that fire and if you don't watch out, next time I'm gonna burn you."

She'd been moving menacingly toward me, her shoulders hunched up to her ears in preparation for a fight, but my words stop her short. Uncertainty flickers across her browned face. Her eyebrows draw down again over the bridge of her nose. Her shoulders drop. She eyes me in search of weakness, like a wildcat hunting the weak link in a herd of antelope.

"If you come any closer to me, you can be sure I'll burn you when you're least expecting it."

She stumbled back a step, and stutters. "You're bl-bluffing."

"You might kick my ass today, but you'll never knew when I surprise you and light your hair on fire," I hear myself speak as if I'm listening to another Marlayna, an alternate Marlayna. "Better yet, maybe I'll just burn you with one of my lit cigarettes. Oh wait, it looks like somebody already did."

When I see the hurt I'd been hunting, I dismiss her from my view and lay back down on my stomach. I place Barbie back in the pool to continue her evening swim as if Diana didn't even exist. It's only when I hear the faint click of the pool gate close behind her departure that I notice my hands are shaking so hard that Barbie is having a convulsion in the swimming pool.

Regardless of my physical affectations, I've won big and I know it.

Chapter Twenty Four

Win: A winning hand pays out.

Summer finally arrives and my mother announces that I'm going to Hawaii to visit my Aunt Ana and Uncle John. They've left Palm Springs after doing quite well with their hotels and dry cleaning businesses and moved permanently to Maui. I'm invited to stay with them for the entire glorious summer. When my commuter plane lands on the island, gone is the asphalt and pavement of my daily life, replaced by rows of burning sugar cane fields. During the drive from the airport, Uncle John explains how the farmers burn the old crops to make room for the new crops. "Out with the old and in with the new, you know."

I roll down my window and stick out my head. The air smells at once both sweet and acrid yet wet like the ocean. I can taste the ocean salt on my tongue. It's a beautiful summer afternoon in June of 1975, and I marvel that in the morning I'd been at the Cambridge Apartments and now I have my head out the window from the back of my aunt and uncle's Charger racing past Hawaiian sugarcane fields. Elton John sings Philadelphia Freedom on the Charger's AM radio, and I already wish I will never, ever have to go back to Las Vegas again.

Their condominium is located beachfront in the city of Kihei and towers over the sea on one side and a fragrant garden of jasmine, plumeria and honeysuckle on the other. The steps and floors and elevator buttons are wet with the sea's moisture, and the sounds of the waves echo throughout the open hallways of the building. I draw the sea air into my lungs with deep, gulping breaths. Hawaii is one of those places you can feel, see, feel, smell and taste all at once. The condo has a balcony with a wrought iron bistro table. After setting my bags in the guest room, we gather on the balcony and I feel like an elegant adult, drinking Seven-Up and listening to the waves crashing on the rocks below.

My aunt and uncle aren't used to entertaining a ten year old so I stay busy during the days exploring the buildings and the gardens. I follow snail trails along the sidewalks. I examine the insect life. I pick plumeria flowers and string them along yarn to make leis. Leis multiply quickly in the condominium: I make them for my aunt, uncle, myself, the doorknobs, and the posts on the balcony until my aunt asks if I think we have enough leis yet? Recognizing my urge to create, she takes me to the bead store and I pick out twine, beads, and shells and macramé anything I can. Tying square knots and granny knots, I fashion bracelets, necklaces, plant hangers, belts and wall hangings. Soon my creations replace the dying leis, and begin to decorate the condominium.

Ana introduces me to the condominium's Paperback Library, a small, remodeled, shelved closet where residents borrow and lend paperback books. I spend much of my time in that dusty little closet, inhaling that delectable smell of old books while choosing the summer's novels. I start with Stephen King's Carrie, then move on to Peter Benchley's Jaws and William Peter Blatty's The Exorcist. After I pick my way through the horror books, I work my way though other genres, including the one that included Erica Jong's Fear of Flying. I guess my aunt noticed at this point what I was reading and enrolled me in hula dancing lessons.

Hula lessons take place twice a week on the rooftop under the black, black night. The instructor is a heavyset, white-haired woman called Ray who laughs at everything, and I do mean everything. She stands directly in front of me to demonstrate the graceful movements of the dance with her large, undulating hips. When I try to imitate her I feel my own awkward clumsiness.

Overlay – A Tale of One Girl's Life in 1970s Las Vegas

"Shake your hips like you're using a Hula Hoop," Ray booms, demonstrating by moving her own hips back and forth and around and around in undulating spirals. The grass skirts rustle and shake around her ample figure. There is no denying my hopeless movements and she laughs out loud, "You'll get it dear, you'll get it!"

Hula dancing for me is incredibly difficult, regardless of how easy it looks. Frustrated by my own stiff awkwardness, I feel increasingly resentful that I haven't been encouraged to play sports or join classes or do exercise of any kind. I don't even know how to move! Even though I'm one of a few participants, Ray spends most of her time with me during the lessons, laughing and smiling her contagious smile. I jump when she places her hand on my shoulder from behind during one of our classes, turning around in time to see a strange look pass between Ray and my aunt. A strange protectiveness over my mother and our dysfunctional life sprouts in my heart and spreads throughout my body, followed by a volatile combination of confusion, anger and guilt. Guilt for enjoying myself, anger at my mother for not providing anything pleasurable in my life and confused at how you can both hate and love a person at the same time.

I sleep late most summer mornings and no matter when I wake my aunt prepares breakfast for me. My uncle makes Sanka, and I am very grown up to be included in the act of drinking coffee with Uncle John on the balcony overlooking the sea. We walk down to the beach in the mornings, and my aunt reads magazines while I alternate between reading and bodysurfing. Though I've been instructed not to go to the ocean by myself, sometimes in the afternoons I leave the gardens and sneak down to the sea to climb the rocks and collect the empty, abandoned shells of the crabs.

After the paperback library the crab shells are my favorite thing about Hawaii. Crabs wear their skeletons on the outside, instead of the inside like humans. As they outgrow their smaller skeletons they simply step out of them and leave behind perfect skeletons of their previous selves. I am completely fascinated by these skeletons and collect all the crab bodies I find. Back at the condominium, I arrange them on a little table my aunt has set aside for my growing collection. Even more fascinating to me is the risk the crabs take during the period of transition from one skeleton to another. The crab is quite vulnerable and unprotected after it sheds one skeleton and hasn't yet grown the new one. I lay in bed at night listening to the waves break against the rocks below and try to imagine what I would become if I could likewise shed myself in this way. It's challenging to imagine being anything other than what I am, because that's all I know. It must take a huge leap of imagination, faith and courage to create a new existence and leave the framework of your old life behind.

My aunt and uncle often go to dinner in the evenings and are at first perplexed that I refuse to go. I patiently explain that I'm concerned they will get drunk and I'll have to sleep in the booth. Instantly I regret letting one of my mother's secrets slip from my mouth, and nervously place my fingers on my lips. "I mean, it's only happened twice, or really, only once, but just the same, I don't want to sleep in the restaurant," I backpedal, but it's too late. I've said it and now I can't unring the bell. The secret is out. Fortunately my aunt and uncle don't make a big deal about it and I'm allowed to remain behind while they go to dinner alone. Although I'm happy with our arrangement, the look that passes between them when I explain my reason for wanting to stay home shames me deeply. I don't like when people feel sorry for me because it only reminds me to feel sorry for myself. I resolve to be more careful in the future.

A few weeks into my visit aunt Ana announces that they've enrolled me in a day camp on the beach. The nausea builds instantly in my stomach like a miniature tidal wave. Even worse than the thought of going to camp are the eyes of my aunt and uncle watching me with an elevated concern. Why must I be so transparent?

"I don't understand why you don't want to go, Marlayna. It's a fabulous opportunity for you to meet other kids. Surely you're bored staying home with us all the time?"

"I'm not bored at all!"

"It's not normal for you to read so much, and spend so much time alone, darling. You need to be around other kids," Uncle John adds.

No matter how much I beg, cry, pout and manipulate, they are steadfast in their decision. The following Monday they walk me down the beach to the camp as my stomach flips and rumbles around so violently I'm sure I'm going to vomit in the sand between my new pink rubber flip flops. In between fights with the nausea, I continue begging my aunt and uncle to remain with me but they say no. When they depart, I walk forward into the group of kids and force a smile on my face. "Hi, I'm Marlayna," I say to the first girl I see and quickly sit down right next to her.

She looks at me with a mixture of shyness and relief, and I think I might just be okay.

A large Hawaiian man steps in front of the picnic tables and introduces himself as Matt, and says he is our head instructor. He says he'd tell us his Hawaiian name but we wouldn't be able to pronounce it properly anyway. This brings a few laughs from the group of kids. Next he introduces several older Hawaiian boys as his assistants. He gives a brief history of Hawaii, and says we'll be learning sports and crafts associated with Hawaii during our time at camp.

During the subsequent weeks, we spend most of our mornings in the ocean, learning how to surf. Balancing on the board is a lot more difficult than Matt and his assistants make it look, and the first week I think I'll be as dismal a failure at surfing as I am at hula dancing. At first I'm content to sit on the board and paddle. With the constant help of Matt and his assistants, I stand on the board one day and awkwardly ride a wave. I won't be gracing the cover of Surfer's Monthly, but I can officially surf.

On Friday mornings we don't surf, and go to a different beach at the bottom of a long, winding walk down a steep path. We learn to snorkel and I'm happy to finally find one activity that's as easy as it looks. During our snorkeling sessions, Matt brings along 'JawsKilla,' a small baseball bat with long nails pounded into the batting end. While he says it's unlikely we'll come across a shark, we should remain calm while he uses his makeshift weapon to drive the shark away. If a shark approaches us directly, we should punch it in the nose as hard as we can. Matt explains that the punch isn't to win the fight but to stun the shark. This is a curious thing – fighting not to win but just to buy time to escape.

"Don't worry about no shark eating you," Matt laughs his big loud, openmouthed, belly shaking Hawaiian laugh. "Hawaiian sharks aren't interested in Haole meat. You don't taste as good as Hawaiians and the sharks know it. Not one of you has enough meat on your bones to interest a Hawaiian shark. Especially you, you skinny little thing," he points at me.

While some of the campers opt to skip the snorkeling expedition after they see JawsKilla, I can't wait to get underwater. Underneath the surface is a different world of complex and fascinating characters. I kick along the water's surface, watching the colorful schools of fish darting around me.

Overlay – A Tale of One Girl's Life in 1970s Las Vegas

Plant tendrils wave back and forth with the movement of the ocean. Fish scatter in and out of the coral's recesses. Away from the reef, the sea urchins scatter along the ocean floor, their spines long and sharp. The sound of my breath through the snorkel draws in and out. I'd prefer to spend all my camp time in the undersea world, but the afternoons are for learning crafts like glass staining, decoupage and macramé. So flows the rhythm of my Hawaiian summer. By the time the month passes and camp ends, I'm as distraught to leave as I had been to arrive.

By the end of the summer my clothes no longer fit. My aunt says it's amazing what can happen when you eat. The day before I leave we drive into town and go shopping for school clothes. Even though I'm only ten years old, I know enough to appreciate her time, thought, energy and money that went into helping me choose what fit and what is more important, what fit appropriately. No longer are my shorts so tight my belly squeezes out on top of the waistband like an exploding muffin.

The night before my departure I can't sleep and can't concentrate on the novel I'm reading either. I try to concentrate on the sound of the waves breaking on the rocks below, but that won't happen. I leave my bedroom and bring my book to the living room where I hope to read on the couch until I fall asleep. Instead, I hear my aunt and uncle talking in their bedroom and put the book down altogether.

"We can't just send her back there, dear. I mean, look at the state she arrived in! We've only just cleaned her up, cut her hair, took her to a doctor and bought her some clothes. She finally looks presentable again," my aunt is saying.

My uncle replies that I'm not their daughter, and that I do have two parents of my own. Furthermore, my mother may not give up custody so easily.

"We could pay my brother's legal fees to fight Sandy and take custody of her, and he would let her live with us, John, don't you think?"

My uncle is silent while my aunt continues to talk. "She's so alone out there. Her mother pays no attention to her at all. We both know my brother's incapable of taking care of her because of his alcoholism. She's no problem at all. All the poor dear does is read and draw. She doesn't even like to go out to dinner, for crying out loud."

I am openmouthed on the couch in the dark, my unopened paperback book still in my hand. I know it's wrong to eavesdrop on their conversation yet I can't just go back to my room while my future is being decided. Is there really a chance I could live in the paradise that is my aunt and uncle's world? My head reels and I feel a strange feeling welling up inside my heart that I realize is hope.

My uncle John relents and says that yes he will pay my father's legal fees as long as it's agreed that I will be permitted to move to Maui and permanently live with them. He says it's probably a good idea to wait until I visit again at Christmas break. "Let's give the idea some solid thought, dear. We need to buy a bigger house first, and furnish it appropriately for a young girl."

I say nothing the next morning to my aunt and uncle about the conversation I overheard the night before. I hope my aunt talked my uncle into keeping me and perhaps I won't be sent back to Las Vegas at all. During breakfast I watch for a sign – a secret smile to pass between them perhaps. I slowly eat the oatmeal with fruit my aunt has prepared, remaining very quiet just in case they want to tell me I'm not going home. I drink my Sanka, being extra careful not to slurp. When my uncle carries my luggage to the car, my hope flags a little. I'm probably not going to hear anything about their decision just yet. I don't give up total hope even through the hugs and goodbyes. It isn't until my plane leaves the ground do I accept that I have to go back to Las Vegas.

My mother is waiting for me at the airport, and when I see her I have two immediate thoughts. I'm disappointed because I'd hoped she wouldn't show and the police would have no choice but to put me on the first plane back to Maui. Second her shorts have become shorter while I was away. She doesn't hug me or touch me, which isn't unusual for her but very different from what I'd been used to at my aunt and uncle's home.

At least there is no news that we moved or she'd gotten married while I was away.

Win!

Chapter Twenty Five

Discard Tray: A tray on the dealer's right side that holds all the cards that have been played or discarded.

Back at our apartment I take my bags to my room and lay out my new school clothes for the year. My mother comes in during this process, looks at the clothes and says nothing. "Aren't they pretty?" I ask, probably a little too smugly. The clothing on my bed is proof that somebody loves me, and this unspoken message flickers back and forth in the silence between my mother and I. She doesn't say a word.

I have difficulty falling asleep. It's only Thursday and this means I have three long days to pass until the start of fifth grade. Our Siamese cat, Kiki, hops onto my bed. In the darkness I can just barely make out her small movements as she slowly crouches down at the end of the bed near my legs. I reach out my hand and ruffle her fur. Under my hand, I feel her body tense and shift ever so slightly backwards. A low guttural growl builds in her throat.

When she rears back and lunges at my face, I sit up in shock and try to fling her body away from me. She digs her front claws into my scalp. Too stunned to cover my eyes on her first jump, I scream and place my hands across my eyes when she rears back for another leap. With each leap Kiki digs her back claws into the tops of my shoulders, hooking deep into my skin. Then she tears into my scalp with her teeth, using her front claws to scratch and dig at my head and my face. Each time she slips off, her claws rake down the sides of my head and along my forearms and make deep gouges in my flesh. When she slips off entirely, she repositions herself quickly on the bed to prepare to crouch and leap again.

My bedroom door flies open and my mother yells, "What in the hell?"

Through the haze of growling, flying fur and pain in my head I realize this must be bad because it's the first time in my life I've heard my mother swear. She rips Kiki from my head with one hand and runs out holding the spitting, growling cat by the scruff of her neck. I hear the front door slam open and Kiki's body hit the wall outside with a sickening whump.

My chest is tight with choking sobs. The darkness in the room grows around my head. My mother returns and pulls me into the bathroom. She makes a few attempts to clean the blood from the still-bleeding cuts and bites. Almost immediately she says we're going to the hospital emergency room. She grabs my hand and pulls me down the hallway, grabbing her purse and car keys as we run to the car. I have a towel that grows red as I dab it on my numerous bleeding bites and scratches. At the emergency room the doctor peers closely at the deep wounds that cover the top of my head, the backs of my ears, my shoulders, and the deep gouges running down my upper arms and back. He says he's never, ever seen a house cat attack in such a manner. "It's perplexing, considering this is the way a wild cat would bring down prey – with a systematic assault to the head."

As the doctor continues speaking I tune out and consider my reflection in the mirror behind the doctor. My Hawaiian-bleached white hair is bloody and matted, hanging in pink strings from my punctured scalp. I turn slightly to view my shoulders, grimacing at the sight of my tanned skin marred with deep gashes and scratches. The doctor calls other doctors into the examination room and they cautiously circle me like I'm prey, collectively shaking their heads. Nurses dab me with

Overlay – A Tale of One Girl's Life in 1970s Las Vegas

Mercurochrome-soaked cotton balls and apply various sized bandages and wraps to my orange-stained wounds.

Still somewhat in shock, I fall asleep that night thinking it's the first time I've ever felt that my mother cared for me. Even considering my burning skin, I don't quite regret the night's experience. The unwavering attention of the doctors, nurses – and my mother – is almost worth it.

The following Monday I start fifth grade at Ruby Thomas Elementary. I set my alarm for the morning, get dressed and walk to school. I don't see my mother and don't know if she's already left for work or hadn't come home from the night before. Still armed with the bravery of my summer experiences, I join a theater club and write a soap opera episode for kids called, "As the Stomach Turns." I star in the production, and it airs on our school's television channel for the entire school to see. I also join the dance club. We make up dances and perform them in a group on the stage overlooking the lunch area.

When creating artwork for a banner to be displayed at our school, my language arts teacher suggests I enter a local art contest. The theme of the contest ironically is "Family." Using colored pencils borrowed from school, I draw a very detailed forest scene depicting a family of deer. Having practiced drawing horse haunches and cat faces for years, the deer anatomy comes easily to me. I detail the set of horns on the father deer who stands tall and proud, front and center, watching over his family. The mother deer stands next to him, protected yet strong. Her large warm eyes watch their baby who grazes nearby, safe and unconcerned. Their idyllic world is full of trees and flowers and grass to eat. I draw families of birds in the trees, and families of bees hovering over the flowers. A stream cuts through the corner of the drawing, and I pencil in faint images of families of fish. The sun rises above the distant snow-covered mountain peaks, and its rays stretch across the entire scene bringing light and illumination and life.

A few weeks later my teacher announces to the class that I've won first place in the city's art contest. My piece will be displayed at the local mall for the next several weeks and she urges us to take our families to see the display. I try to get my mom to go to the mall, but she's never free to go. Each weekend my friends and I walk to the mall to visit my piece. When the exhibition ends, my piece returns to the classroom with a large, blue First Place ribbon attached to the top right hand corner. One of the judges has written 'Amazing humanistic aspects aptly captured by the artist' on the back of the ribbon.

The Artist! The judge called me The Artist! After painstakingly rolling the artwork into a tight tube so it won't smudge or bend, I carry it carefully home to share my good fortune with my mother. I try hard not to get my hopes up, but I even let my imagination go as far as imagining she will take me out to a congratulatory dinner. She doesn't come home after work or at all that evening. Though I want to have my picture professionally framed and displayed in our living room, I tack it onto my bedroom wall instead. Eventually I discard it.

By the time I see my mother again my enthusiasm for my win has diminished to the point that I never even mention my prize-winning portrait of Family.

Chapter Twenty Six

Fold: In poker, when a player declines a hand and drops out of a bet.

One fall evening I run through the dusk to reach my apartment. I stop short when I find my father sitting on the curb outside of my apartment. His head hangs low, and he brings a cigarette shakily to his mouth. As I walk forward from the gloom, he lifts his head. "Penut, my mother died."

"Are we going to her funeral?" I ask, excited that her death might mean a new family experience for me. Although I haven't been to a funeral, I often watch people on television attend funerals. They wear black, cry and pull their hair at the burial, and afterward go to a big house where many people bring platters and casserole dishes of home-cooked food to assist the bereaved. They gather around the food table and whisper good things about the deceased. Families attend funerals together, traveling from far away to pay their respects to the departed. I wonder how many of our family members will be there. Will I get a chance to meet new family members? Other cousins? Great aunts and great uncles?

"She's already buried, Penut. She died a few days ago, and John already buried her without letting Ana and I know."

Now just what kind of family burial is this? Just like that my grandmother is gone, swallowed by the earth, and taking all chances for connection and understanding into the casket with her.

My father suggests we go to the Sizzler, brushing the back of one hand across his wet eyes. At the restaurant my father's in the mood to talk, so I listen. He says his own father had been the type of man you would want as a friend. The oldest of seven children, Kenny Glynn spent a hardworking happy childhood as the handsome football star of the small Kansas town in which they lived. Most of the inhabitants of the town were related to the Glynns in some form or fashion. Amazingly enough, the Glynns were known for their big families and even bigger parties. Relatives would travel from far away just to spend the holidays with the Glynns. All the uncles knew how to play real Irish 'seconds', and Kenny and his siblings grew up dancing, singing and enjoying a good life in America, adored and loved by their tight knit Irish clan. Kenny showed promise in academics and his teacher begged his father to reconsider his decision, but Kenny was forced to leave school to work the farm in support of the big Irish family. After a few years of tilling the soil, Kenny made the unorthodox decision to depart for California, as his ancestors had left their country in years past to make their way in the states. He'd known nothing but success as a boy, and had no reason to think success wasn't his birthright wherever he went. He told the family he had big dreams of entering the real estate market, and would send for them once he was successful. The family couldn't wait that long though. That winter my great grandfather tired of tilling the frosty Kansas flatlands. One early evening he walked into the family home, pulled off his gloves and announced they were all moving to California after Kenny.

As the Great Depression settled across the states, Kenny began his life in California by marrying one of his neighbors, a half-Irish, half-Italian beauty named Marguerite: my grandmother Marge. He began his contracting business, and they built their first home around the corner from their two sets of parents. He later designed several other developments in the neighborhood where he lived. Two children were born, my aunt Ana, and my dad, John, or "Buddy" as he was called after the actor Buddy Rogers, who was a childhood friend of my grandfather's. Buddy's success in Hollywood was one of the reasons my grandfather Kenny left Kansas for California.

Overlay – A Tale of One Girl's Life in 1970s Las Vegas

When the kids were 4 and 2, the 30 year old Kenny had to make a quick stop one evening. He was driving a delivery truck, a temporary job he'd taken while riding out the Great Depression. The short stop caused a can of paint to fly from the back of the truck and strike him on the back of the head. Other than informing his wife about his injury when he returned home, he said no more about it. He died in the middle of the night on October 1, 1933 of a spontaneous cerebral hemorrhage, holding his head and screaming while his wife looked on, horrified and unable to help. He passed quickly, in full view of his two little children who stood crying in the doorway of their parent's bedroom. Marge found herself a widow at the age of 23 in the midst of the Depression with two small children and no way to support her family. What choice did a woman have back then but to remarry? The lucky man was a friend of her husband's, John Juneman. He did Marge a big favor by marrying her and saving her and her children from certain starvation. He also helped himself to the sexual favors of her four year old daughter, my aunt Ana, while he was at it.

My father explained that when growing up, his was the kind of house where you didn't invite anyone to visit. When he began rebelling he was shuffled from relative to relative during his childhood. The favored son of the favored son was just too big of a trouble maker for John Juneman's household. My father joined the Marines before he was 16 as an attempt to find stability and security – and a home. By the time he left the service four years later, he had developed an affection for Kool menthols and good Irish whiskey. Both would prove to be his undoing, and he would spend the rest of his life alone. His life was a byproduct of the lack of a father's love and presence, and his resulting addictions. The remaining members of Kenny's family were all dead, having developed drinking problems of their own. Cirrhosis of the liver was the number one cause of death of the siblings.

I lay awake in bed for a long time that night, alone in my dusty, now-faded canopy bed. I could almost hear the laughter and fiddle-playing of the extended family I almost had. I imagine my Irish uncles and aunts and cousins and great aunts and grandparents. For the first time in my life my father is a human being to me, born into what should have been the kind of family I have long imagined. Perhaps through a series of tragic and unfortunate circumstances he'd instead become a victim of untimely death and addiction. He became something new and different in my mind that night, not just 'my father – the alcoholic.' I wonder how life would have been different if Kenny had lived and John Juneman had not entered the lives of my father and Ana. What if Kenny had weathered the Great Depression and continued building the houses and apartment complexes in his neighborhood. Would my father still have become an alcoholic? Would having a father around have saved him from the life he'd made for himself? I fall asleep dreaming of Christmas, when I will again travel to my aunt and uncle's condo in Hawaii. I'm patiently counting the months until I can be with them again.

In November I return home at dusk to find my mother sitting on one of the no longer new red velvet couches. She has a serious look on her face and asks me to sit down. When I do, she tells me that my uncle John has died. The air rushes forth from my mouth as if I'd been punched in the stomach. Not my uncle John! John of the easy smile and the constant laugh and the pressed slacks and short-sleeved flowered Hawaiian shirts. John, who taught me the meaning of the word 'contradict' and that annoying habits such as saying, "Nuh uh!" in response to everything was annoying and should be ceased immediately. John, who was always ready with a quick joke or a clever play on words. John, who took me out to breakfast one day and told me how lucky I was to receive my own personal mini scoop of ice cream, then laughed with his wide open mouth when I took a big bite of that whipped scoop of butter.

"Are we going to the funeral?"

"No."

I try not to think about what John's death means for my own future. Sitting cross-legged on the floor in front of the television that night, I stare at the shows and I stare at the commercials. Where is John now? Is his body in the ground? Can dirt fall through a crack of the coffin and land on his face? Can he feel it? Does he know he is dead? I think of a time when my mother had taken me to a junkyard on the outskirts of Las Vegas. A palomino horse was lying on the side of the road, as if he'd just fallen over dead. The smell emanating from that horse was so thick and pungent, it carried over the junkyard and I'd had to pull my shirt up and cover my face just to breathe. I wonder about John. The smell of death. There is something so sickening about death. Something embarrassing about decomposition. Your body just ceases to exist and there's nothing you can do about it.

I don't hear anything at all from my aunt in the subsequent months, even though I write long letters when we have stamps. She doesn't respond. That Christmas Eve and Christmas Day my mother works, or just isn't home or is on a date or dead in an alley somewhere. She leaves a wrapped gift for me under the little green plastic Christmas tree. I wake up alone on Christmas morning, open the present and find a record player. She'd stuck in a few 45s to accompany the record player; instrumentals from Disney movies I'd long ago ceased to find of any interest. A better choice would have been disco 45s like Taste of Honey or Ohio Players, but that would have required my mother know something about me and my interests.

I place the record player in my room, grab the 45s to take with me and go outside to try to find some other kids. I knock as I go from door to door and apartment to apartment. All the other latchkey kids of the Cambridge Apartments must be somewhere else with their own families.

As I work my way back home with my hands stuffed in the pockets of my cheap high-water sweatpants to guard against the wind's chill, I again consider the violin-playing Glynn uncles and mourn a life I don't lead. I thread my way to the end of the apartment complex to the cinderblock wall.

Taking one record at a time, I fling it as hard as I can against the wall. I pick up the pieces that are still big enough to throw again, yelling, "Fuck you Bambi! Fuck you Pinocchio! Fuck YOU Sleeping Beauty!" I throw them repeatedly again and again until all that's left are tiny fragments of record vinyl that I leave lying on the ground.

I return to my apartment and fold for the day.

Chapter Twenty Seven

Hit: In blackjack, to take another card. The card received is also called a hit.

As anyone who knows will tell you it can be a curse to be awake in this life. If you're paying any sort of attention to what's going on around you, you might understand that you can be either cursed or blessed and hope it's nothing less than equal measures. If it isn't equal, you better hope you're blessed more often than cursed. That spring day in my tenth year when I stayed home from school I didn't know that the scales had just tipped. My entire life was about to fly off the cliff because the road had just run out from underneath me.

Late in the afternoon I take a long bath. It's one of those perfect baths taken in the perfect solitude of a perfectly silent house. Mr. Bubbles surrounds me and I make bubble bouffant hairstyles and bubble beards. I wash my hair. My hair's grown very long, and all the television commercials emphasize the importance of good Conditioning so I slather on the No More Tangles with reckless abandon. Afterwards, I wrap my body in a towel and am thinking of giving myself a pedicure when I open the bathroom door and gasp in surprise to find my mother directly outside the bathroom door passionately kissing a tall jean-jacketed man. At least this is the order I interpret what's before my eyes: mom, home, kissing, man, jean-jacket. She laughs in that too-happy way I've come to know is a sure sign of impending danger and says, "Marlayna, this is your new father. We got married today."

My stomach is a hard little ball. I mumble something and escape through the open door to my bedroom. I meet my new father in a towel, and I don't even know his first name! I pull on a tee shirt and sweatpants and slide quietly into the living room where my mother is sitting on her husband's lap. A gallon of pink wine is on the coffee table with two glasses. I sit alone on the fading red velvet love seat and ask my new father what his name is.

"Dean Parker," he says, squinting at me through the haze of his cigarette smoke. His small, square teeth are nicotine-stained. He says I might just be pretty enough to be a model.

I say I want to be a model and despite my reserve, feel a smile slide across my face. I flip my wet hair off one shoulder for good measure.

"I know some people. We'll see what we can do about that."

I look at him and a glimmer of hope sprouts in my heart. Maybe, just maybe I dare to hope, Dean Parker will turn out to be all right. Just all right. I don't dare hope for more than that. That night my mom drives our old car to the trailer park where Dean stays and we help pack what little he owns, just as we had several years before with Mr. Nice. Dean doesn't own much other than clothes and a few record albums so I don't ask him for anything. On the way home he sits in the passenger seat of our car, smoking cigarette after cigarette, repeating, "I can't believe I have a wife and a daughter!" as if he's just won the grand prize at a carnival.

I bounce up and down in the back seat, singing out loud because I'm lost in the mania. I forget to act dignified. I want to believe that Dean Parker is good and that the unexpected entrance of this newest stepfather will be the answer to everything. I wonder if he plays the fiddle or makes good linguini or has children of his own or parents with a house in the country. I've always wanted grandparents with a house in the country and surely Dean brings something new and wonderful to this arrangement.

What he brings is a whole lot of stories and the truth is a vague goal at the end of a tunnel. Dean is a prolific songwriter, or at least that's what he claims. Every now and then when the radio is playing he turns up the volume and says he wrote that particular song. He says he didn't make a penny for selling these songs that he penned on napkins and matchbook covers. Dean Parker is from Louisiana - a mysterious place he claims is full of wild gators and unusual foods. To prove it Dean makes a big pot of Gumbo shortly after he moves in. My mother's stereo is on in the living room while he cooks.

"Wrote this song," Dean calls from the kitchen as he chops ingredients for the Gumbo.

"Did you make a penny for this one?"

"Hell no, Mary."

"It's Marlayna."

"Say what?"

"My name is Marlayna. Not Mary."

Dean just continues singing over the chop-chop of his knife.

Gumbo is a strange stew with slimy vegetables called okra. I don't care how slimy it is though because it's real food and not a TV dinner. Maybe Dean will cook like Mr. Nice did. Unfortunately, the home-cooked meals don't become a habit, because consistent is one thing Dean is not, and no amount of storytelling can hide this fact.

Dean is consistent in one area - he doesn't work. At all. My mother continues to work her bar tending job during the day while Dean stays at our home watching television, smoking cigarettes and drinking vodka. With the addition of another person's expenses, our financial situation grows steadily worse as the months pass. Where there used to be just enough or mostly enough for two, now there is not enough for three. The differences are evident in our empty refrigerator and in the full liquor cabinet.

Where I was again used to being alone and enjoying the solitude of our little apartment, now there is Dean at home every day. When I wake up in the morning, he is snoring in the bedroom. When I come home from school he is sitting in a hazy cloud of smoke in our living room. When I go to sleep at night he is telling loud stories in our living room.

I spend as much time as I can away from the apartment by running around the Cambridge Apartments with the other kids. When the sun dips down I hope I'll be invited to come inside another friend's apartment to spend the night. When I'm not invited, I just ask. When I'm refused, I regrettably return home and go straight to my bedroom. Sometimes I eat whatever dinner there is, but usually just stay in my room with the door closed and my television turned up for company.

As a newlywed, my mother spends her evenings at home again. While this may sound like an improvement, the new assortment of strange characters that visit our apartment is not. They lounge about on our red velvet sofas, spilling red wine onto our carpets and exhaling their smoke into our living room.

As the noise for their laughter and storytelling increases each night, I have to turn up my television so I can concentrate on my homework. Since my bedroom shares a common wall with the living room there's little I can do to get away from the ruckus.

I've been hit and I know it.

Chapter Twenty Eight

Proposition Bet: A one-roll bet that's also known as a center bet.

"I'm Rick," calls a man's voice one evening through my closed bedroom door, "Can I come in?" I open my door and he is standing in the encircling gloom of the hallway. He looks safe because he is smiling. Since I assume he is the guest of my mother or Dean, I move aside and he passes into my bedroom, trailing a scent of patchouli, sweat and smoke. With one hand, he reaches up over my head and pushes my door closed behind him.

Comfortably reclining his body upon my canopy bed, his limbs relax as if he belongs there. He looks up at me from under his long blonde lashes and smiles. He asks what I'm doing in my room all alone. Looking into the blue of his eyes, I explain that I'm reading and with a wave of my hand indicate the novel bent open on my bed. Instead of acknowledging my book as I expect him to do, he stands up and walks to my window overlooking the front parking lot. From my windowsill, he gently lifts one of my tiny potted cacti and turns it back and forth with his long, elegant fingers. He asks if I know that you can make drugs out of cactus.

No, I didn't know this.

"You make peyote from it. Peyote takes you to another plane where anything's possible." He returns distractedly to sit next to me on my bed, now closer to me than he was the first time he sat down. "You can turn into a real animal when you take peyote, like a cougar or a mountain lion. It's wild shit."

Images from the anti-drug movie I'd just watched in health class called 'Dead Is Dead' pop in my head, and I tell Rick about the movie and how it showed a woman throwing up cottage cheese all over a dirty staircase.

"Nah, that shit ain't real, girl. Drugs are fun. They just make that shit up because they want you to think drugs are bad."

"Drugs aren't bad?"

"Not if you know how to use them. Did you know that you can inject anything into your veins to get high?"

Canned laughter from the Carol Burnet show in the background grabs my attention. I glance over at my little black and white television to see Carol dressed as a maid. "What do you mean by 'get high'?"

"Getting high means to feel good. Like if you don't feel like drinking wine, you can just put it in a needle and inject it straight into your arm."

"Why would anyone want to do that?"

"Because it feels good. You could even inject milk in your arm if you wanted to."

"That's just crazy."

Overlay – A Tale of One Girl's Life in 1970s Las Vegas

"The whole world is crazy, little one."

"I don't think so."

"You'll understand when you're older." Rick lifts one of his skinny arms and shows me a long scar line of needle marks. "See? I know how to feel good."

"I hate needles. That doesn't sound like feeling good to me."

"I can show you sometime how fun it really is."

Since I don't say anything, he qualifies his offer by adding, "After all, I am your brother."

He looks nothing like the smiling dark eyed boy whose picture used to grace my mother's bedroom mirror. "My brother?"

"Dean's my father. That makes me your stepbrother."

"You're too old to be Dean's son."

"Well, not his real son, I mean, but we like say I'm his son."

"Saying it doesn't make it so."

He is silent for a moment. "So have you kissed a boy yet?"

My face heats with the sudden rush of blood. "I'm not telling you." I know from the way his lips turn up in the corners to a smile that I shouldn't have blushed. That I've indicated something I didn't mean to indicate. He places one of his hands on my upper thigh and squeezes. His opened hand encircles most of my thigh. "I could teach you to kiss. I'm a good kisser. Want to find out?"

I look down at the size of his man's hand on my little thigh, and out of sheer nervousness a giggle escapes from my lips. While I know his hand on my thigh isn't a good thing, I'm more afraid to be rude and push it off like my brain nudges me to do than to let it rest where it is.

In the momentary silence, drunken laughter erupts from the living room. Someone yells, "Aw, hell, you mother fucker, if you would've told me first, I wouldn't have run!" More laughter. The clink of a wine glass on the table. "Fuck you!" someone else yells in return. Guffaws. Snorts.

Rick leans forward then and I sit as still as a stone as his blonde mustache draws near. His eyes are blue, so blue, and in my statue state I watch his eyes grow bigger and bigger as his face nears mine.

"Come on back to the party, Rick," my mother says then from where she stands in the open door to my room. She motions for Rick to pass by her. Her voice is flat, yet it lifts at the end when she says his name as if she questions his existence. Her hand is in front of her throat as if guarding her words.

Rick stands and saunters slowly out of my room without a word. I'm both relieved and disappointed by his departure, and the realization that I liked his attention scares me. How could I want him to kiss me, know he shouldn't, want him to like me, yet want him not to notice me all at the same time? Later that evening I leave my room and walk through the living room on the pretense to get water from the kitchen. As I pour water into a glass, I lift my eyes casually to search for Rick in the crowd, acting as if it's an accident that I happen to look at him. My mother watches me, and I feel an unexpected appreciation for my mother. Rick looks at her, drops his eyes, and doesn't look at me again.

I see Rick one other time, a few days after the first time I meet him. I sit on my bedroom floor with my legs crossed, memorizing the nines of my multiplication tables. As I pore over the numbers... nine...eighteen...twenty-seven....thirty-six... a discordant thumping erupts in the living room, growing louder and louder.

Forty-five...fifty four...sixty-three.

Loud grunting and the rising voices of people in the living room alerts me to open my bedroom door and run the short distance to the kitchen. A group of men and my mother are watching two men circle each other around our small dining table. One is Dean and the other is Rick. Both men have steak knives taken from our kitchen drawer clasped in one hand, and as one lunges the other ducks, two drunken ungraceful jousters.

"I'm trying to memorize my NINES! Can't you kill each other somewhere else, PLEASE!" I return to my room when no one pays any attention to my proposition.

Chapter Twenty Nine

Craps: To crap out.

I may have escaped Rick, but there's no escaping Dean or the growing list of incidents that now regularly plague our home. One evening I carry a big bag of trash past Dean. I set it down on the living room carpeting to open our front door so I can carry it to the dumpster. Dean watches me and makes no move to get up and open the door for me. The overhead light outside our apartment has been burned out for so long that when I open the door I know to hesitate for a moment to let my eyes adjust to the inky darkness. Out of the gloom rush two men so quickly that I instinctively hold the bag of trash up as a shield and push against them as they push forward. Then I slip between their two bodies. Dropping the garbage bag, I run forward into the darkness. As I round the corner of my apartment building, I look behind and see they aren't following me but I keep running anyway. I run to the manager's apartment and pound my fists upon her door, puffing and panting. I remain there for a long time, even though she doesn't answer. I have nowhere else to go.

It's a bitterly cold winter night, and I have no jacket and am just thinly clothed in the T-shirt I put on to take out the trash. I don't want to go back to the apartment in case the men are still there. Nor do I want to wander around in case the men are also wandering around looking for me. I don't even know who they are, what they want or why in the world they charged into our apartment. So I sit on a lounge chair at the swimming pool. Since it's a moonless night, I'll be safe in the darkness and no one will see me while I try to figure out a course of action. Over the next few hours, I weigh my options. Should I go to friend's house and tell their parents what happened? No, it's too embarrassing to talk about my circumstances with adults who I already believe don't like me. Should I knock on a stranger's door and hope I get lucky and find a decent person? No, the risk is too great that the person answering the door is a pedophile or a murderer. Later that night, I check the parking lot and see my mother's car. I knock on my apartment door and she answers and doesn't ask where I've been. Instead she leads me to the bedroom where Dean is lying in bed, smoking. "Look what they've done to him."

Dean rarely wears a shirt, so it's easy to see the already developing green and red bruises decorating his ribcage. "They stomped my ass with waffle boots," he mumbles over the cigarette in his mouth. I don't know what waffle boots are, or why those two men would stomp him with them. Asking the questions doesn't bring satisfactory answers from Dean or my mother. So I stop taking the trash out in the evenings, and always make sure the front door is locked after that night.

In the beginning, Dean is like a giant playmate. He lets me apply gooey face masks to his bristly, unshaven face, and then lets me peel them slowly off in an attempt to keep the mask intact in one piece. His face always messes up the mask, as the rubbery pieces cling to his stubble. He lets me give him massages with mint-scented alcohol. "Just don't get the shit in my eye," he says as I carefully drip the alcohol over his back. When I finish the massages, he asks me to walk across his back, around and around. My mom sits on the couch drinking wine, and doesn't leave the room even once to use the restroom. Then there is the Gumbo, which is worth more than a few points in my book because it's real food: warm and fresh. Sometimes he makes special Louisiana sausage called "boudin" or 'blood sausage, preparing them in a way he'd learned from his mother who lives somewhere in Louisiana. The food leads me to hope Dean is the beginning of something new and good for my mother and me.

I am wrong.

Overlay – A Tale of One Girl's Life in 1970s Las Vegas

Within a few months of his living with us, my feelings about him morph from a mild annoyance to an impossible-to-veil hatred I didn't know I had the capacity to feel. While my years spent watching television taught me that vampires sucked blood from you and then you pretty much died immediately, I didn't know there were more frightening monsters in the world. Real monsters that could drain your blood little by little, day by day. In this way, you died a slow and ignorant death, and you might not even know it was happening until it was too late. While you might avoid the trauma of a bite on the neck or knife in your belly, the long, slow and silent death seemed to be far worse that being quickly put out of your misery.

For example, Dean began making up arbitrary rules to be the authoritarian stepfather. Though I'd had free run of the apartment complex since we'd moved in, Dean now said I was no longer allowed to go to the third floor of our building because drug dealers lived there. In our three story apartment building, the third floor was the only place worth going because all the buildings were connected in one long breezeway on the third floor. Kids regularly raced each other along the length of the breezeway and gathered above for games and contests. If there were drug dealers up there I had never seen one. So I pay no attention to Dean's rule and continue to do as I please, fairly confident he will never know where I go or what I do. What right does a cigarette-smoking, vodka-drinking stepfather have to tell me what to do? One night when I return home, he surprises me when he asks if I've been on the third floor of our apartment complex.

"Yes."

"I told you that you're not allowed to go up there."

"It's a stupid rule."

He looks at my mother, then back at me. "I'm going to whip you with a belt."

My mother looks down at the matted shag carpeting. I've never been hit in my life, and think surely she will tell him so but she is silent. Instead, Dean tells me to follow him to my room, where he and my mother sit next to each other on my fading canopy bed quilt. I'm instructed to take my pants down and lay over Dean's lap. He whips me with a belt three times, and I slide off his lap and angrily jerk my pants back up, not saying a word. I won't give him the pleasure. The next day after school I go up to the third floor, as usual. When I return home, I'm questioned and again I answer truthfully that I've been upstairs. I receive four whips and still don't say a word. The scene is repeated on the third day as well, and the whips are harder and I lose count of how many I receive. Still, I am silent.

Perhaps Dean figures out on the fourth day that I won't deny what I've done regardless of the consequences, and that I'll simply continue to do as I please. He stops asking me about my visits to the third floor and the beatings cease. I continue to do what I want and he stops asking me about anything at all. He stops talking to me entirely. If I'd had any lingering doubts whether my mother was really taken away by aliens several years ago, I'm now absolutely convinced she was. I stop talking to her apart from any communication that is absolutely necessary. Our house divides in two: the two of them and me. I spend any time I have to be at my house in my room alone with my door locked.

Dean Parker and I don't waste a whole lot of time learning on which side of the line we stand – and so, in my tenth year, the battlefield lines are clearly drawn. He refuses to concede that I've won, and I begin plotting how to force his hand.

No one is as patient or as stubborn as I am.

I'm learning how to gamble.

I will make sure he craps out.

PART FOUR

(1976 – 1978)

Chapter Thirty

True Odds: The ratio of the number of times one event will occur to the number of times another event will occur. The odds posted in a casino are usually not the true odds.

I'm not sure exactly when, but one day I realize we are poor.

We are poor and unhappy: a double serving of nastiness.

Although I fight this awareness with every iota of my being, our circumstances have crept inside and become a part of Me. I can no longer see anything else through this murky veil of misery. I can't escape the way our poverty hangs over and around us like a buzzing cloud of gnats. It's reflected in my worn clothing, our empty refrigerator and the lack of funds to pay for anything I want to do. What bothers me in particular is that we hadn't been poor before, in which case I wouldn't have known the difference. We're poor out of sheer embarrassing laziness. If Dean would work, we'd have more money than when my mother and I had been alone. There would be three of us sharing the salary of two, rather than three of us sharing the salary of one.

If I think too much about our arrangement, the choking feeling works its way up my throat and tightens its grip. Like a fervent and desperate prayer, I remind myself that I'm one of the lucky ones, and so begins my habitual comparison of my circumstances to the other kids around me. I have a whole host of children with whom to compare myself, as there is no shortage of similarly disadvantaged children in the Cambridge Apartments.

Take Angela, who lives with her single mother and three little brothers in an unfurnished apartment with very little food and no adult supervision. Her mother is never at home, and this leaves Angela tasked with caring for her three little brothers without much in the way of supplies. Though my situation isn't all that great, I have much space in my consciousness to truly feel sorry for Angela and her brothers. I feel a strange sort of responsibility for them as well.

The first time I spend the night at their apartment, I'm just happy to be away from Dean. As dinner time rolls around we search the kitchen and find one single box of dehydrated mashed potatoes. There's no milk or butter to add to the mix as the directions suggest, so Angela adds hot water to the potato flakes. Then she shakes salt and pepper to the mix. "It helps with the taste," she says as she stirs a wooden spoon around the pasty looking clump. Her brothers eat the reconstituted potato flake mix without a single complaint. I dip a spoon into the portion Angela allotted me, hesitantly tasting the crunchy-dry mix. It's truly disgusting, but I don't want to be rude and not eat with them. I briefly consider running home to my own apartment to see if we have any food I can contribute to the meal, but quickly think better of this idea. I didn't know who or what I might find there....and it could potentially be much worse than tasteless potato flakes.

They don't own a television, so when night falls Angela suggests we have a talent show. Their apartment living room is empty other than one naked mattress, so she says the performer will do their act on the mattress while the audience watches from the floor. One audience member will hold a flashlight. Angela's brothers take turns jumping on the dirty mattress and singing for their performances. None of her brothers can pronounce their Rs properly, so we're treated to song versions of "Whinestone Cowboy" and "Boogie on Weggae Woman" and "Philadelphia Fweedom." I hold the flashlight as they dance and play the air guitar, their skinny little legs kicking and their long stringy hair lifting and falling as they jump up and down.

Overlay – A Tale of One Girl's Life in 1970s Las Vegas

When Angela's turn comes, she jumps onto the mattress and hesitates for a moment in the lighted cone of the flashlight. The upward angle of the light creates shadows on her thin frame that create a facade of curves on her skinny body. She slowly bends forward, and quickly snaps her long hair back. Spreading her legs, she moves her hips around in exaggerated circles, swiveling and circling as if she were using a Hula Hoop in slow motion. Breath skitters from my mouth like gravel, and I nervously laugh and ask, "Angela! What is THAT?"

She doesn't stop her bizarre movements to answer my question, instead lowering her eyes and half-closing her lips. Angela's three younger brothers sit Indian-style before the mattress; rapt, silent and focused on the movements of their ten year old sister. "It's sexy dancing," Angela finally whispers in between hip-swivels. "Haven't you ever sexy-danced before?"

My discomfort at Angela's dance grows so that I feel sick inside and want to believe it's the dry mashed potatoes rolling around disagreeably in my stomach but I'm only trying to fool myself because I know the movements come from a place I know nothing about. I shake my head when she suggests we do a Sexy Dance together, so she reaches down and grabs me and pulls me to her tiny frame to grind her hips against mine. I back up, wondering why her brothers still don't react to this strange behavior, and stumble backwards pulling us both down on the hard floor.

"Let's take off our shirts and sexy dance!" Angela squeals in laughter.

I sit down Indian-style next to one of her brothers for protection and say I'm too tired. Angela throws off her little T-shirt anyway, and she doesn't have just the little hard buds of breasts that most of us ten year old girls are sporting, but real tiny roundish lumps. She waves her skinny arms around, continuing the grinding movements of her hips. Her long brown hair trails around as she bends over, and whips her head back and forth. She appears to be completely oblivious to us.

I desperately wish her mother would come home. It doesn't occur to me to just go home to my own apartment. I don't know how I can keep these four children safe, or from exactly what, but something about Angela and her brothers makes me feel I am supposed to protect them. So I stay the night with Angela and her brothers, and sleep with them on the mattress in the living room. We cover ourselves with dirty sheets. I go to sleep hungry. Her mother doesn't come home at all that night.

Walking home from school a few weeks later, Angela tells me that she and her brothers are going to spend the night at her ex-stepfather's house the next night, and invites me to come with her. She says it's fun at his house.

"What's fun about it?" I imagine an oversized swimming pool or a horse stable. I'd visited a friend a few years back who'd moved from the cinderblock apartments. Their new house was gigantic, and the back yard was stacked with activities like a pack of dominoes. Directly behind the house was the swimming pool. Behind that was the pool house. Then a large field of grass for soccer and football and then the best part: the horse stables and riding ring. I'd gone home that night so sick with jealousy I couldn't even eat my TV dinner.

"You'll see how fun it is if you come," is all Angela says, a secret smile playing at her lips.

Her mother drives us across town the next afternoon in her old station wagon, a cigarette hanging from her lipsticked lips. She deposits us in front of a small, old house, honks once and drives away. Families of weeds are doing their very best to escape the chain link fence that leans at odd angles around the property. I'm disappointed to see there is no pool or horse stables at this run-down place.

Begrudgingly, I follow Angela and her brothers up the steps and when I walk into the ex-stepfather's house, I know from the drop in my stomach that something is terribly, terribly wrong at this place. Although plenty of daylight remains outside, little of it penetrates the damp gloom of the house. As my heartbeat accelerates, I look outside through one of the dingy windows and begin the now-familiar argument with myself that I'm imagining danger where no danger exists. The house is just dirty, I argue with myself. So what if there is nothing to do in the darkened inside? We could go outside and find some other kids to play Red Rover or Red Light Green Light.

I hear the backfire of the station wagon as it chugs away from the dank little house at the end of the cul-de-sac at the same time that the front door slams behind me. We have been shot, catapulted, fired into this house. A strangling sense of abandonment pushes up from my belly and threatens to explode from my throat in a primal scream. My chest begins a slow heave for breath. Turning toward the sound of movement, Angela's stepfather lifts his girth from the well-worn easy chair where he has been sitting and moves toward us. He's a very big guy, with unevenly cut graying hair and a belly that greets you from over the top of his shorts. "I'm Big Ray," he says to me and extends a meaty white hand that I don't know what to do with other than politely shake even though I shrink inside at the thought of touching him. He eyes Angela at the same time as he offers us peanut butter sandwiches. I have no appetite and politely decline, but the other kids eagerly accept his offer.

A teenage boy enters the kitchen wearing only white underwear and begins spreading peanut butter across pieces of white bread he arranges on the countertop. Having no siblings of my own and not knowing if this is the way older brothers dress at home, I turn my head away so I won't look. After all, it's the middle of the day. Shouldn't he be dressed by now? Who is he? The real son of Big Ray? Why is he not introduced? I try not to look at him or Big Ray, but can feel the burning pinpricks of their eyes on me.

I consider leaving the house immediately but feel a conflict building. Big Ray and the underwear-clad boy are much bigger than me. What if they chase me down? To further complicate matters, I don't know exactly where we are. I'm too afraid to ask to use their phone to call my mother, and who knows if I can even find her? Conflicted between being an obedient child or saving myself, I just stand in the living room pushing my cuticles back with my thumbnail. If I leave, what will happen to Angela and her brothers? Perhaps my being there will make a difference.

As the teenager continues wiping peanut butter back and forth across the bread in the kitchen, Big Ray returns to his easy chair and asks Angela to sit on his lap and say hello.

"Let's go play hide and seek outside," I say, and everyone ignores me. Angela's brothers are lost now in the screen of the big television. The teenager spreads peanut butter. I turn my head slightly, enough so that from the corner of my eye I can watch Angela approach Big Ray and fold her little body sideways across his lap. He leans forward and sticks his tongue in her mouth. Angela's beautiful long hair falls back across Big Ray's arm as the pressure of his kiss pushes her head backwards. Angela's brothers continue to watch television, completely oblivious to this abuse of their sister.

I stand in the same spot I'd taken when I'd first entered the house, and still haven't moved either of my feet a single step. Overtaken by the sudden idea to blend into the background so I won't be noticed, I move in what I hope is an imperceptible way toward Angela's brothers, joining them on the floor to gaze at the television set. I needn't have bothered to be discreet as Big Ray pays no attention to me as I slip past him. Eyes wide yet seeing nothing, I listen to the slurping noises of Angela and her stepfather behind my back over the noise of the cartoon characters. As the boys sit motionless and unconcerned I'm sick to realize that the behavior of Angela and her stepfather is nothing new or unusual to this group.

Angela gets up behind me and I feel Big Ray's eyes on my back. "Come here."

I turn around and look directly at him. "No," I answer in what I hope is a firm voice. Angela stands next to his chair, smiling at me.

"Come here for a minute. I want to tell you a secret." He's still sitting in the chair, with his legs spread and his big belly straining the front of his white T-shirt. There's a big brown stain where his belly button is.

"I don't want to hear the secret."

"You have to come here. I said so."

"No, I don't."

"If you know what's good for you, you'll come over here right now. Come on, I won't hurt you. It's just a little secret."

His voice drops a couple of notes, causing the little blonde hair on my arms to lift in alarm. My heart pounds so loud I'm hoping it will stir the boys from their television show. I imagine it will call them to action. They'll hear the sound of my pounding heart and know that nothing about this is right and if we all band together and run out as one group we stand a good chance at making it to another street and knocking on someone's door and having them shut it behind us and keep us safe. Then we can call my mother and have her pick us up. Angela and her brothers can live with us in my room. Dean will move away....

None of this happens.

The eyes of the boys remain glued to the television, their mouths open and slack, their faces and necks tipped back and relaxed. They are oblivious to the sound of my pounding heart. I look from side to side and take in a deep, rattling breath. I can see the teenager in the kitchen putting the sandwiches together and slapping them down on paper plates.

After much cajoling and several direct orders from Big Ray, I stand. Not because he orders me to do so, but because I figure if I give in and allow this, then I will avoid that. It's a conscious decision. A choice between two evils. I want to think that my way of eyeing him and the teenager will communicate to them that regardless of the fact that I arrived on the crazy train at this horrible place, I am not their victim. Instinctively I know it's very important that I don't appear weak or too obedient and I have to straddle the line in between. So I do as I'm asked, and sit on Big Ray's lap and when he inserts his salty tongue in my mouth, I taste eggs and tobacco and the Glow-pop Angela had sucked on during the drive to Big Ray's house.

None of us are allowed outside to play that day. We fall asleep on the living room floor, the television still blaring the too-loud, inane laughter of cartoon characters. When I awake in the middle of the night and reach out my hand to make sure Angela is still safe next to me, I feel nothing but sticky fabric. She isn't there. Even worse, her little brother Phillip is not there either. I know from the coldness of the blanket that they haven't been there for a long time. In that awful darkness of Big Ray's house, I lay on his living room floor and know where they are and what they're doing, and feel sick for Angela, for Phillip, for me, and for her little brothers who can't even yet pronounce their Rs properly and no one cares at all. I must be the only person in the world who cares about the Sparks children and this thought makes me spitting angry. Rage fills me at her mother for sending us there and not protecting her own children, and endangering me. The rage burns and spreads throughout my body until it encompasses Angela and her brothers and the teenager and Big Ray and my mom and my dad and Dean.

The question burns in my head so fiercely I can't sleep for the rest of that awful night. Why aren't the adults in our lives protecting us?

I don't tell my mother what happened the night before. I'm too embarrassed to tell her that I allowed that fat nasty man to stick his tongue in my mouth. Truthfully, a small part of me is afraid to tell her the truth. What if she doesn't do anything with the information? She isn't protecting me from Dean....why would I think she would call the police on Big Ray? It's easier to remain quiet and optimistic and think that if I had told her then maybe she would have become enraged and driven to his house and cracked him over the head with that blaring television set. Although I can't imagine my mother capable of that level of passion, part of me holds out hope that that's exactly what she would have done if I'd told her. By not telling her I'm able to stay safe within the well-ordered boundaries of my own imagination.

What I also don't do is forget the fact that Angela knew what Big Ray would do and brought me to that house anyway. And on a warm evening a few weeks later, while running around the complex with the other apartment kids, Angela and I get into an argument. It starts over something small, something silly. It turns when she kicks me hard in the stomach. I sink down against the wall behind me, trying hard to suck in a breath. I want to cry out in pain, but I can't draw in a big enough breath to force out a sob. A small child stands nearby, repeatedly asking me if I'm okay in a nervous, tittering voice. I can only nod as I wait for the pain to pass. When my breath finally returns, I allow the rage that has been brewing inside me since the night at Big Ray's house. I let it take me.

Howling with my mouth open as wide as I can stretch it, I run toward Angela as she stands and laughs with a group of kids. Her eyes fly wide and her mouth opens as she turns to run. When I see that she's afraid I fire up and run even faster. Both of us now screaming, I chase her up the three flights of stairs toward her apartment and leap on her back like a mountain lion before she can open her apartment door. I take her down hard with that leap, pummeling her with my fists as she falls to the ground. I punch her back, head, neck, and anything my fists can reach. I smash her face into the Astroturf that lines the floor outside her apartment door, holding it down and pressing it back and forth to muffle her screams. Then I stand up and kick her in her sides as hard as I can until she curls up in a fetal position like a tiny shrimp. When she lifts her arms to try to fend off my blows I kick them too. Then I grab her by her long brown hair and drag her back and forth across the ground, oblivious to her screaming. She flails her arms around and tries to fight me off, but she simply cannot match my rage. When she finally stops trying to fight back, I release her hair and stand panting over her as she crawls past me and knocks feebly on the bottom of her apartment door, sobbing in uneven fits and chokes. Phillip opens the door and quietly helps her in without uttering a word.

Satisfied that she's gotten what she deserved for the circumstances of my first kiss, I return home, my rage spent. Later that evening I knock on Angela's apartment door to apologize. Phillip answers the door and stares at me from the hollowness behind his two big, sorrowful brown eyes. I've already steeled my two feet solidly on the ground in my best imitation of a prizefighter because I fully expect him and his brothers to jump on me in defense of their sister. "She can't come out. She has a headache. Sowwy," is all he says, and he quietly shuts the door.

I know Angela's mother won't make an appearance at my apartment that night to defend her daughter and I'm not wrong. Deep inside I want her to show up in defense of her daughter, and I want to be punished for my attack on my friend. I want our mothers to get together to berate and punish me, because then I could have told them about Big Ray and the teenage boy in his underwear. I could have said that Big Ray and the teenaged boy took Natalie and Phillip away during the night. Nothing is ever said or done about my attack on Angela, and my own guilt that I feel is surely worse punishment than anyone else could have inflicted upon me. But my guilt does not help anymore. It does not solve the core problem for Natalie and her brothers.

Our friendship ends that night, and when Angela's mother moves her family away to a trailer park on the outskirts of town I breath a huge sigh of relief. I never see her again, but I continue to hate her for not fighting back – against Big Ray or me. I hate her more for not protecting herself, than I do how she endangered me.

Perhaps I am no better than the predators that surround me.

I've become an Underlay.

A bad bet.

Chapter Thirty One

Stiff: In blackjack, a hand that is not pat and may bust if hit once.

Thank God for sixth grade ... if only to kill the long uneventful summer. Contrary to what one might believe, there is only so much swimming one can do during a summer.

I hope my Aunt Ana is feeling better so my Christmas vacations with her can resume in a few short months. Now that Uncle John's passed away, I'm hoping my aunt will be even more inclined to want me to move in. I could keep her company, and keep her mind occupied while she grieves. I write to her often, describing in great detail my life and my friends, but I'm very careful to leave out the negative parts because I don't want her to feel any sadder than she already does. When I finally receive a letter and read that she is very sad and misses her mother and her husband very much, I respond with my favorite story. I fill several pages of the scented purple flowered stationary she'd sent me with my perfect cursive loops and lines with the story about how whenever she looks to the sky and sees beams of sunlight streaming through the clouds, she is seeing God take souls to heaven. Her next letter says she cried all day after reading my last letter. She says the idea of God calling Marge and John to Him was so comforting that she'd taken to watching the sky whenever possible to see evidence not only God but her mother and husband. She sits on her patio in the afternoons and again in the evenings, watching for evidence of God. She is comforted now by the cloud formations, as well as the flights of birds which seem to her like posses of angels breaking the monotony of soul-taking. She thanks me for reminding her of such a beautiful thing, and says that she's pinned my letter to her refrigerator so she can read it many times throughout the day.

I try to squelch the thought that going to her refrigerator many times a day means she is drinking a lot of wine, but it rises up and pierces the idyllic image I knows she's trying to create for me. If my beautiful Aunt falls prone to the curse of alcoholism that plagues my family, I don't know what I will do. She is the only beacon of light I have left.

In the meantime the school boundaries have been redrawn and most elementary schools on my side of town no longer offer sixth grade classes. One school is now designated to hold only sixth graders, so the sixth graders catch buses from all over the city to attend this one school. There are several upshots to this new arrangement. Having to move so many times means that I have many old friends all at one place at this new school. It's like a reunion of sorts as I meet up with kids I haven't seen since my first years at elementary school. I'm super excited about my new class, and when we have the first spelling bee of the year, I easily win on one of the most misspelled words in the English language: sergeant. Another upshot is since I take the bus across town and back I am out of the house for very long periods of time. What a relief!

The upshots almost make it okay that there isn't any money for school clothes, so I make do with the tight, faded shirts Ana bought the year before and the two pairs of pants that mostly fit me. A week into the school year, I ask my mother for a pair of white Keds, and I return home from school to find a large black pair of imitation Keds placed in the center of my bed. With one angry look, I can see they are way too big. I lift the shoes from the bed and turn them over in my hands and my stomach fills with acid. They are new and clean, their laces still tied together in a double knot and a bow, but the Salvation Army tag is still attached.

A bubble of fury detaches from the floor of my consciousness and explodes into my hands. I don't have socks. I don't have underwear. My mother's refusal to provide the one thing I've requested for the school year suddenly sends me over the edge. I pull my arm back and slam the shoes against the side of my bedroom wall. The release feels so good, I do it again, and then again. The white walls of my bedroom mar with black scuff marks from the tennis shoes, as I repeatedly slam them into the wall. Tears of relief stream down my face and I'm surprised to find I have been yelling, "I HATE HER I HATE HER I HATE HER I HATE HER," without even realizing I am saying a thing.

My bedroom door opens and Dean looks in to find me panting and sweating with the shoes in my hand, my arm cocked back for another throw. "Just what in the hell do you think you're doing?"

"The shoes….they don't fit me."

"You spoiled selfish brat. Look what you've done." He leans against my doorframe and points one long, skinny arm toward the black scuff marks on the wall.

I glance quickly at the wall and know to be silent. I stare back at him with my chest heaving.

"If I hear one more noise coming out of this room, I'll be back."

The little white clock on the table next to my bed indicates it's only 5:30. My mother won't be home for at least two more hours. I say nothing more, but look directly at him and refuse to drop my eyes. I quietly shut my bedroom door and lock it after he walks away and I don't come out again until I hear my mother's voice, even though I had to go to the bathroom so bad I nearly peed in my water cup.

That fall a new friend invites me to spend the weekend at her house. After school I run to my apartment where I plan to tell my mother that my friend's mother will be picking me up soon. My mother hasn't been working for a while and is home all the time now. Our front door is open and as I approach the living room I see the packed boxes.

NO!

My mother is in my bedroom, packing my books into a box. My bed has already been dismantled, the ruffled canopy lace lying crumpled on the ground.

"What's going on?"

"We're moving today."

"Who's moving?"

"What do you mean who? You, me and Dean, that's who."

"NO! I just started making new friends! Why do we always have to keep moving?"

"It's time to go, that's all. Put down your backpack and start packing."

"But I've been invited to spend the night at Rachel's house! Her mother's going to be here soon and I have to go!"

"Not anymore you're not. Call her and tell her you can't go."

"Mom, she's rich!"

"Now you're definitely not going. That's no reason to have a friend."

"She just happens to be rich! It isn't WHY I'm her friend. I want to see her house. She has a game room and a maid and-"

"Get packing," my mother says in the voice that ends conversations.

I hear Dean snoring from the master bedroom. I wander in and see a forgotten cigarette burning in the green glass ashtray beside the bed. I know why we're moving. It's because Dean doesn't work and my mother doesn't work and there is no one to pay for the three of us anymore. I have the sudden urge to take that cigarette and smash it in the middle of his Frankenstein forehead. I imagine it burning through his skin, his muscles, his tendons. I see it burn through his skull until it reaches the soft, pulpy brain. Surely if his brain is burned, he would die.

"Get packing," my mother repeats as she passes the bedroom door.

How I wish I could drop this stiff hand and pack for Aunt Ana's house instead.

Chapter Thirty Two

Vigorish: The fee or commission taken by the House.

Our rent house is so far from Aunt Ana's beautiful, light-filled condo that I revert to my childhood fantasy that this latest turn of affairs is a dream. It has no windows in the front – only crooked greenish clapboard tiles, some of which are hung askew. Watching quietly from the back seat window of our car, I deduce that the house must have been carelessly dropped by a giant hand from the sky onto the gravel lot. It looks a lot like a little green Monopoly house, set far back on the lot and learning mostly toward the left. There's no foliage except for one bare-limbed anorexic tree that leans to one side as if cocking its head to see who we were and why we are stupid enough to live in this house. When my mother pulls to a stop, I get out of the car and walk around on the gravel. Black widow spiders line the underside of the leaning wooden fence that borders one side of the property. I squat down and poke a stick toward one just to see what it will do until my mother calls me to help move boxes inside.

Since the house was advertised as 'furnished,' we've left all of our furniture behind or sold it or something. Furnished isn't an appropriate description for the wood and fabric we find in the new house. The couch and love seat are a sad mix of beige, brown and a yellow that might have once been white. No matter where you sit, you sink onto the broken springs beneath the tattered fabric. The spindly legged coffee table and plasterboard end tables hardly look sturdy enough to hold a half-empty glass of water. The small living room is a box and one corner serves as a tiny eating area. Faded green shag carpeting mats down all the walkways. Cheap, dark wood paneling covers the tiny living room walls. One pink-tiled bathroom will be shared by the three of us.

At the end of a short, dark hallway are the two small bedrooms. I carry my first box into the dark paneled room that is my bedroom on the left. The smell of stale cigarette smoke greets me as I eye the one bed, one end table and one cheap dresser. I set my box down on the end table and begin to cry. "It's so ugly," I cry into the filthy, naked mattress, then instantly regret insulting the sad furniture. "I'm sorry…it's just….it's just...so ugly...everything..." I quickly run out of words for how I feel. My life isn't under my own control and I hate the choices my mother makes for me, leaving me to bounce around behind in her mistakes.

After the boxes are brought in from our car my mother and Dean leave to explore the neighborhood, code for 'check out the bars.' I organize the few things I have in my room and then wander around the dirty little house. Even though the Cambridge Apartments were certainly not luxury villas, I know that moving to Jefferson Street drops us down a few ladder rungs below respectability. I make my bed and lie down, wishing there was a way to reverse the last few hours and instead go to Rachel's house, play in her game room and have her maid make snacks for us.

Monday I start sixth grade at my newest school, the sixth school I've attended in six years. As I walk to the school I take some comfort in the thought that I'm getting better at starting anew. I don't throw up once, and fall in step with the other kids streaming down the street. I find my way to the head office and announce to the secretary behind the counter that I'm a new student. The secretary asks if I have a transfer slip or a parent with me.

"No slip," I answer with the sleepy indolence of having gone through this process repeatedly.

"Where's your parent?"

"No parent. They're sleeping."

She purses her lips and drops her eyes in the way that flustered school secretaries are known to do. She doesn't seem to find my parentless situation all that unusual. "Well, here then, fill these papers out, and I'll send you to class. Have you registered yourself at school before?"

"Yes, I know what to do," I answer and ten minutes later I walk into my newest class. Looking around from the safety of my seat, I see that even with the number of times we've moved, I know no one in this classroom. It's easy to determine which girls are popular by the way they angle their bodies in their chairs, and I make mental notes of who they are. At recess I walk up to the girls I'd noticed and introduce myself.

"You're so cute!" Donna says with a confidence I wish I had.

I smile in return, secretly admiring her shiny black braids. "Thank you."

"Come with us," and they grab my hands and we spend recess flipping around on the uneven bars. They show me how to do cherry-drops, and double-spin drops. Rainie is tall, with a short Dorothy Hamill haircut. She wears neat little braces on her tiny, perfect little white teeth. Dawn has a pageboy cut and a sweet smile. Red-haired Kim is built like an athlete: short, stocky and strong. Donna is so happy and outgoing that I can't help but like her best of all.

I walk home with my new group of friends one day the following week. They all live in the neighborhood next to mine, which is definitely higher-end, judging by the neat, compact collection of homes that are perfectly apportioned along the streets. This contrasts sharply with the strange mismatched buildings dropped onto lots in my neighborhood. Every house in their neighborhood has grass around it instead of gravel or dirt. We say goodbye one by one to each friend as we reach their house, until we reach Donna's house.

She breezily invites me inside in a way that tells me she never has to worry about what she'll find when she comes home from school. Her house is small but tidy and the couches are covered in plastic film. She introduces her brother as Leon as he walks through the living room. I turn to stare at him as he passes. Leon has a gigantic afro that moves in rhythm to his steps. He's tall and thin, dressed in bell-bottomed jeans and a T-shirt from "Good Times" with "Dyn-O-Mite" emblazoned in sparkling letters across his chest. I follow Donna into her bedroom and she asks if I want to help style her braids. Taking a big glob of Vaseline in her fingers, she works it through her hair. I help her rebraid her hair, delighting in the mushy feeling of the Vaseline.

Donna cues one of her 45 records on the little turntable in the corner of her room. She dances around for a moment, and I sit perfectly still on her perfectly neat little twin bed, completely entranced by the way she moves. She is cute and alive, and her dancing is simply nothing like the sexy dancing I'd watched Angela perform. She grabs my hands and pulls me up to dance with her when she finally notices she is dancing alone.

"You have about as much rhythm as a tin can rolling down a hill. Didn't nobody ever teach you how to dance?"

"Not really. No."

"I will, then." And Donna whirls me around and forward and backward in the mottled afternoon

146

sunlight of her bedroom. My entire being fills with a ridiculous happiness as I watch her twisted braids flipping back and around as we twirl around her bedroom. Donna is so tiny like me, yet light and upbeat and happy, so very unlike me. Clasping her two cool hands in mine and whirling around her room feels about as every bit as perfect as I can ever remember feeling. I think of Angela for a brief moment and then push the thought of her out of my brain. Perhaps this move to North Las Vegas wasn't so bad after all if it includes Donna.

Several days later the kids want to walk me home. I do my best to shrug them off, telling them I'll just see them at school the next day. Collectively they insist on knowing where I live. "It's only fair," Dawn says as she wraps her arm around my bony shoulders, "you walked with us the other day. We want to see where you live now."

The very last thing in the world I want is for my new friends to see where I live. I'm prepared to do whatever it takes to keep them away. As we stand on the street corner in the after-school sunlight, my mind races with ideas on how to handle this latest turn of affairs. If I argue or tell them no, perhaps they won't like me anymore. I could make up an excuse. I could lie. I could pretend I am sick. I argue back and forth with myself, finally resigning myself to fate in deciding the lesser of two evils. They can see where I live and decide if they still want to be friends with me once they see how poor I am. As we walk the few blocks to my house, my confidence wanes and I try to develop a last-ditch plan to tell them at the corner that it's far enough, that I'm not feeling well or my stepfather has a contagious disease. If we get close enough to my house maybe they'll feel sort of satisfied to know approximately where I live. Otherwise I worry they'll want to come in, and I'm way too embarrassed for them to meet my mother and Dean or see the awful cheap furniture in our house. The girls are laughing and chattering as we walk while I'm so sick and distracted with thoughts of how I can extricate myself from the situation that I can't concentrate on the conversation at all. The stale unwashed scent of sweat rises from my body and I hope they can't smell me. The hairs on the back of my neck lift as waves of anxiety pour acid into my stomach. I didn't need to plan an excuse to keep them away after all, for I'm still praying when I hear the first siren, even before I see the fire trucks.

Please God, don't let those fire trucks be headed to my house. Please, don't make this emergency be about my family. Don't let me be embarrassed in front of Rainie, Dawn, Kim and Donna. I just met them, and what if they don't like me if they find out there is something awful going on at my house today?

As we turn the corner where I'd planned feigning sickness, the two big red fire trucks are parking in my front yard, which is not the green manicured grass carpeting of my friends' neighborhood, but poor gravel.

"I wonder what happened at that house," someone murmurs.

".....it's my house..." I mumble, running forward and letting my books fall from my hands. I know that Dean has killed my mom while I was at school. That she's bleeding out on the living room floor while I worry about being embarrassed and keeping the girls from seeing how poor I am. What a terrible daughter I am. My German Shepherd, Charlie, meets me at the front door as I charge in, whining and trying to lick my hand. Inside the crowded living room, my mother is indeed lying on the floor as I'd imagined, paramedics working furiously all around her.

"Doesn't he look like the Wolfman?" she cackles when she sees me, turning her head toward the bearded paramedic kneeling at her side. She is not dead. She is not dead. She is not dead.

Overlay – A Tale of One Girl's Life in 1970s Las Vegas

The paramedic looks up at me and in his eyes I see the dark, pitying look I tire of seeing in the eyes of others. I know that he understands my humiliation and I hate it. Suffering alone is one thing, and suffering in the eyes of someone else is something else entirely. Something I don't much like at all.

"What happened?" I ask the room.

"She's cut an artery, and we're trying to staunch the bleeding," Wolfman answers, speaking to me like I'm the adult and it hits me then that I am the adult and I've been the adult for some time.

I squat down next to Wolfman and see the deep gash running across my mother's palm and down her wrist. "What happened? Something like this doesn't just happen!"

"I was trying to knock on your window and I put my hand right through it. Wasn't that right, Wolfman?" my mother slurs and with another sickening lurch of my stomach I know that she is completely drunk at 3:00 p.m. in the afternoon.

Dean. Just where is Dean, I wonder? There he is, sitting at the tiny kitchenette table, wearing only a pair of ridiculously short jean shorts which are probably my mother's, and calmly smoking a cigarette as if he were a captain surveying the stormy seas.

"Wolfman!" my mother laughs. "You're so handsome, Wolfman!"

"Ma'am, you've got to remain still so we can stop the flow."

That's when I hear the cough.

"We brought your books...." Donna says from behind me.

I freeze. My back stiffens. The absolutely very last thing in the world I want to do is turn around. From where I'm kneeling on the ugly worn green carpeting next to my mother, I turn my head in slow motion to hope not but to see Rainie, Dawn, Kim and Donna huddled in one corner of our living room. There can't possibly be a God. What sort of God would allow this type of embarrassment to be inflicted upon a child, especially after I'd prayed for it not to happen?

"We'll see you at school tomorrow," Donna says, setting my books down on the wineglass stained plasterboard coffee table.

I watch them leave, but it takes me a moment to find my words in the muddle of my brain. "You ruin everything," I say to the drunken alien-mother on the floor. "I hate you! Why can't you make cookies? Or drink tea, for God's sake?"

I could swear Wolfman strangled a small smile but I can't be sure. It could have been my hopeful imagination. It may have been just a weary grimace. I don't come out of my bedroom for the rest of the evening. I'm too busy struggling with my wish that my mother had died, freeing me to go live somewhere else with someone else like Ana, or my dad, or even Donna. I want to be anywhere but here in this ugly little clapboard house on Jefferson Street.

I don't want to face the humiliation of going to school the next day, but the thought of staying home with my mother and Dean is even worse than facing the girls. My head is low as I walk in my classroom the next morning until Donna smiles brightly at me and asks if everything is okay.

148

I tell her yes.

"Good. 'Cuz I want you to come over after school today."

I could have cried. Not only is my home life never mentioned again with the girls, but I don't have to suffer them wanting to come to my neighborhood. They never ask again. From that point on, I'm always invited to their homes. Although I'm happy to have met my new friends, I still miss my friends from the old neighborhood and often call them in the evenings when my mother and Dean are out at the bars. One day I pick up the phone and there's no dial tone. My mother explains the next day that the phone has been disconnected.

"We don't even have a phone now? Everybody has a phone! What if there's an emergency?"

"We'll run next door and use theirs," she answers in that maddening way she has of not addressing the reality of a situation and instead scurrying around it.

Another afternoon I arrive home from school and notice that our dog Charlie doesn't meet me at the sidewalk. I ask my mother what happened to Charlie as I set my books down on the table.

"He had rabies. We had to call animal control to take him away."

"Rabies? He was perfectly healthy yesterday!"

"He woke up this morning convulsing and frothing at the mouth," Dean says. Just like that Charlie is gone. That night I think of my big, lovable Charlie and know he'd really been euthanized because we're too poor to feed him. His body is probably lying on a heap of other stiff dog bodies at the pound. If only I'd been given the opportunity to help. I could have contributed baby-sitting money or washed cars or mowed lawns to feed him.

A few weeks after Charlie's disappearance I arrive home from school and don't see our old green car in the driveway. Happily thinking no one's home, I walk inside and am surprised by my mother and Dean sitting on the couch, drinking wine.

"Where's the car?"

"It broke."

"Let me guess...rabies?"

The vigorish has grown quite steep, I'm afraid.

Chapter Thirty Three

Holding Your Own: Breaking even.

One Saturday afternoon my mother says she and Dean are going to the store, which of course means heading to the local bar. I ask to go with them, only to be obnoxious. When Dean says no, I tell them I hope someone will kidnap me while they're gone. They're unmoved by my bluff and shut the front door behind them. When I hear their footsteps traversing the gravel of our front yard, I jump from the couch and open the front door with a noisy flourish so the kidnapper can come right in. It will serve them right if someone kidnaps me. They don't appreciate me anyway.

Sitting back down on the plaid love seat, I pull open the newspaper to read Dear Abby's column. I enjoy reading about all the strange problems people from all over the world describe to Abby – a scratching post of human experience. Reading Dear Abby's column makes me feel just a bit better about my own world. Yesterday's letter had been from a young bride who complained that her new husband, a mortician, only wanted to have sex with her after she'd laid in a bathtub full of ice for twenty minutes. She wanted to know if this was normal behavior for a newlywed husband. Even I knew it wasn't, and wondered how you got to be of marrying age and had to ask such a thing. I find Abby's column and begin reading. Today's letter is from a sad girl in a wheelchair who wonders if she will ever find love.

Lost in the world of this lonely young woman, I look up just as a tall skinny man walks through the front door and takes one step into the living room. I throw down the newspaper and run the three feet to the back door so fast I probably look like the blur of the cartoon Roadrunner being chased by Coyote. I place my shaking hand on the knob, but don't turn it. For some reason it seems important that I don't run down the alley behind our house.

"Where're your parents?" the stranger asks, craning his skinny neck toward me. His long hair falls away from his neck as he swivels his head. He remains standing just inside the front door.

I am shaking furiously from the unexpected rush of adrenaline that flooded my body at this invasion. I lift my arm and point down the hallway, stuttering through my shaking jaw, "Th-th-they're in there..." Even though I'm stuttering fiercely, I know to maintain eye contact with this man to let him know that I'm startled but unafraid. I really am very afraid that he will see through my façade and know I'm alone in the sad, ugly little house.

He looks at me, looks toward the hall, and looks again back at me. I am fully conscious of the fact that my future is being determined in that head of his. He stands motionless for a moment as if deciding what to do, moving his mustache around as he chews his bottom lip. Then he simply turns and walks out without a word. I don't know how much time passes before I feel safe enough to unclasp my hand from the safety of the back doorknob and run to the front door to lock it. I'm sure it was a long while.

When my mother and Dean return later that evening, I unlock the door and tell them what happened. My mother doesn't believe me, and I almost can't blame her. I know the story is almost too incredulous to be true - I say I hope I'm kidnapped and a man walks straight into the house? She threatens to call the police and report the invasion in a mean-spirited attempt to call my bluff. I beg her not to, fearing that the stranger might come back again. What if he's watching our house this very minute and waiting for them to leave because he knows I am unprotected? Knowing how often

Overlay – A Tale of One Girl's Life in 1970s Las Vegas

I'm alone, I don't want to take the chance of alerting the stranger. My refusal to call the police only confirms to my mother and Dean I'm lying, but I don't care. I gladly lose that battle to win the war.

Since our move to Jefferson Street, not only are our possessions disappearing at an alarming rate but my mother and Dean drink all day and throughout the evening now. I don't know how we have any money at all since it's been months since my mother worked, but I worry it won't be long before we don't have enough money to survive. I figure they're getting the money to afford the jugs of wine, gallons of vodka and cartons of cigarettes which arrive in steady supply by selling off our possessions. Very little food is purchased for our house, and if it weren't for the free lunch program at school, I wouldn't eat at all.

As before at the Camelot apartments, a motley crew of characters find their way to our living room. Considering the neighborhood where we now live, this group is far worse than the one before – the true muck at the bottom of the barrel. There is old, toothless Mary from next door, who sits in a stained housedress with her legs apart and her baggy knee-high nylons pulled up in uneven lengths to her knobby knees. She alternates between drinking wine from a plastic cup and sucking on her lipsticked cigarettes. Her hair rises from her head in a perfect imitation of a white-haired Heat Miser. Mr. Ornelas from the corner stops by occasionally, bringing his own beer. His English is accented and sounds particularly amusing sputtered between the holes where a couple of teeth used to be. Most of the others I don't know, and don't want to know.

Then there is Gary.

I immediately notice him sitting on the couch one afternoon as I return from school. As I cross the living room toward my bedroom I turn around to look at him in response to his wolf-whistle. I stop short. He is the most handsome man I've ever seen in our living room, and perhaps even my whole life. He smiles a crinkly blue-eyed smile at me when our eyes meet and asks, "How old are YOU, beautiful?"

While I turn my chin toward my mother I can't drag my eyes from Gary's face, surprised as I am by his unabashed flirting with me in front of my mother. She doesn't hear his question and is talking to somebody else so I answer that I'm eleven years old.

"Well, darling, in a few more years, I think I might just marry you!" he has a big laugh that displays a dazzling array of white teeth. "I'm 32. Would you marry an old man?"

I smile shyly before slipping into my room. "I'm almost twelve," I whisper to him once I'd shut my bedroom door.

Secretly I hope Gary will visit our house again and I eagerly scan the faces of the drunks on the couch as I pass through the living room each day. He's rarely among the visitors, but when he is I make sure to take frequent trips to the kitchen, pretending to search through our cupboards for food. He can't see from where he sits that our cupboards are completely empty. For all he knows I'm taking my time choosing from the caviar, salmon, soups, gourmet cheeses and fancy crackers in our cabinets. Each time I pass him, Gary never fails to give me an exaggerated wink, and I smile a shy little smile in return. It's as if we are the only two people in the room. The laughter and murmurs fall into silence. The other people disappear from view. There is Gary, sitting back with his bell-bottomed legs spread and his fingers interlaced behind his long-haired head. And there is me, walking slowly across that looooooooong length of our living room, smiling and smiling and smiling.

Overlay – A Tale of One Girl's Life in 1970s Las Vegas

The only time I pay the slightest bit of attention to the conversations in our living room is when Gary is visiting. Instead of turning on my little black and white television set to drown out the drunken murmurs, I crack open my bedroom door so I can clearly hear his contributions to the conversations in the living room. I hope to glean information about Gary's life from his various comments, but he doesn't brag or repeat himself in the way that the rest of the living room denizens often do. So my curiosity about him grows.

One afternoon as I walk home from school I'm overtaken by an impulsive desire to go to Gary's house and knock on the door. I don't know what I'll do when he answers, as I have no plan. I'm slightly relieved when he doesn't answer my knock. I peer through the dirty window next to the front door, cupping my eyes with my hands to shut out the sunlight. I can just barely make out the shape of a couch in the living room, and a guitar resting against one of the walls. Other windows reveal a similar lack of furniture or personal items. Two dusty basement windows are close to the ground. Looking around to see if anyone is watching, I lay down on the dirt and peer through those windows too. The basement is empty except for a few boxes and a lawnmower. Gary's lack of possessions is every bit as curious as he is to me. It's almost as if no one lives at the house on the corner of Jefferson Street.

I sit down on his front step to wait for him. There's no reason at all for me to go home so if Gary returns soon enough he can invite me inside his empty house. At least I know there is room inside for me. If he would marry me, I could move in and clean up the place. I imagine washing the windows, scrubbing the floors, and adding a few plants. I would macramé plant holders and doilies for the couch. I imagine Gary coming home and opening his eyes wide at all that I'd done to our home, beaming at me with love and pleasure. Gary and I could be happy together, and our marriage would be an easy way for me to leave the house I shared with my mother and Dean. Beginning my walk home, I decide that when I turn twelve in several months I will visit his house again and accept his proposal. After we marry my mother will come live with us and Dean will just conveniently disappear and fade into oblivion.

Maybe he will disappear back into the Louisiana swamps.

Bonus points if he gets eaten by an alligator.

No breaking even allowed.

Chapter Thirty Four

Raise: In poker, a player raises by matching the previous bet and then betting more to increase the stake for remaining players.

Dean becomes increasingly combative as the months pass on Jefferson Street.

He argues with my mother during visitor hours, which has the upside of washing the drunks off the couch and back to their own hovels. I quickly learn to become sorry to hear them leave because a familiar pattern emerges. Dean's voice rises and then my mother's rises in return. Their arguments stem from nonsensical things such as why my mother dated a particular boy when she was a teenager to what happened to the last cigarette.

The first time he punches her and I hear my mother cry, I tear out of my room like my hair's on fire and launch myself at Dean to pummel him with my fists. "Don't you hit her! Don't you hit her! Don't you hit her!"

Taking one arm to easily fling me backwards into their bedroom dresser, he eyes me in that crazed drunken way in deciding what to do about this unexpected turn of events. Raising his elbow, he prepares to backhand me when my mother lunges forward and grabs his arm.

"No!" she grunts, hanging firmly onto his arm as he works it viciously back and forth to fling her away from him. "Get out of here, Marlayna!"

"No!" I don't move. There is absolutely no way I am going to move.

Their wrestling continues until Dean finally extricates his arm from her grip and shakes her off like a bad habit. "You two deserve each other, you fucking tramps." He leaves the bedroom. The front door slams a moment later. Then the screen door follows suit.

I look at my mother expectantly, hoping this is the final incident in a long line of offenses and that I will be sent on a surprise vacation tomorrow to visit my aunt Ana and when I come home I will find that we've moved back to the better side of town and that Dean has gone the way of Mr. Nice. After all, he hit her this time and was about to hit me, and surely this is enough to incite the raging parenting instinct that even the mammals on the educational shows on television exhibit. She looks back at me, her chest still heaving, then turns and runs out of the bedroom. I hear the front door slam and then the screen door slam a moment later.

Her frantic footsteps sound down our gravel driveway, punctuated by her calling his name in the night. I go to bed and vow not to involve myself again. Unfortunately for me this means that I endure the continually escalating noise, fighting, grunting, yelling, slapping, punching and crying from the other side of my bedroom wall.

One blustery afternoon around Thanksgiving I arrive home from school and find two strangers sitting stiffly on the ugly plaid couch, a man and a beautiful, petite Japanese woman. I am told that these strangers are my brother and my sister in law. The tension in the room is so heavy I imagine that if I reach out my fingertips I can feel a physical shimmery sickness undulating around us all.

Dean is smoking and saying stupid things that I tune out of my consciousness. My mom is obviously very embarrassed at being surprised by such an unexpected and important visit. My brother is quiet and serious and I can see he is at a complete loss to reconcile this bloated woman with the beautiful mother he had last seen when he was a small boy of five years old. He stares at her with a look that questions whether she is even real. I'm reminded of my belief that my mother had been taken away by the Body Snatchers. I am fascinated with the platform shoes my pretty sister in law is wearing and ask to try them on more than a few times. To have a female in my home that is well put together is a treat I can't quite fathom. I know there is something seriously wrong and uncomfortable going on between all the adults in the room and I fill the silence with chatter-sound that embarrasses even me. They don't stay on the plaid couch for very long. And unlike my sister's visit from years before, we do not walk them outside, shake hands and say goodbye. They are on the couch one moment and then they are gone the next.

Christmas break draws near, and I check the mailbox for an invitation from my aunt to come spend the holidays with her. Since she can't call me, I write to tell her about the dates of my Christmas break and wait for a response. When I find her letter in our mailbox one early December afternoon, I drop my books in the dirt and open it where I stand. She begins the letter by apologizing for not having written to me in such a long time, and explains that something very exciting has happened in her life – she has gotten married! She spends all of her time with her new husband and his children, and has been so busy lately that she hadn't had much time to think about her sadness at losing her mother and John. She hoped I was enjoying school, and looked forward to receiving a letter from me soon. There is a check for $50.00 addressed to me, and an admonition that the money is for me to spend on myself.

I drop my head back and sigh to the heavens, releasing all the breath I'd held as I read her short letter. My last chance for a normal life and childhood evaporates, and with it goes my optimism. I have a hard time sucking in enough air to continue breathing.

The first night of Christmas break, a girl from my class named Antoinette invites me to spend the night at her apartment. It's a cold night, but we have no choice but to walk a very long way to a row of tiny light-blue apartments. After I've been at her house for an hour she brings out a board game and we begin setting up the pieces. There are two 'crickets' included in the game, tiny boxes of metal that you click with your fingers to make loud popping noises. On an impulse I put one cricket up to each ear and vigorously pop them back and forth. Instantly my head reels as a fierce ringing noise sounds in my head. "Oh my God," I lay back down on the living room floor. The ceiling reels around overhead and I close my eyes. I don't feel good and ran to the bathroom. In the silence of Antoinette's bathroom, I hear a strange buzzing sound that's so loud it makes me sick. When I realize the sound is coming from inside my own head I vomit into the toilet.

Antoinette's mother is able to reach a neighbor of ours who goes to my house and tells my mother she need to find a way to come pick me up. Vertigo-bound on Antoinette's couch, I take a weak look at my mother when she arrives. I don't have the strength to wonder how she drove to come and get me since we no longer have a car. Back at our house I run a hot bath, hoping and praying that when I turn off the water, I will no longer hear that awful tinny noise. It's still there when I shut off the water and after a few minutes in the tub I can no longer tolerate silence because it only seems to intensify the ringing in my head. I spend a restless night flinging my body around on the mattress and crying miserably for silence.

The next morning when I return to consciousness and the first thing I notice is that the sound was still echoing in my head. As the day progresses I'm unable to concentrate on anything other than the ringing in my head. I have no appetite. I leave my bed in the afternoon and stand in front of my mother, who sits on the plaid couch. With my hands clasped tightly around my skull I say I can't stand the noise.

"Just lie down and get some rest. I don't know what else to say."

"Can't we see a doctor? Rest doesn't make it go away. It's driving me crazy!" I return to my bed and sob my frustration into my pillows.

Christmas morning arrives. I leave my bed to open the few gifts I receive. I'm weak and apathetic from days lying in bed without food. My mother bought my presents from the Salvation Army, and managed to not pick one thing I either like or need. When I open the wrapping containing the black faux-leather miniskirt, I gathered enough strength to say thank you, barely able to acknowledge my fleeting frustration that she would think I would ever wear such a thing. I have two pairs of underwear, one pair of shoes and several mismatched socks. Why in the world would I need a black mini skirt? Christmas afternoon she brings a big plate of turkey and stuffing to my room. My little black and white television set is on to distract me from hearing the ringing but I still can't concentrate on the programming. My eyes follow my mother as she walks through my bedroom door with the plate, sets it down next to my bed and leaves. I turn to my side and drift back to sleep again.

Some afternoon my mother opens my door to tell me that she will cash my $50 check from Aunt Ana for me. I don't respond.

Death would be better than living, seconded by deafness and blindness, so I plan to starve myself to death. After the first week passes and I continue to wake up alive in the mornings, I start holding my ears and trying to blow out my eardrums to deafen myself. I stare at the overhead light to blind myself. Morning after morning, I continue to wake up to the sound of horrendous ringing and screeching in my head. Though I grow weaker, I don't die.

New Year's Eve arrives. Though our living room fills with the usual drunken characters, I'm too weak to feel any sort of frustration. I don't even think of Gary, or wonder why he did or didn't show up. I never even check if he's there. I wake briefly when I hear the drunken yelling from our living room accompanying Dick Clark's Rockin' New Year's Eve Countdown, and drift back into my stupor as the people yell in unison, "HAPPY NEW YEAR!"

A few days before school is to resume my mother barges into my room in the afternoon and demands I get out of bed. I try to stand at her insistence but my head is whirling around inside my skull and I fall to my knees. My mother is mad at me and I wish she would just go away and let me die. I know I'm close. It's been two weeks without food and I know from Science class that I have at the most one week left to go. A human being can live only three weeks without food, three days without water and three minutes without air. Seven more days and I will be gone. I sit on the ground since my legs are too weak to hold me and make a sound that would have been a cry if I had the energy or the water in my body to make it happen. My mother brings a pair of pants and insists I put them on. Leaning against her I have just enough energy to lift one leg and then the other into the black holes of the pants.

She holds me up with one arm while using her other arm to adjust the pants around my ankles and pull them up around my hips. When she removes her hands the pants slide back down to the floor. I don't own a belt so it's clear my meager wardrobe no longer fits. The effort of putting on pants is too much for me and I beg her to just leave me alone. Then I half-step, half fall out of the pants around my ankles, return to bed and sleep for the rest of that Sunday. I no longer wish to be awake.

Monday morning arrives and when my mother tries to wake me up for school, I'm too incoherent to function. She returns with a wet washcloth and gently wipes my face. She says she's taken a job as a maid at a nearby motel, and that I'm coming with her to work. Too weak to cry, I just moan in response. I haven't eaten or showered or changed clothes in nearly two and a half weeks. So my mother dresses me in clothes that hang on my body. I'm already like a corpse. I sit on the bed and wish for death or sleep. I can't follow her words. I'm too tired.

She goes away and returns with some sort of food and places it in my mouth. The nausea rises and I close my eyes against the food, her face, the light, the morning, life. Why won't she just go away? I know I'll be dead in a few days and it will all be over. All I want is to lie back down until it's time. I know I'm not wanted in our house. I know I'm not loved. So why won't she just let me die in peace? Is her conscience preventing her from letting me go? Why the rush now to come in and save me at the end?

She insists I accompany her to the motel, and it doesn't matter what I say, I have to go. Since we still have no car I have to lean on her the entire two mile walk to the motel. I pray to die along the way and wish it was summer and that the searing Las Vegas heat could zap me into irreversible dehydration. It's January and it's cold, and instead the wind breaks through whatever it is she's dressed me in. I imagine this is all a dream and that if I make it through today I won't wake up tomorrow.

Disappointed when we make it to the motel, I'm unresponsive when my mother tries to get me involved in the cleaning. I merely move from one motel bed to the next, laying motionless in each room that she cleans. I'm so sick I don't even care if she's changed the sheets or not. I don't care who laid in the sheets before me and so I lay in the dirty sheets, on the dirty pillowcase of whoever had rented the room the night before. My mother tries in vain to talk to me but I can't hold a conversation. I eventually stop offering feeble one word responses and just ignore her. I drift in and out of consciousness. Dreams fade into the reality of the motel room and then back out again. I'm lying on the beach in Hawaii and then I'm back in the motel room. At other times I'm with John and Ana and when I wake up and remember John is dead and Ana remarried I go right back to sleep. The day progresses. At the end of the day my mother buys me a candy bar from the $10 she made on the shift, and insists that I eat it before we walk home. The sugar is like a shot of adrenaline to the heart of my depleted body. After several tentative bites, I quell my rising nausea and shove the chocolate into my mouth with gulping, hulking bites.

"I feel a little better now," I say and immediately vomit on the sidewalk. We walk back to our house with me again leaning on my mother. Later that evening I experience a small increase of energy. My mother brings a plate of rice and chicken to my room and it almost smells appetizing so I pick at a few pieces of chicken and eat several pieces of white rice.

"You are going to school tomorrow," my mother says when she returns and eyes how little I've eaten as she picks up my plate. "Even if I have to walk you in there myself."

After the Wolfman incident there is no way I want my mother at my school. I ask for the plate right back and when she leaves I choke down two more bites of cold chicken. I scrape the rest of the food into the trash and quickly cover it with balled up pieces of notebook paper.

Overlay – A Tale of One Girl's Life in 1970s Las Vegas

Looking in the mirror the next morning I see a face of two giant eyes on top of sharp angular cheek bones and jawline. When my teacher sees me, her mouth falls open in an unrestrained gasp. "Marlayna! My God! What happened?"

I say I've been sick and refuse to say anything else. Nor will I answer the questions of my friends and classmates. I can't join the conversations about what I got for Christmas or where we went on vacation. At recess I don't have the energy to play on the bars so I sit on the low wall encircling the sand area and watch Rainie, Donna, Dawn and Kim spin around on the bars. Watching the spinning makes me feel sick and I settle for drawing circles in the sand with a stick I find nearby.

I don't concentrate in school because it's already a habit to monitor the ever-insistent ringing. The noise of the other students is painful to my ears and causes me to squint and hunch my shoulders.

I have such a small appetite and since my stomach has shrunken considerably I continue to lose more weight. I ask my mother for the $50 that Aunt Ana sent me for Christmas. I desperately need clothes, as nothing I have fits. Unfortunately, while I was sick the money was spent on groceries I didn't eat.

So I take a needle and thread and sew crooked inseams along my pant legs and take in the waistlines. I'm only eleven years old but I'm worn out from the continuous raises. The stakes keep rising as my energy, hope and enthusiasm dim.

Overlay – A Tale of One Girl's Life in 1970s Las Vegas

Chapter Thirty Five

Sevening Out: Rolling a seven after the point has been established causes the shooter to seven out and pass the dice to the next shooter.

A new family moves onto Jefferson Street: Daisy Hernandez and four of her five children. Karen becomes a friend out of convenience more than anything else for we have absolutely nothing in common. Karen's at least a head taller than me: strong, tall, healthy and confident. Since Daisy works nights as a cashier at a topless dance club, Karen cares for her three younger brothers at night like Angela from my last neighborhood. There ends the similarity between Karen and Angela. Karen is strong in every way that Angela had been weak.

Karen isn't smart but she's powerfully alive and outgoing in all the ways I wish I was. She likes loud music and dancing, often turning the stereo up loud and pulling me up by my hands to dance with her. She laughs all the time and I'm fascinated by the way the laugh rises from her belly and explodes into the room from her oversized mouth. Karen's family gets Food Stamps and Welfare and this means there's always food at their house. Karen makes dinner for the four of them (plus me) every night while her mother's at work. Though the meals aren't elaborate, she's adept at whipping up simple dishes like macaroni or hamburgers, adding a salad with bottled dressing, and baking a cake mix for dessert. After dinner Karen turns on the stereo in the kitchen while we work together with the boys to clean the kitchen and vacuum the living room. Then we sprawl together on the living room floor to watch Charlie's Angels or the Bionic Woman, Karen's favorite shows. Karen loves female superheroes and I learn not to talk to her while she watches or she will say, 'Shhhhh!' with an angry gesture of her hand.

I fall so preciously into the fabric of their routine and relish the orderliness of their household. Karen's mother expects the house to be cleaned and vacuumed every evening before bed and I enjoy helping so I can feel like part of the family. Her brothers don't understand my willingness to do work that's required of them and not me and they often make fun of me. I don't care. I would have done all the work just to stay at their house, eat dinner, enjoy the company of happy kids my own age and be out of my own house.

As much as I want to I know I can't spend every night at Karen's house. When I do go home I'm so miserable between Dean's existence and the ringing in my head I can barely stand to exist. I read a lot and escape into the characters. I fall asleep most nights with a book on my chest, obsessed with why I can't have the kind of family I read about in my books. I picture my once-beautiful mother, younger and thinner, the one Frank Sinatra had asked out on a date. Her stomach is not fat and bloated from the alcohol and cheap food. Her hair is secured with one of the lovely colored scarves she used to wear, and she's smiling in the easy way she had when I was a child. I make up a father from scratch out of a conglomeration of men and fathers I know. I imagine a Jewish father who works during the daytime (the most important quality), but arrives home every evening promptly at 5:00 PM, briefcase swinging from one hand. He looks like Michael Landon. He's stern yet loving, and my siblings and I run in a pack to greet him in the driveway when we hear his car's engine. I'm neither the oldest nor the youngest sibling – ensconced safely in the middle. My dream family eats dinner together, laughing and talking about the day and our futures. Though we have chores we aren't responsible for every detail of our very existence, and after having bathed we're tucked safely into our beds, secure under the sensible and watchful eye of our two loving parents. They kiss us good night on our foreheads, a safety blessing every child wants and deserves. We don't worry about whether there will be enough to eat or if our stepfather will spend so much money on alcohol that we won't be able to pay the rent. My ears don't ring. My dream family sleeps peacefully and always awakens to yet another perfect day.

Although I fall asleep at night in the company of my perfect family, I'm usually awakened by the grunts and screams from the real family in the bedroom next door. When I place my pillow over my face to drown out the noise, I'm locked inside the excruciating noise of my own head. It's better to hear the fighting than the ringing. I soldier on. Late one evening I'm awakened by fighting so loud that I break my vow to remain uninvolved and creep down the short darkened hallway toward the kitchen. Peering around the corner, I unexpectedly lock eyes with Dean. His eyebrows drop as he lurches toward me then unexpectedly falls sideways when the cast iron skillet clasped in my mother's hand lands on the side of his skull. He falls to the ground with a whump and doesn't get back up.

Ticking interrupts the still-reverberating clang of the skillet with Dean's skull. On our wall is the cheap plastic clock we'd inherited from Mr. Nice, a black cat whose eyes roll side to side and a tail that swings back and forth with each tick of a second. It's 3:42 in the morning, the cat ticks.

Dean makes no sound from where he lays crumpled on the dirty linoleum floor. For such a big man, he'd fallen into a position that made him look like no more than a rumpled flesh-colored sheet. He's nearly flat: nude and defenseless. I clench my jaw in hope that he will no longer be breathing and we will be free from him at last. The heavy breathing of my mother behind me now drowns out the sound of the ticking plastic cat.

Please let him have sevened-out. Please.

"Is he dead?" my mother asks, and we stare together at Dean's back, watching the rise and fall of his breath.

"No, he's not dead."

"I think he'll be quite harmless for a while." My mother replaces the frying pan on the stove, then opens a cabinet underneath the countertop and shoves the frying pan towards the back. "Just in case."

"In case of what?"

"Go to bed. It's late."

"It's early."

"That too." She flips off the kitchen light and Dean lies alone on the cheap linoleum floor, crooked and askew, just as in real life. I crack my bedroom door open and stay awake for as long as I can in case Dean tries to kill my mother while I sleep. When my alarm sounds in the morning I creep into the kitchen and gaze at the empty linoleum. Glancing behind me, I see he isn't asleep on the plaid couch either. I pad back down the hallway and turn the knob of their bedroom door very slowly. I hold back a gasp because I'm surprised to see Dean sleeping peacefully next to my mother. Their faces are turned toward me in sleep, openmouthed and vulnerable. My mother has one arm slung over Dean's shoulder as if in protection. Dean's blackened cheekbone contrasts starkly with the bleached white of the sheet pulled up beneath his face. My mother's hand, the one that delivered the blow, is slack on top of the sheet near his face. The room smells of exhaled alcohol and cigarette smoke, moist, pungent and stale.

I slowly close the door.

Chapter Thirty Six

Baccarat: When baccarat was introduced to Nevada in the late 1950s, casinos tried to instill the glamorous aura associated with the European game. In most casinos, baccarat was played in a roped-off area, was closely monitored and sometimes even guarded.

Winter gives way to spring and I gain a few pounds back thanks to Karen's cooking. I no longer have that haunted, hollowed look that was me in the mirror. Though he'd been there all along, one day I notice Danny and Danny notices me. Danny is popular and laughs a lot, dropping his head back and laughing to the sky in a way that makes his brown bowl-cut hair flop back and forward again on his forehead. I can't imagine what Danny could possibly see in me. My hair isn't cut right or fashionably styled like the other girls. I have so few items of clothing that I have to repeat my combinations several times each week. The underarms of my shirts have developed unflattering black stains and although I devotedly rub store-brand stain remover on the stains and wash my shirts by hand, there is only so much I can accomplish. I never look quite clean. I'm so small and skinny I have the physique of a five year old. My teeth are donkey-big and coming in crooked. They grow in all different directions, up down and sideways, as if searching for enough food.

Inexplicably Danny likes me anyway, and when we have a party in our class one afternoon Danny pulls me out to dance with him. I'm still a little weak from my illness that winter, but am strong enough to yank my hand from his grasp. I don't know how to dance. I lack the confidence to dance. I sure as heck won't be caught dead dancing with the cutest boy in the world in front of my entire class.

S-A-T-U-R-D-A-Y NIGHT!

S-A-T-U-R-D-A-Y NIGHT!

"Come out here, silly!" Danny yells to me from the center of the room. He throws his arms up in the air and twirls around.

I watch him from where I now stand at the back of the room wishing I could be somebody other than who I am. I want to be the girl who jumps out in the middle of the room. I want to be the free and happy one. I want to yell and sing with my mouth wide open. I want to take his two hands in mine and twirl around the room until our teacher says, "Now, now, you two! Settle down!" In my mind I'm spinning around on the floor with Danny, happy and free. My body is rooted at the back of the classroom near the science posters where I hope no one notices me and wonders why I'm not dancing. If I had the ability right at this moment to change places with any one of those happy 11 year old girls dancing on the floor I would do so regardless of the consequences. Even if I knew that doing so meant I would die next year.

On the last day of school I walk toward home with the girls as I usually do, although we always part at the corner and go to our different neighborhoods. Danny approaches us from behind and asks if he can talk to me alone. Donna raises an eyebrow at me in a wicked way and I raise my eyebrows to glare at her to stay with me. She winks and moves away instead.

"Would you be my girlfriend?" Danny whispers in my ear as we fall in step behind the girls. The sweet smell of Doublemint gum accompanies his request. My ear feels wet and warm from the force of his sugary breath.

Overlay – A Tale of One Girl's Life in 1970s Las Vegas

I whisper, "Yes!" and watch his hair whip back as he runs ahead to catch up with the girls and when they turn left at the corner and head to their neighborhood we all yell, "Have a good summer!" to each other and I head home alone to my neighborhood. I float along on a cloud of glorious disbelief.

I have a boyfriend!

I have a boyfriend!

I have a boyfriend!

I want to tell my mother. I wish I had the kind of mother that I would want to tell. I want to run into the house and fall into the arms of this mother and hug her and tell her all about Danny who danced to the Bay City Rollers and asked me to be his girlfriend. I want her to ask questions about him and suggest we invite his family over for a barbecue so we can all get to know each other. I want to sneak away from overprotective parents who sip martinis on the back deck, distracted by their discussions of the stock market and the opera they'd all attended last week. I want Danny and I to sneak away to a secret place like my closet that's chock-full of clothes and he'll sneak a kiss and I'll giggle and say, "Oh you shouldn't have done that!' and then we'll laugh and do it again. I want so much. I want knowledge and imagination outside of the life I live. In the end, I tell no one my fantastic secret. Not even Karen. There just isn't anyone I trust enough with this glorious information.

My twelfth birthday arrives a week later and I throw an impromptu birthday party for myself. I call some friends from Karen's phone and invite them over. My mother and Dean aren't home so I arrange a 'make your own pizza' lunch with English muffins and spaghetti sauce. We don't have enough cheese for the 'pizzas' and several of the girls including me end up with a disgusting mix of plain spaghetti sauce on a muffin. Even baking it can't render it appetizing. The only game I have the supplies to play is bobbing for apples with the few old apples I find in our produce drawer. I locate a big metal tub in our shed, wash out the dead spiders, fill it with water and place the apples inside. One immediately sinks to the bottom and we all watch it disappear. I reach in and pull it out and toss it over the fence. We take turns bobbing for apples and I run into my house after each successful bob to return with a gift. Since I wasn't able to buy anything for my party, I hand my personal items to my guests: used mascara, a pair of green earrings that had once been silver, a mini pad of paper with a few pages missing.

My guests look embarrassed and in those looks I see that even among the poor, I am now the poorest. No longer do I have the other kids on the lower rungs to compare myself to as I had at the Camelot Apartments. I'm feeding at the bottom. Sandra says she has to leave early and asks to use my phone to call her mother. I say our phone's out of service and see Karen trade a quick look with Sandra. When Karen offers to let Sandra use her phone the other girls ask to come and call their mothers too. I'm left alone, relieved that my party's over. I empty the tub of water and vow never to celebrate my birthday again. Only as the hours of the day crawl by does the humiliation subside.

A letter from my aunt arrives with another check for $50. My mother says she needs it for food and will pay me back. The summer seeps along and the days grow increasingly hotter. I no longer have free access to a swimming pool so there isn't much for me to do. I take a job babysitting for the single father across the street, charging him $1.00 per hour to watch his two little boys. My mother says I'm not allowed to charge him at night when the boys sleep on my bedroom floor, since I'm not really watching them. This means I "watch" them for ten hours and make only $2.00. I'm

166

grateful for what I make though and use the precious dollars for any personal items I need like shampoo, conditioner, socks, underwear, blush or mascara. Shopping takes me hours as I painstakingly choose what I need the most and what I have to do without. I tabulate and re-tabulate the amounts in my head, attempting to maximize the smallest amount of money to buy the largest number of items I most need.

After one such shopping spree, I return from the drug store and stop short in utter horror. Danny is circling his bike in front of my house. I make a quick dive into some nearby bushes and even though it's hot and I've scratched my back against a branch I remain there until I'm sure he's gone ... and then for a few minutes longer just to be sure he doesn't come back. What in the world is he thinking coming over to my house? Who told him where I lived? Boyfriend or not, the last thing I want to do is to run into him during summer vacation. What mortification! From that point on I am very careful to peek first before I leave and return to my house.

I spend most of that summer with Karen and her brothers. We stay up late, playing records and making up dances in her living room. We sit outside on an old car parked in her driveway while Karen pounds out drumbeats on the weathered hood. I soak up her energy and drown out the noise in my own head. Another girl, Pat, moves into an apartment down the street. Pat's from California and has a personality every bit as strong as Karen's. Karen and Pat are very different from me in many ways and when the two of them are together they often exclude me. There are so many things they naturally understand that I don't. They have older siblings and their exposure to the bigger, normal world far surpasses my chaotic and limited experience. They both start their periods that summer and talk about all they have to do regarding having periods. They make fun of me for not being as physically mature as they are. They talk about boys and what they've heard about sex and drugs. Karen says her grown up sister smokes pot and tells Karen it makes her feel relaxed and happy. Her sister also tells her that taking LSD makes you see things that aren't really there. While Karen and Pat think this might be fun, secretly I think it sounds horrible. I have enough trouble managing what really is there without worrying about what seems to be there but really isn't. What if it's worse than what really is there?

When we can collect enough money for the $.50 entrance fee for the neighborhood pool and Karen doesn't have to babysit, we go swimming on summer afternoons. Ashamed at my skinny body compared to the other girls, I enviously eye Karen and Pat's breasts and hips. Easily a full head shorter than the two of them, I look more like their much younger sister than their friend. Sometimes Danny and his friends are at the pool, and he chases me around the edge until the lifeguard yells, "Hey, you two! No running!" I spend those afternoons trying to avoid him and never confess to either Pat or Karen that I'm his girlfriend.

Karen and two of her brothers go to spend a week with their father toward the end of summer. Since their youngest brother has a different father and won't be going with them, Karen's mother asks if I'll stay with her and watch him at night while she's at work: a glorious offer. It's strange to be in the silent house all alone with the baby minus the noise of Karen, Jimmy and Ricky. I imagine that I live with Daisy and the baby and we have a quiet peaceful house without a couch full of drunks keeping me up at night. I enjoy taking care of Stephen that week and discovered a delectable peace in caring for another human being. It makes me feel better about myself to care for someone else - a tonic to escape my own life.

Daisy pays me $50 for the week, truly a small fortune for me and perfect timing for the onset of the new school year. Catching the city bus to a clothing store the first thing the following morning, I spend nearly six hours choosing clothing, tabulating and re-tabulating my purchases over and over to make sure I have enough to pay for what I've chosen. A pair of jean capri pants, matching vest, two tee-shirts and a pair of pants are the five items of clothing I have for the school year. Since I don't have money left over for the bus, I walk the ten miles back home, clutching my bag of clothes and sweating in the heat of the Las Vegas summer.

In the first week of seventh grade I break up with Danny when I notice Pat walking down the hallway between classes. Pat has braces and long, feathered brown hair that moves when he walks. When I smile at Pat in the classroom, he looks at me with a measured and undeniable disgust. He must not realize I'm smiling at him, so I repeat my smile as I pass him again in the hall the next day at school. He doesn't smile in return.

While sitting at my desk in my next class, I look down at my body and try to see myself through Pat's eyes. I know my hair is ugly and stringy, but as I finger the scratchy split ends I reason that it's always mostly clean. Since I cut my own hair I know it's not perfect but it's fairly even. Running my tongue across my teeth I can feel they're dirty. I'd noticed in the mirror this morning that I have some rather unattractive kitten scratches on my face. I've recently begun plucking my eyebrows and sometimes I don't get them quite even, but surely Pat won't notice such a minor thing. I make up for my eyebrow issues by applying two bright circular patches of blush on the dead center of each cheek. My matching capri and vest outfit is certainly very stylish, and sniffing my armpit note that I still smell new and clean. I've only worn the Capri outfit two times this week, so it can't be my clothing that repulses him. Continuing my gaze down to my shoes, socks, and shins, my legs are scabbed and scarred and cut from my numerous learning-to-shave incidents. Once-white socks fall around my bony ankles, accentuating the stained, ripped tennis shoes I wear. They're too small and they hurt my feet, but they're all I have. My big toe nail pokes through the canvas of my left shoe, cracked and dirty. Gross. No wonder – it's definitely my shoes! Pat must have noticed my shoes. That afternoon I ask my mother for socks and underwear and shoes explaining I don't even have enough to last me one week.

"I wish I could help you, but I can't," my mother says, her expression inscrutable.

Dean takes a long drag on his cigarette, eyeing me through the exhaled smoke.

"Mom, you haven't bought me school clothes in two years."

"I've offered to take you to the Salvation Army."

"I don't want clothes from the Salvation Army! I need underwear and socks and new, clean shoes!"

"Seems the last time she bought you a pair of shoes you just threw them at the wall like a spoiled brat," Dean interjects.

"That was two years ago! I need a new pair of shoes! I have one pair and they're too small. Look, my toe pokes out!" I would like to say I got somewhere with them, but if I said that I'd be lying.

That night during the evening's drunk-fest, I pore over my history book and catch sight of my dirty socks. A slow burn of anger fires across my stomach and I hold my hand to my stomach to ease the burning pain.

I'm not even asking for glamorous items. I will be happy with the necessities. But how I want glamor too.

Chapter Thirty Seven

Any To Come: Term used to describe when all or part of returns from one wager are automatically reinvested on a subsequent bet.

I'm not afraid of Dean. The distance I keep is more from my instinctive awareness that he's just so much physically bigger than I am. I regard him warily like one would a junkyard dog on a long and potentially unreliable chain. I know to stay well out of his reach. In a purely physical confrontation I assume he would win. The realization dawns that I need to be much smarter than he is to survive.

However, the beatings and yelling and crying at night on the other side of my bedroom wall are taking their toll on me. I'm not spending as much time at Karen's house anymore because all she talks about are boys and drugs. When all I can think about is survival, I'm hard pressed to listen politely to the silly conversations that pass between Karen and Pat. So I'm usually exhausted and having difficulty staying awake in my classes. Rather than concentrate on the words of my teachers, increasingly often I find myself daydreaming about how I'm going to handle what I now refer to in my head as 'the Dean situation.' I plot and plan ways to permanently eliminate him from my life and release my mother from his spell.

I usually start out by thinking that the best possible scenario is for Dean to die: it's the only guarantee that he will be out of our lives forever. If anyone ever did, Dean has murder victim written all over his face. He practically begs for it. Could I be the one to kill him? Was I capable of such an act, physically or psychologically? I picture my mother hitting him with the frying pan. Hit in the proper place, a blow to the head could be fatal. I can't even reach his head unless he's sleeping, and I'm unsure of the perfect place for frying-pan-to-skull impact. If he doesn't die when I hit him, I most certainly will when he comes after me. I'm sitting in math class and through the noise in my head I hear my teacher say, "If not x, then y. This is the formula."

Perfect: if not me, then who?

I've just finished reading "Helter Skelter" so I consider Charles Manson and Squeaky Fromme. People kill people all the time. Where does one find these people? How do you recognize a killer – is there a secret mark? Is there a place where these people congregate – a killer's bar, for example? How do you find it? I imagine people probably don't kill for free. I imagine it must be a career and I have no money to offer a potential killer. The murder plan fizzles out around this part of the reasoning process.

If not x, then y.

If not me, then who is not the solution. I must have the wrong answers for x and y.

What if x = death?

If not death, then….what?

What's a substitution for death?

Coma? Sleep? Locked away?

Overlay – A Tale of One Girl's Life in 1970s Las Vegas

The bell rings to signal the end of class. I gather my books and now I have my answer: the closest thing to death is prison.

The next time I hear Dean say he's going to the store I ask to go with him, thinking that if I'm alongside him when he has money in his pocket I can get some of the things I need. He denies every request I make for food and instead starts tucking whatever he can fit inside the pockets of his jean jacket.

"What are you DOING?" I whisper, horrified.

"Shut up. Do you want to eat or not?"

Yes, but no: not under these conditions.

At the cash register he pays for one carton of cigarettes and a gallon of the cheapest Rose wine. I wonder how a wine could have such a flowery name and wreak such havoc on my family. I hope some of the stolen loot will slip from his jacket when he reaches inside to get his wallet, but this doesn't happen. We exit the store and instead of heading to the right as we should, I follow Dean to the left and to the back of the store. He sets the bag containing the wine and the cigarettes on the pavement, flips open the lid of a large dumpster and pokes his hand around in the trash. Tossing me a bag of spoiled cabbage, he says to make room for more. He adds several other bags of spoiled vegetables to my outstretched arms, then moves to another dumpster. He tosses heads of lettuce and an odd piece of smushy fruit to me.

"I'm not carrying this!" I'm mortified by the thought that someone from school might drive past this back alley and see me with my arms full of rotting food.

"You'll do what you're damn well told. You won't tell your mother where I got the food from if you know what's good for you."

What's good for me? What does it matter what's good for me? Nothing about life is about what's good for me, but only what's good for everyone else. So that evening my mother makes stir-fry with one of the bags of spoiled cabbage. Though I swear to myself I won't touch the garbage food I learn that night that when a person is hungry they will eat anything.

Even rotten cabbage floating in soy sauce.

Apart from being a lazy drunk, abuser and chain smoker, Dean's also a thief. Rather than get an honest job he steals mail and forges the welfare, unemployment and retirement checks of our neighbors. I hear him laughing to my mother one evening about how the entire neighborhood is supporting us.

While he finds this amusing, I consider our next door neighbors, Jose and Hilda Gonzalez. They've been very kind to me when I'm particularly hungry. The elderly Hilda has waved me inside on more than one occasion when she sees me walking home from school. She gestures for me to sit down at her tiny kitchen table and pats me on the head. She prepares a simple meal, places it on the table in front of me and drinks coffee while I eat. Sometimes she invites me to help her work in the garden, loading my arms with part of her meager take-in.

How can my mother allow such a thing to happen to Mr. and Mrs. Gonzalez when they've been so generous to me? It's the last straw - I can't stand the humiliation of Dean abusing those around

172

us any longer. I'm afraid my mother won't survive Dean's next attack.

The next morning when I see both of my mother's once beautiful blue eyes black and swollen shut into tiny slits, I call upon every bit of strength I have to remain cool. I decide to use Dean's vice as a weapon against him. "Dean, we're out of Kool-Aid. Do you think you could go to the store today?"

He grunts in reply, not wanting to seem agreeable in doing something that's directly asked of him. I have time so I wait and later in the afternoon when he exhausts his supply of Marlboros he says he thinks he'll go to the store.

"I'll go with you," I add, not asking for permission. I say a silent prayer in my head that my mother won't ask to come along. Lately, she's made a strong effort to not allow me to be alone with Dean so I fully expect her to say she'll be coming along. It won't do to have her come along today and I hold my breath. She's silent for a moment and I imagine that probably because her face is so battered her vanity won't allow her to be seen in public – and she declines to come along. Dean and I begin the long walk to the store.

My head is full of cotton, my thoughts fuzzy and erratic. The slap of our feet on the pavement keep a half-time beat with the thick thud of my heart. I can barely breathe because my chest is so tight with anxiety I have to force myself to take deep breaths. In. Out. In. Out.

At the store, Dean doesn't take a shopping cart which is a sign he's going to steal most of the items. Trailing behind him as he cruises the aisles, I keep my eyes on his hands as they deftly secret away small items into his denim jacket: Ramen noodles, sugar, powdered spaghetti sauce mix. When I see the Kool-Aid disappear into his jacket pocket I say, "I'll be right back."

He turns around at the sound of my voice and looks down on me as if he's just noticed I'm with him, "What's the matter with you? You're acting weird."

"Nothing."

"Hurry it up, then."

Once I leave him I walk-run along the aisle, anxiously looking for a store employee to report his shoplifting. Once he's arrested and sent to jail for the rest of his life, my mother and I will be safe again. I picture the store clerk tackling Dean to the ground and searching his pockets. The crowd will gather around, shaking my hand and patting me on the head. The police will arrive and thank me for doing my civic duty and congratulate me on never having to see Dean again. Dean will rot in jail for the rest of his life.

I find an older grocer in the produce department. He doesn't look strong enough to protect me from Dean and this could be a problem if something goes wrong with my plan. "Excuse me," I say to him, and my voice already shaking.

The grocer turns toward me, a watermelon balanced in one hand. The thought runs crazily through my mind that he could throw the watermelon at Dean if something goes wrong, and I can run away during the distraction. I would have to then run home and warn my mother of the impending danger. We would throw a few things in a shared bag and hightail it down the street where we would find a pay phone, call my dad and he would rescue us from this existence.

Overlay – A Tale of One Girl's Life in 1970s Las Vegas

"Help me."

"Help you? What can I help you find?"

"See, there is this man-"

"This man?" he cocks his head to the side, turning one ear toward me.

"Yes. There is this man. And he's stealing!"

"Smiling? This man is smiling?"

"No! He's not smiling! He's stealing. He's stealing from your store!" My heart thuds so thick and hard I can feel the force of blood coursing through my body.

"From this store?"

"Yes! From this store!" I pant with fear, knowing time is running out. "Please have him arrested. Have him taken away. Forever. Please! You've got to hurry!"

His eyes move up from mine to a spot several feet above my head.

"Ready?" I hear Dean say from behind me as he places one hand around my neck.

The grocer looks at me and I cry inside for him to see, to help, to do something; to notice my fear, my dejection. Just save me! I scream in my head.

The grocer will not be my savior today.

My mouth pinches into a tiny O. I debate whether to just calmly say to the grocer, "The man behind me is shoplifting. If you check his jacket you'll find all the items he has stolen." All I have to do is say it. Just say it. Open my mouth and say it. Move. Do something. Speak. Say it.

"Everything okay?" the grocer's eyebrows draw together.

Dean squeezes my neck and forcibly turns my body away from the grocer. "Everything's just fine."

I fail.

On the walk home I collapse as all the adrenaline that rushed through my body thickens and pools and then dissipates, leaving sickness and exhaustion behind. I fall sideways into a bush and lose consciousness.

I have neither the strength nor the stamina to stay alive anymore. And I know that every beating of my mother after that afternoon in the grocery store will be my fault. I had the power to save her and fear held me back, and now I will aid and abet her future suffering. I halfheartedly return to planning Dean's elimination. It doesn't eradicate the guilt I experience in the meantime.

I know I'm running out of time.

The ticking time bomb plays a drumbeat in my head, ringing in my ears and beating in my heart.

It becomes an automatic reinvestment in every piece of me...every cell conscious of the ominous ticking of time.

Chapter Thirty Eight

Giving Odds: An additional bet used to back up a Don't Pass or Don't Come bet after the point has been established. This reduces the house edge on your action.

There's a boy in school and his name is Oliver. He has white-blonde hair that he wears straight and long, under which peeks light blue eyes and a peaceful, easy smile. One afternoon as I'm heading home from school he appears alongside me and nervously asks me to be his girlfriend. I mutter a quick yes and scurry away since it doesn't occur to me that I can say no.

When Karen and Pat find out about my new boyfriend (which they think is my first), they relentlessly pressure me to kiss him. For all their talk of boys and sex, I wonder why they push me to kiss a boy? They talk about it so often I stop walking home with them in the afternoons just to avoid the conversation.

A week after Oliver asks me to be his girlfriend, Karen and Pat plead with me to stay after school with them, claiming that Karen left something in the art room. I should have known better. I want to walk home alone and work on the "Dean situation" in my head and don't see why they need me to remain behind. However, they're so insistent I agree to wait for them. When we near the corner of the building where the art room is located, I stop walking when I see Oliver standing outside the art room door nervously kicking the toe of his white tennis shoe on the cement.

"I left my notebook inside, Marlayna. Would you get it for me?" Karen asks.

The conundrum I face is that if I don't go into the art room, I will look shy and stupid in front of Oliver. If I do go, I'll fall victim to some plan I'm sure they've devised. I decide to take my chances since they're all looking at me and I'm beginning to sweat. That familiar rancid smell is seeping from my pores. I step into the art room and flip the lights on. Immediately Oliver walks in behind me. He turns off the lights and locks the door.

My name whispered from his mouth floats through the room. I can hear a smile in his voice. There are no windows in the art room and therefore no light. I put my hands out to blindly feel around for the desks, attempting to move away from him as silently as I can. I shuffle around, carefully placing my feet on the ground one after another in desperate silence. I hear Oliver following the noise of my footsteps. I hit my shin on a misplaced chair and the subsequent clang surely gives him a general idea of where I am in the room. My leg is smarting, and my heart is pounding and I'm really sweating now. I can hear Karen and Pat outside the door, laughing and talking in complete normalcy. If I can lead him in a complete circle and reach the art room door before he does I can unlock it and run home.

As I feel my way around the darkened room, Oliver's hand reaches out and grabs my forearm. "Don't be scared," he whispers at the same time I'm thinking that we're locked in the pitch-black of my art room where I'd happily sculpted a purple octopus from clay just that morning. My stomach recoils at the thought of physical contact with another person, let alone a boy.

Oliver wraps his skinny arms around me in the dark and says, "You don't need to be scared. I won't hurt you." He reaches toward me, searching for my lips. We open our mouths to kiss and after a few face bumps, our lips meet. He doesn't use his tongue like Angela's ex-step-father Big Ray had, and instead moves his open mouth around mine like a dying fish gasping for air. After a moment I pull away and in the dark I wipe the salty wetness from my face with the back of my forearm.

The afternoon light is searing, and Pat and Karen are black against the light of the day. Oliver says goodbye and bestows one of his easy smiles on me before he slips away. Karen and Pat pester me with questions all the way home, but the only thing I will say is, "That wasn't very kind of you."

Days pass and I'm getting very little good sleep and am more exhausted than I've ever been. I work successfully to avoid Oliver before school, during school and after school. After some time passes, I hand him a note asking him to meet me on the football field after our last class of the day.

Oliver is already waiting, and my heart pulls in my chest when he sees me and smiles.

"I want to break up," I blurt even as we are still walking toward each other.

His smile cracks on his lips and when he tilts his head to the side his straight blonde falls across his forehead, "Why?"

Why?

Why? Why? Why? Why?

Why indeed?

How can I possibly explain the complications behind my decision? That I can't handle the additional stress of having to kiss my boyfriend? That I know I'm poor and my clothes are cheap and ugly and I'm not even pretty and our dinners come courtesy of the grocery store trash bin and that it's so much easier not to be noticed at all than to be confronted with all the things I wish I had when I would have gladly settled for just having the things I need?

How can I tell him that I sometimes cry myself to sleep because I'm so hungry and if I have to see another Kentucky Fried Chicken or McDonald's commercial I will kill myself? How can I share that I'm often woken by the sounds of the physical abuse of my mother? That when I wake up on time in the mornings and prepare myself for school I'm upset that I haven't been asked to babysit enough lately to earn enough money for toothpaste or hair conditioner?

Now that Oliver has noticed me I've noticed myself and my tremulous position in the world. My spiraling abject poverty and inner despair is a force that carries me through my days now. This isn't just what is going on in my life. This IS me. How can I have someone in my life when I can't be ME? I don't try to explain any of this. I know I would be unable to articulate these dark thoughts.

Big tears roll down his face and I stare at them in horror. The thought that he likes me enough to cry is way more emotion than I'm prepared to handle. I turn on my worn-down heel and bolt. Big, hulking sobs break from me as I run toward my house.

Pumping my arms to run as fast as I can, I cry for Oliver and the way I wish things could be, as well as the way they aren't ... but mostly for the way they are.

The bets and losses are growing. I must figure out a way to give odds and change the direction of the game.

Chapter Thirty Nine

Battle Royale is played between one player and a dealer. A regular deck of 52 cards is used, with one card dealt face up to the player, and one card dealt face up to the dealer. The game is very simple in that whoever has the higher card wins.

My mother takes an evening bar tending shift that November, bundling up in a Salvation Army jacket for her walk to the bus stop. It's a cold night in the Las Vegas desert, and she seems nervous before she leaves. Her eyes dart around the smoke-filled living room like a cornered rabbit. After she shuts the front door, the resultant silence that falls upon our house is a distant cousin to the days when I was alone in the house with my real father. Only it's Dean and me this time. I hide in my room, sitting cross-legged on the floor and watching my little black and white TV. I'm also writing my first book: a first person account of a 12 year old girl who will survive the Black Plague after her entire village is wiped out, including her own family. She will have to find her way to another village to start anew. I drop right into the character:

At the sound of her mother's cough, Cathryn again places her hand on her mother's forehead. Burning. Wringing her hands, Cathryn reluctantly thinks of the one person who can help. She eyes the small cot in the corner of the hut where the still body of her little sister has laid dead these few hours. It is already too late for wee Elizabeth.

"I will be back. I'll go to the house of the Witch," Cathryn whispers into the ear of her fevered mother.

"No, child. No. The price is too high."

"I will make a trade. I have something of value the Witch will surely want...."

"Promise me you won't help me," Cathryn's mother coughs. "Save yourself, child. There is only death in this hut. Leave. Never come back."

Cathryn kisses her mother's fiery forehead, grabs her shawl and leaves the hut.

There isn't any food in the house which isn't an unusual situation, but tonight I am so hungry my stomach is clenched in knots. The fast food commercials draw tears of frustration down my cheeks. Steaming fried chicken. Salty, greasy French fries. Big burgers with cheese oozing down the sides of fluffy buns. Thick milk shakes. Opening my bedroom door, I listen for sounds in the living room. Hearing nothing, I foolishly hope Dean has left for the night, perhaps to join my mother at the bar. I walk down the short hallway and enter the living room. There I see the cherry of his cigarette, where he is sitting in the gloom and smoking a Marlboro. A bottle of vodka rests before him on the coffee table.

Looking down and away, I move to the kitchen to search the cabinets. Amongst the packets of sugars and spices, I'm gloriously rewarded with one overlooked single cube of bouillon. I place it in a teacup, add hot tap water and scurry back to my room. I feel Dean's gaze on my back as I pass through the living room. As much as I want to boil the water, I don't want to spend any more time near Dean than I absolutely have to.

Outside the hut, Cathryn runs past the freshly turned soil and roughhewn cross marking the grave. The body of her older brother lies three days in the dirt, buried by she and her mother before her mother caught the Fever. I am nearly alone, Cathryn fears -

It's longer than I expected when I hear my door handle turn and find Dean taking up the big space in my doorway. Instantly I regret retrieving the bouillon. I should have gone hungry, I scold myself. Stupid, stupid me. Now I've attracted his attention.

"Where's the cat?" Dean has long regaled me with his tales of slamming doors on kitten bodies and cutting them in half. I know better than to let him anywhere near my cat. Living with Dean requires a constant vigilance to protect my animals, and tonight is no exception.

"Under the bed." Thinking, planning, plotting, panicking.

"Get the cat out," he orders, a cigarette bobbing from the side of his mouth. Then he's gone, slamming my door behind him.

I quickly consider my limited options. If I put the cat outside my bedroom window, he will trail around to the front door. Once he scratches on the screen door, Dean will kill him. I know this. If I personally carry my cat outside and try to take him to Karen's or Pat's house, Dean will grab the cat from my arms as I pass his armchair. I know this too. I know I'm not strong enough to withstand much physical violence from Dean. I've seen what he's capable of doing, and I know my cat will likely be squashed in the ensuing struggle.

The door to the Witch's hut creaks open. "Come in, Cathryn," a raspy voice says.

"How did you know it was me?"

"I am a Witch, Cathryn. I know all."

"Then you know why I am here, Witch?"

"Of course."

"And will you help me?"

"There is a price for help. It is not free."

"I have no money, Witch. My brother and sister are dead. My mother is dying."

"There is no hope for your mother, Cathryn. I cannot help her. She has the Fever."

"You must, Witch! Oh please! I will give you anything you want. Just please save my mother!"

"I can only save you, Cathryn." With that, the Witch coughs and Cathryn knows.

"How much longer do you have, Witch?"

"A few hours at most. The Fever takes its victims quickly. It does not tarry."

"But how can you help me, Witch?"

"I have one vial of medicine left. It is only enough for one person. It is too late for me, but it will save you, Cathryn."

Overlay – A Tale of One Girl's Life in 1970s Las Vegas

"Witch, what shall I give you in return?"

"Your promise that you will drink this medicine and run to the next village. You will not return to your hut. You will never come back here again."

The door opens again and Dean repeats his demand. I realize his intrusions into my room aren't about my cat at all, and true fear begins coursing through my body. I calmly assure him I will take the cat outside but he kicks over my cup of bouillon with his toe anyway and together we watch it bleed brown across the pages of my Black Plague story. "Get the cat out," he says before he leaves the room.

"The vial is here, Cathryn," and the Witch places the small bottle into Cathryn's outstretched palm.

"Thank you, Witch."

"Make your promise to me, Cathryn. You will not split this medicine with your mother. It will not work for either of you if diluted. You must make the decision now to swallow it whole and run to the next village."

"Witch, 'tis an impossible situation to leave my mother to die alone!"

"Not impossible, child, just difficult." The Witch coughs. "My price for your life is your promise. Pay it and be on your way before I change my mind."

"Witch, please! I cannot leave my mother. I am all she has!"

"She no longer needs you. Now pay it."

Cathryn sobs, knowing she awoke this morning a child and would end this day a woman.

I am calm. I am cool. I show no emotion. My best option is to take my cat and climb out the window, but I have nowhere to go once I escape into the winter night. I'm still trying to figure out what to do when Dean walks into my bedroom again.

"I'll kill the fucking cat!" he yells and throws himself on the floor of my room, reaching under the bed with his long arms.

"Please, Dean, don't!"

My bedroom door is open and I know all I have to do is jump over his long legs and run straight through the doorway. What will he do to the cat after I'm gone? Helplessly watching him flail his skinny arms underneath my bed, I wring my hands and will him to stop this craziness now.

He does stop, miraculously enough, and pulls himself upright. I'm considering the idea of feeling relieved when he stands towering over me and I see something in his eye I haven't seen before: a sick gleam of desire. I jump onto the end of my bed so that I'm only a foot shorter than he is. It happens quickly. He lunges for me and I reach back with every bit of strength I have to pull my arm around and punch him firmly in the nose just like I'd learned to do in the oceans of Maui if faced with an attacking shark.

Momentarily stunned, he recovers quickly and takes his large hand and slams my chest with the force to send me flying backwards from the end of the bed to the wall behind me. As I slide down the wall trying to grasp a breath, he's already moving toward me, staggering side to side. If I had had any doubt what the evening is about, that doubt is eradicated on the spot. I duck to the side as he lands on my bed and I almost escape his grasp. I really almost do. Although I turn to the side quickly it isn't quickly enough and one of his large hands grips my upper arm.

I wrench forward but he holds me with a strength I didn't know he had considering his drunken state. I scream at him to let me go. I yank and jerk my arm away from him, but he is bigger and stronger and just as I had always feared, my efforts to twist away from him are futile. He holds my little arm firmly, effortlessly, his hand completely wrapped around my arm. When I look into his eyes I know I have one last chance to get away from him before he takes me around a corner I won't survive.

He laughs then, a chuckle that builds into a snicker. "You're not so tough now, are you little brat?"

That is when I swing my free hand around and punch his cigarette straight into his mouth. With a girly-like squeal he reels up and backwards and the second he releases his grip on my arm to clasp his hand over his mouth I scramble to my feet and run. I run through my bedroom doorway, down the hallway, around the corner, through the screen door, down the walkway, over the garden gate, across the gravel driveway and don't stop until I reach Pat's house several blocks away.

Cathryn swallows the entire vial in one swallow, surprised by her greediness, by her will to live. She wanted to save half for her mother, but knows the Witch is right. Her mother is beyond hope and cannot be saved. No one in the village survives the Black Plague. Wrapping her shawl tightly around her shoulders, she faces the Witch. "Thank you, Witch."

"You are the future, Cathryn. Take your memories with you and go to the next village. There you will make a new life for yourself. Leave Death behind in this village. Do not take it with you."

Mrs. Rodriguez opens her door to find me heaving, panting, babbling and unable to string two sensible words together. When she sees me turn my head to make sure I'm not being followed, she grabs my shoulder and pulls me into their apartment. Locking the door, she places her two hands on my shoulders. "Mija, what's wrong?" she asks, her breath warm and sweet, a savior's sweet hope.

Mr. Rodriguez enters the room as his wife holds my heaving shoulders. I'm conscious of their concern and pity, which exacerbates my feelings of shame. I feel as if I'm floating overhead and above the whole scene. I watch this happen from some far off place. Another planet. Another galaxy. I wonder if I died and just didn't know it yet. If I am alive, I've taken the first step ever in reaching out to another human being to ask for help and I need to move forward. I won't let shame stop me. I won't remain silent anymore. There is no going back to the village this time. My head is full of cotton and I struggle to gather my words, concentrating on slowing my breathing. I try to explain the evening's events by telling them I'm afraid Dean is coming after me.

"Patricia," Mrs. Rodriguez calls, "take Marlayna into your room, Mija, I need to speak to your father."

Pat and I lay on our stomachs on her bed and she hands me a crossword puzzle. I try to concentrate on the words before me but the letters skip around the page. Heated Spanish passes between Mr. and Mrs. Rodriguez in the living room. Pat doesn't translate and the yelling escalates.

Overlay – A Tale of One Girl's Life in 1970s Las Vegas

When I hear my mother's voice I go to the living room and approach the backs of Mr. and Mrs. Rodriguez as they stand together at the front door. My mother is not invited into the sanctuary of the Rodriguez home. She stands on the doorstep looking angry and indignant as if this entire evening is one giant embarrassing inconvenience. She has the decency to look embarrassed as Mrs. Rodriguez berates her. When she turns to leave I come out from behind Mrs. Rodriguez and entreat her to stay with us.

"She can stay can't she, Mrs. Rodriguez?"

"Your mother is a grown woman. She can do as she wishes."

My mother turns and leaves, her heels clacking down the cement walkway. Behind me Mr. Rodriguez is now brandishing a pistol and assuring us all that we are safe. The thought that someone would protect me as a part of his own family is too overwhelming for me to absorb.

"Should I go to the house, Norma?" Mr. Rodriguez asks his wife.

"Norbert, she made her own choices. All we can do is protect this child. The mother's on her own."

Mr. Rodriguez turns the gun around in his hand, examining it with a look that says he is disappointed not to have been able to use it.

It's a long and horrible night punctuated with thoughts and images of doom and disaster. I can't sleep knowing my mother has gone to face Dean's anger. Tiny, young and malnourished as I am, I know my presence in my mother's life guarantees at least some small degree of safety due to my role as a witness. It also helps her maintain at least a small degree of normal living. If I'm not in the house who will prevent Dean from killing my mother? At least I am there to pound on the bedroom door when I hear the pummeling get out of control. Who will save her now?

Cathryn leaves the witch's hut and turns North on the well worn foot path. She wonders briefly if she should go back to her hut and see if her mother is still alive, even as her feet travel North and carry her from her village. In the end, she figures it's best not to know. In this way she is free to imagine her mother and sister and brother as she best remembered them: happy, laughing and alive.

'A journey of a thousand Miles starts with one Step,' she says out loud to herself, and repeats it as many times as she can as she makes her way to the next village.

And finally, Dean Parker loses the Battle Royale to yours truly.

Overlay – A Tale of One Girl's Life in 1970s Las Vegas

Chapter Forty

Blackjack: In blackjack your objective is to beat the dealer in one of two ways. You can either accumulate a higher score than the dealer without going over 21, or sit on a lower score and hope that the dealer goes over or busts.

The next morning Pat and I walk past my house on the way to school. In the early morning winter sunlight our house appears quiet and peaceful. It is difficult to imagine the chaos the house regularly encloses when it's bathed in such a cool blue and calming light. She could be dead already, I think and stop walking.

"No," Pat pulls on my arm, annoyed. "My mom says you are to go straight to school. If you don't, I'm supposed to call the police. Don't put me in that position."

A change in my living environment is now beyond my control: as I pass my house to go to Pat's after school I see my father's car parked in our graveled yard and know I will be leaving Jefferson Street that very day. I say goodbye to Pat who continues along the street not knowing I will not see her again. My handsome father is sitting on the couch next to my mother inside the house. Dean is conspicuously absent and for this one thing I am enormously grateful.

"Hello, Penut," my father greets me in his crisp, sober voice.

"I won't go live with you."

"You have no choice," my mother says.

"No! I won't go! Who will protect you?"

"That's not your job. Marlayna," my father says next: two separate, punctuated sentences.

"You're going with your father today. That's final."

"There are a gazillion other ways, Mom!"

"You can't stay here anymore. It's just not safe for you."

"Get your things together," my father directs. "I'll be outside this dump."

My position is futile. That much is clear. I walk down the short hallway and look around my bedroom. There's really very little I want from my bedroom. I grab the story I'm writing about the Black Plague from my night table, and stand in the center of my room, looking around and not seeing anything else I want to take with me. I have no photographs or records, and I certainly don't want any of the clothes outside of what I have to wear out of here. Carrying only the pieces of paper that hold my story, I walk outside to my dad's yellow Chevy Nova. He's absently smoking a cigarette, standing next to the open trunk. Looking at my hands holding my papers, he asks, "That's all you have?"

"Yes."

He shakes his head.

Overlay – A Tale of One Girl's Life in 1970s Las Vegas

When I walk into the house to say goodbye to my mother she's standing before my bedroom window with her back to me. As I move closer to hug her, she shakes her head and waves me off with one hand. I back up softly, and join my father in his car. As he backs the car down the graveled driveway, I wonder why she has deserted me. I can't understand this. She has busted.

PART FIVE

(1978 – 1982)

Chapter Forty One

Blackjack Bet: What makes the game of blackjack more entertaining is sometimes you can increase your bets in mid-hand if you have a good opportunity to win. When presented with the opportunity to make these bets, you should take advantage of them because they help eliminate the house edge.

My father rents a beautiful furnished townhouse on Topaz Street, far from Jefferson Street. I don't go to school for the rest of that week and instead accompany my father on various errands. I get my first professional haircut at a real salon, marveling at the smooth, no-split-ends feel of my hair. We shop for a new wardrobe which includes to my great relief, underwear AND socks. I haven't had new clothes for so long that I have to stop myself from repeatedly opening the bags and smelling the new-clothes smell. It is deliriously intoxicating. Even more fun is buying all the home items we need to decorate our new townhouse: new floral-printed sets of stiff sheets and green towels and plates and silverware and plates and cooking utensils.

My joy in receiving all of these wonderful things is however consistently undercut by two things: fear for my mother's safety and annoyance at my father's continuous complaints about my health and appearance. "The judge warned me that I should have never let her have custody of you. He took me aside in his chambers and told me she was unfit to be a mother. He told me if I were to let her raise you that I may as well shoot you in the back of the head. Look at you, you're filthy, your teeth are rotted, and you have no idea how to keep yourself clean. What was I thinking leaving you with that lunatic? I knew she was crazy, but ever since she had that hysterectomy her hormones whacked her out. I should have killed that trailer trash Dean when I made the plan to do so..."

"Killed Dean?"

"I knew he was bad news, and though I wasn't surprised at all that your mother married that piece of garbage, I'm sorry you had to deal with him. I planned to just kill him outright, and spend a few years in jail to get him away from you."

"Why didn't you just take custody of me? Wouldn't that have been an easier solution?"

"It wasn't possible back then, honey, it just wasn't possible. I had to sober up first. I've got a few months under my belt now."

I hope. I hope. I hope.

When Monday morning arrives I leave my house to take the bus to my eighth school. I vomit in the dirt during my short walk to the bus, wipe my mouth with the back of one hand and continue on my way. The good thing about moving so many times is that I end up in the same place I'd started. I pass kids in the halls I've known from years past, and from the different schools I've attended all over the city. I see many familiar faces in the hallways, including one I hadn't imagined I would ever see again.

We pass each other in the hallway between classes, and although we certainly recognize each other, we do not speak. Christine, the girl that Mr. Nice had raped four years earlier, has grown much taller but is easily recognizable to me even though her stringy hair nearly covers her face. Even with the dark patches under her eyes I know her immediately. Our eyes meet, and possibly both sets of our pupils dilate in recognition and shock and then immediately slam shut. Seeing her shadowed face reminds me of times I no longer want or have to think about. Inside, I am annoyed that I must see her again. She is a reminder of all that I want to leave behind. After a few days, I no longer see her again and am not sure why. I can admit to myself that I am relieved.

Though I immediately get busy with the process of making friends, inside I am achingly lonely. My heart hurts. I miss my mother but have no way to contact her since she doesn't have a telephone. I rely on her sporadic calls to learn if Dean has killed her yet or not. When she does call she's usually drunk, and though I want to hang up at the sound of her slurred voice I fear I won't hear from her again. So I suffer the drunken calls from her, hating them and hating her, yet loving her in fluctuating measures. The guilt is overwhelming. If I don't take her call she might die. If I do take her call, my stomach suffers. It's a no-win situation.

The twice weekly trips to the doctors, dentist and orthodontist begins. I have 25 cavities and most of my teeth have to be filled. There's a discussion that I might need bridges due to the advanced stage of decay of many of my back teeth. The dentist and hygienist are incapable of hiding their disdain for the state of my teeth, and look to my father in askance.

"I just took custody of her. Don't blame me," he says defensively, placing his hands on his hips. He is embarrassed and angry, towering nearby as I sit in the dentist chair feeling like a failed science experiment.

The hygienist spends a long time cleaning, scrubbing and polishing my teeth on my first visit. She teaches me how to brush and how to floss by demonstrating the exaggerated movements in the mirror as I mimic her. "How often do you brush your teeth?"

"Not really ever, but I will now." I think of my mother and the Dental Hygienist career she never had. Would things have been different?

I visit a doctor for the ringing in my ears. After a thorough examination that consists of peering into my eyes, peeking into my ears, up my nose, and down my throat, he listens to my heartbeat with his stethoscope. He asks many questions. Afterwards, he asks me to go to the waiting room so he can speak privately with my dad. On the drive home I ask what the doctor said. My dad is silent for so long I think he isn't going to reply. When he does speak it is with the grace of having carefully chosen his words.

"The doctor told me that after the death of his daughter his ears began to ring. He said it's a condition called tinnitus, brought on by immense stress. No doubt you had it because of what went on in that poor excuse for what your mother called a home."

"Is it ever going to go away?"

"Probably not."

I settle back down onto the car seat, realizing that I'd pulled my entire body up in hope that I could anticipate a day when I would no longer hear the cacophony inside my head. My father tells me I am going to have to avoid stress as much as I can for the rest of my life, saying it's the only way I'll be able to manage the condition.

My mother calls and asks me to come visit her. She and Dean have moved to a trailer park in a northern part of town rumored to be even more disreputable. I take down the directions to her house, and promise her I will try to get my father to take me to see her. Surprisingly, he agrees to take me that coming Friday after school. I have no way to let her know I'm arriving since they don't have a telephone. I dress purposely that morning in my new jeans and tee-shirt that reads 'Foxy' in red letters across the chest. My hair is styled and perfectly blow-dried in waves of feathers. Half of my cavities have been filled and I absently wonder if my mother will even notice my shiny teeth.

As we park outside her trailer I see the outline of her head when she parts the dingy blue curtain that tries its best to cover a front window. My father and I step from the car and into the bright spring sunshine, and he walks with me to the battered trailer door. My father looks wonderful. He still has a full head of jet black hair, clean cut and perfect. I am proud of him, proud of his looks, proud to be seen with him. He smells of shaving cream and Irish Spring bar soap.

When my mother opens the door, my father and I both gasp at the sight of her face. Both of her eyes and her chin are black with bruises. One eye is swollen completely shut.

"I'll be in the car," my father says with a curious lack of emotion. "You have five minutes." That clean, fresh scent of him lingers briefly as he walks away.

I don't want even five minutes inside the tiny trailer, and instantly regret my decision to visit. The furniture is worn and the chair seats are blackened from where the butts of the previous tenants met the fake leather. The wood paneled walls are decorated with cheap, knock off prints. Nothing from our previous house is visible, as if my mom and Dean had just simply walked into the previous tenant's decorating scheme. Tenant in. Tenant out. Tenant in.

I cannot look my mother in the eye. I look long enough in her general direction to be polite when she speaks, until my eyes burn with the desire for movement. I let my eyes roam the room in the pretense of examining the surroundings. Though I foolishly hope for the answer I know I won't hear, I ask where is Dean and do my best to hide my disgust when she says he's at the store. I have a momentary flashback of watching him tuck food into his jean jacket.

When my father honks the car horn I am flooded with gratefulness. I hope my mother doesn't hear my exhale of relief as I stand. I don't want to hug her but I do anyway from an internally forced sense of obligation. I remind myself that her face is a good indication that Dean could very well kill her soon. I don't want to feel bad that I don't hug her the last time I may see her. The anger grows that I am continually wrestling with these feelings and emotions.

"Maybe you can come again soon," she suggests and I lie and tell her I would like that very much.

As we pull out of the trailer park my father says in a shaky voice that I am never going there again. I am never allowed to see her again. "Never," he repeats for good measure. I want to argue and even feel I should argue....but I don't. Instead I ask to be dropped off at the roller skating rink.

Somewhere at the roller skating rink between "Boogie Fever" and "Always and Forever" I let my mother go. I can't protect her any longer and I just want to be a child for the first time in my life. So what if I'm already twelve years old? Twelve is still young enough to be a child, isn't it? Recalling the crab shells I'd collected during my summer in Hawaii several years ago, I imagine that I'm shedding the self-image I've carried on my back. The self-image I developed during the years spent sliding down the hill of respectability with my mom cracks and crumbles around me.

Overlay – A Tale of One Girl's Life in 1970s Las Vegas

As I skate around the rink that evening with my new friends I feel the rush of air blowing back through my styled hair, blowing away my previous identify. I know I look good in my new bellbottom jeans. I flip around and skate backwards, moving my hips from side to side. When boys ask me to slow skate I accept, and I get my first hint of the power a woman can have over a man. I make a promise to myself that day that I am going to live only for myself from that point on. With each circuit of the skating rink, I consciously leave my past with my mom behind. I will reinvent myself with my dad in my new village on Topaz Street. This is my time now to step out of my old shell and grow a new one. No one needs to know about my past.

When I'm dropped back at home that evening by one of my friend's parents, I find a sight I'm not prepared for: my father's inebriation. "Dad! How could you?" I am thunderstruck that he is sitting in our living room nursing a tall glass of whiskey.

"Penut…." He smiles a crooked grin, a boy caught doing what he knows he shouldn't be doing. I watch as relief washes across his rubbery face. Judging by his appearance, he's probably been nursing a never-empty glass of VO whiskey since he dropped me off at the skating rink. Had the appearance of my mother caused him to fall off the wagon? Was it my fault for asking him to take me to see her?

I run upstairs, feeling at once overwhelmingly sick, hating him, hating my mother, hating everything in the entire world and the universe beyond. Why must I always trade good for bad? If something good happens then something bad always happens to even the scales. What in the world is wrong with just having good for a while? It's now clear I'm not wanted by either of my parents – because whoever I live with becomes a drunk. With a sinking feeling, I consider that my father had been correct all those years ago when he told me I wasn't supposed to be here. Again I know there is no God, as my dad's drinking is a clear indication to me that a God can't exist. I have nearly a decade under my belt of wasting my precious time praying to God that my parents will stop drinking. Yet they continue to drink, regardless of the torrents of prayers I volley to the heavens. That night I quit praying altogether. "I hate you, God!" I whisper aloud. "I had a measly two hours of freedom from visiting my Mom's awful trailer to finding my dad drunk again. TWO HOURS!"

The next morning I wake up hoping maybe my father is just going to binge once and stop drinking again. I'm wrong. He opens the bottle early that day and just keeps on going that first day. I find solace in the fact that although he continues to drink, he also continues to go to work day. Our kitchen is stocked with food and I have everything I want or need. When I arrive home from school in the afternoons I find the money my dad leaves for me to buy dinner at one of the fast food restaurants on our street. He doesn't start drinking until he arrives home from work at eight PM. By that time I'm already upstairs working on my homework so we have very little interaction with each other. As I've already been accustomed to doing, I spend the majority of my time alone in my room.

After attending cheerleading tryouts after school one afternoon, I hear the phone ring as I walk in the front door. It's my mother asking me to spend the night with her for Thanksgiving. She is sober and for a moment I foolishly imagine that I can enjoy eating Thanksgiving dinner in the little trailer with her and Dean. I put down the phone to ask my father because it seems like the polite thing to do. When he says no and reminds me that I'm no longer allowed to visit her, a mix of disappointment and relief washes over me. Picking up the phone from where I'd left it on my bed, I tell my mother I'm sorry but I'm not allowed to see her anymore. She spouts a few veiled threats about going to court and regaining custody of me, but we both know she will do no such thing.

My father works the entire Thanksgiving weekend and I sit alone in our apartment, watching television and eating junk food. During the commercials I think of my mother alone in the trailer with Dean eating rotten cabbage stir-fry. The guilt gnaws at me. I don't hear from her again until nearly Christmas, and when she calls she is so drunk that I can't understand what she's staying. I tell her not to call me when she's drunk, and that if I hear she's been drinking I will hang up the phone. She can't see that my knees are shaking, knocking together like some sort of cartoon character. I'm so glad we're on the phone when I deliver that difficult news. "I can't save you, Mom. You're going to have to save yourself."

The phone clicks in my ear.

Her next call is in March of the following year to inform me that she's left Dean and moved in with Denny, my third stepfather and her fifth husband. They are moving to Arizona the next day and she's called to say goodbye. "You will always have a place to live with us," she says, her voice breaking.

"Thanks, Mom, but I'm really happy here. I've made the cheerleading squad, and I have so many friends." Though I cry a little as I hang up the phone, I feel a huge rush of relief. The pressure is gone, evaporating like rising steam into the heavens.

The House no longer has the edge on my action.

Chapter Forty Two

Black: the most common color used for $100 chips.

Out of all my friends from the old neighborhood, I miss Donna the most. One Friday I call and ask if she wants to spend the weekend at my house. She agrees and I place the phone on my bed to run downstairs to ask my father if we can drive across town to pick her up.

"Isn't she black?"

I'm still at the bottom of the staircase with my hand on the railing, thinking that I've left the phone face-up on my bed. My heart starts to pound as I hope Donna hasn't heard his question.

"I guess she is," I answer, wondering how I could not have noticed such an obvious thing before.

"Then no, she cannot spend the night here. This isn't a nigger house."

"DAD!"

"Your mother may have allowed niggers at her place but they're not welcomed here."

Telling Donna that my father is sick and no one is allowed to come over is seventh grade speak for 'you can't come over because you're black and my father is racist' and we both know it. Donna and I will never speak again. Donna was the first friend to discover the hell I was living on Jefferson Street and like me anyway. How ironic that out of all the people that crossed through my life my father would dislike her in particular based solely upon the color of her skin. Donna had given me the gift of showing me there were people who would like me for me, without disliking me for whom I'd been born to.

Since there is no point in trying to maintain relationships across town I turn my attention to developing new friendships in my neighborhood. On the bus one afternoon I hear a girl's voice say, "Hi, I'm Angel," and look up from my book to see girl with a freckled face with crooked teeth smiling at me over the school bus seat.

I shyly answer a hello back and return to my book. I'm reading, "Flowers in the Attic," a horrible story about a mother who locks her children in the attic of her rich mother's house after the death of her husband so she can pursue other men.

Angel is not to be deterred. "So what's your name?" she asks in between chomps of her gum.

When I answer that question she asks another. Then another. By then we are standing at my front door and she asks, "Well, are you going to invite me inside?"

Angel is not only amazingly outgoing, but kind as well. She lives with her single mother in a house not too far from my new apartment. Her mother is a real estate agent and works much of the time. "Come over for dinner this week," Angel invites as she waves goodbye to me that evening, "My mom's making chicken. Actually, I'll be making the chicken, but come over anyway."

Angel is strong and secure in every way that I feel vulnerable. When anything goes wrong in her life, her standard response is, "Oh, well!" I ask if she cares about anything. "You never seem to get upset about anything. Don't you care about anything at all?"

"Sure, I care, but there's no point in getting upset about the things I can't change. I'd rather concentrate on the things that I can change."

That summer Angel researches and discovers a week long YMCA camp at Camp Fox on Catalina Island, California, and suggests I come along. We board a bus and travel from Las Vegas to San Pedro, California, where we spend the night in sleeping bags on the floor of a giant gymnasium. The next morning we take a ferry to Catalina Island and see our first view of Camp Fox. It has a curious design of cabins with no walls....just a Spartan design of floors, roofs and bunk beds. My bed is on the bottom outside, and I feel brave and secure, knowing I'm not the least bit afraid to sleep out in the open.

Just like that I learn what it's really like to be a kid. We spend our days kayaking, making crafts, swimming, running relay races and traipsing all over the island. During mealtimes we line up and serve ourselves cafeteria-style. After every meal, we sing camp songs, one after another. Angel is always one of the loudest singers. I continually envy and admire how outgoing she is. Nothing bothers her and she is curiously incapable of embarrassment, a condition that plagues me with a haunting regularity.

"So this is what it's like to be normal!" I say aloud to myself continually as I run around laughing with normal girls from all over Nevada and California. They don't seem to suspect that I'm not one of them, and that I haven't been raised with all the privileges they have. I listen to their casual mention of other camps they've attended and just keep quiet that this is my first overnight camp experience. Who here would believe that I could be 12 years old without having ever attended a single camp? Or that I don't know how to ride a horse? Or that we don't have two homes…one in the mountains and one on the beach? Besides paying attention to how the other girls behave, I make a continual effort not to worry. I am so accustomed to taking on adult worries that it's habitual to worry if everything is okay at home. Is my dad drinking too much? Does he still have his job? What if something happens to my mom…how will I know? Who will tell me? Will the world survive without my paying close attention to all that transpires? It is a heavy load I carry, and though I constantly try to shrug it off, I wake up anew with the burden each following day.

Evenings at camp are great fun, as we giggle and tell scary stories from our bunk beds. The nights are cool so we burrow into our sleeping bags in the utter blackness, gradually falling asleep amidst the whisperings and cricket-song. My bed is arranged so that my feet face out toward the edge of the cabin toward the nearby hills. No doubt due to the huge amount of physical activity crammed into our days I sleep as if I'm hibernating. Then on our second to last night I awake from a sound sleep and sense something evil standing next to my bed, just behind my head and out of my range of vision. I know not to move, or even indicate I'm awake. I can't see the thing I sense behind me, but I feel it as clearly as if I have my hands right on it.

I do the only thing I know to do on an inky dark night with a group of sleeping 13 year old girls, which is to break the pact I made to ignore God. I close my eyes, envision white light and pray a sky-full of prayers.

Please please please please God make that thing go away it's really scaring me and if you make it go away I promise you I won't ask for anything again as long as I live just take it away and make sure it never comes back…I'm sorry I said I hated you because I really don't I was just mad at you and people say all sorts of stupid things when they're mad please forgive me and take that thing away and protect me from whatever it is and don't let it hurt me you know I've been through more than most and I just don't think I want whatever that thing is to bother me…

After several minutes spent praying I sense the thing move away and reluctantly fall back into an uneasy sleep. The next morning a single boar's tooth rests on the end of my bed. I pick it up and twist it around on my fingertips in wonder. I try to imagine that it was a boar I'd sensed the night before and somehow managed to project one of its teeth bloodlessly upon my sleeping bag, but I know better. I have no explanation for what happened to me the night before, and eagerly look for Angel to share my news with her.

"It was this big, evil thing, standing behind my bed. No, I didn't see it, but I felt it, and I have no idea what it was, but now I'm scared, and oh my God, what if something terrible happens tonight?"

Angel smiles at me, shrugs her shoulders and says not to worry about it. "What can you do?" she asks, grabs my hand and offers to race me to the kayaks.

That evening is our final night at camp. The sun dips down below the horizon as the directors begin preparations for a giant bonfire. When the fire is good and roaring, all the campers and counselors gather around to sing songs. I'm still shy by nature, and accustomed to doing as I'm told so when the director says we should close our eyes and sing songs to God, I do. I open my eyes occasionally to look across the fire and watch the older kids on the other side of our gathering, laughing and grabbing at each other. The boys and the girls take advantage of the closed eyes of the counselors to sneak kisses and hugs.

The camp leader says we are to pray to God and ask Him to come into our hearts. I do as I'm told in a fervent way. I definitely am not prepared for what happens next when I feel something that can only be described as a bolt of lightning shoot through my body. Starting in my heart, it radiates out in concentric jolting circles. Jumping up, I stare wide-eyed at the fire like one of those crazy people you see on the religious channels on television. Amidst the din of the singing no one hears me yell, and since we're supposed to have our eyes closed no one witnesses my reaction. The kids across the fire are still goofing around and punching and pulling at each other, and everyone else has their eyes shut in dispassionate song.

I reach next to me and grip my counselor's upper arm and whisper, "I FELT IT. I FELT IT happen to me!"

My counselor's name is Sherry, and I think she is particularly ancient because she is eighteen years old. I watch as uncertainty and fear flicker across her fire-lit face. She is afraid of me. "That's … great," she whispers in return.

"Did it happen to you, too?"

"No," she says so quietly that I almost don't hear her, and then she turns her face back to the fire.

The next morning the campsite is brightly lit by the sun, hinting of no trace of the strange events of the last several evenings. We hug our friends and counselors goodbye, promising to stay in touch. Then we board the ferry and begin our journey back home.

Chapter Forty Three

Pit: An area of a casino in which a group of table games are arranged, where the center area is restricted to dealers and other casino personnel.

A few months before I'd left for camp, my dad had allowed me to get a little black and white kitten. When my father picks me up from the bus station that afternoon the first thing I ask about is the kitten.

"It's gone. I took it to the Desert."

I shriek.

I already knew that a week of fun away at camp likely carried a steep price tag, and now is the time for me to pay but I didn't expect this. When we reach our apartment I run from room to room searching for the kitten, not comprehending that my dad would really do as he claims. Her food, water bowls, and litter box are nowhere in sight. I am sick at the thought that my dad could have committed such a cruel act. He sits in his chair smoking as I race around the apartment. A tall glass of VO rests on the table next to him. He is drunk, silent. Engulfed in my own rage I miss the warning signs flash across his drunken face. He has begun a transition from effort to a place of ambivalence.

The next morning after he leaves for work I draw ten signs advertising the loss of my kitten. My teenage handwriting loopily says my cat meant a lot to me, and asks readers to please call or return her directly to my apartment. I include my phone number and address. I walk around several nearby apartment complexes, armed with a roll of tape to hang the signs near mailboxes and laundry rooms. Then I return home to wait. When the phone rings in the afternoon, a man's voice says, "Hello, I have your cat."

"That's great news! Can I come get her?"

"We have a few minor details to work out first."

"Work out? I don't understand."

"See, I brought the cat in my bedroom and she shit on my comforter."

Not quite sure what I'm expected to say, I offer to pay for his comforter to be cleaned.

"DRY-CLEANED."

"Of course. My dad will pay for your dry cleaning. Can I just come over and get her now? I really miss her."

"Not so fast. My comforter wasn't the only place your cat shit."

"Uh, where else?"

"Well, when I saw she'd shit on my bed, I threw her ass into the bathroom. Then she shit all over the bathtub and the bathroom floor. She even shit on the toilet."

"Okay, my dad will help you do whatever it is you need. Can I just please come over?"

"I don't want your dad's help, I want yours. She's your cat, isn't she?"

"Well, yes, but what do you want me to do?"

"I want you to come over and clean the cat shit out of my apartment."

"Okay, where do you live?"

"First, I have bad news."

"What is the bad news?"

"Your cat's dead."

"Dead?"

"Yes. After she shit on my bed, and then shit in my bathroom, she shit in the living room. So I broke her neck."

"Why would you do such a thing?"

"She's stinking up my apartment so I'm going to bring her dead body to you."

"You don't know where I live!"

"Oh yes I do. It's right here on your little sign." In the background I hear the crumpling of paper. "Topaz Street. You're right across the street from me."

"That-that's not my real address. I just put that address down."

"Now you're lying. So you just sit tight. I'll be right over to hang your dead little cat by its neck from your doorknob. It's been a few days, so be prepared. She smells nasty." The phone goes dead in my ear.

My hands are shaking. I stumble to the window in my upstairs bedroom and look across the street to where the caller claims he lives. The curtain trembles in my shaking fingers. No one is crossing the street, yet. So I sit on my bed and hug my knees to my chest and rock forward and backward. I'm still rocking when the pounding starts at the front door. I leap from my bed, tear down the stairs and run out the back door of our apartment, not even bothering to shut it behind me. I run barefoot across the cool, wet grass of our apartment complex, then through the desert to my friend Caroline's house.

When her father, Mr. Mack, answers the door I burst into tears, sobbing an incomprehensible story about madmen and cats. My shoulders shake from the force of my sobs. When I see the care and concern reflected in his eyes I cry even harder. He asks me to wait and returns a few moments later, brandishing a large pistol that he tucks into the front of his pants. He drives us back to my apartment complex, parking right outside my front door. I follow behind him, completely hidden by the sheer bulk of him. He turns the knob, which is thankfully absent the body of my dead cat, and kicks the door open in one motion, blocking it with his foot so it won't slam shut against us. He holds the gun straight ahead in his two beefy hands, aiming into the darkness of my apartment. I am so close to him I'm practically tucked into his armpit and can sense the placid calmness emanating from him.

The back door is still open as I'd left it, and in the murky light of the backyard we can see the curtains rippling silently through the open door. As he stands with legs akimbo and pistol aimed at the back door, we watch the figure of a man walk up the back steps and reach a hand forward to part the curtains. Mr. Mack crouches to fire his pistol as my dad steps through the back door, flips on the light switch and freezes at the sight of us.

The breath I've been holding bursts forth from my body so fiercely that I'm nearly catapulted backward from the force of my exhale. "It's my dad!"

Mr. Mack drops his hands and slowly tucks the pistol back into his pants. Only my dad remains motionless, holding a small blue basket of laundry in front of him like a shield.

"Just making sure she's safe," Mr. Mack says. "She heard someone trying to get into the apartment, and it scared her."

"It was me. I didn't have my house key."

There is a very awkward silence and Mr. Mack leaves and I completely deflate from the adrenaline crash.

The next afternoon brings a bigger surprise to the front door. "Hey Cuz! It's Robert." He's standing on my front porch, looking like a big, dumb dog.

"I know who you are." I would have recognized that big hair anywhere.

He moves so close to me that I instinctively back up as he walks uninvited into the apartment and shuts the door behind him. "I talked to Uncle Buddy, and he said to just come on over and wait for him to get home from work." Robert sits down in my father's armchair, instantly shrinking our living room with his girth. With the onset of manhood, he is now so large that his body spills out from the sides of the armchair. He grins. "You're just a little bitty thing, aren't you?"

"I'm thirteen," I answer with a small degree of indignation. "I'm not done growing yet."

"Either am I."

I want to laugh. I want to throw my head back and revel in the unexpected visit of a favorite relative – a cousin. I want to hear all the good news of our family and hang out with him like cousins do. I want to like him...but I don't. So I sit primly on the couch and wonder what in the world I can do to keep him entertained for four hours. He solves this problem by asking for something to drink and when I get up to walk into the apartment's combination kitchen/dining room area, he is right on my heels. I hold the refrigerator door open, peering inside to see if we have a coke I can give him when he asks, "So have you kissed a boy yet?"

Oh, no. It's already begun. My heart rate accelerates, but I make no outward move other than to slowly close the refrigerator door. I struggle between protecting myself from where I'm afraid this conversation is heading to doing a simple bit of bragging. I turn toward him as if I'm going to answer, but am really only gauging the distance between the area leading toward the front door. Could I bolt past him quickly enough to escape the reach of his beefy arm?

"So have you?" he repeats, grinning as if it's some intimate joke the two of us share: How Many Boys Has Marlayna Kissed? He places an elbow against the wall I need to cross, effectively blocking my escape route.

Instead I move in the other direction, placing the dining room table between Robert and me. "Maybe."

"You have not kissed a boy." He takes a few steps around the circular table toward me. "I can tell."

I move in the opposite direction. "It's none of your business, anyway."

"I bet you don't even know how to kiss," he says next, as if I'm stupid enough to fall for that line. He darts around the table toward me.

"Shows how much you know then."

When he lunges toward me I push away from the table and break for the front door. He's quickly behind me and I hear the breath whooshing from his lungs when I stop to pull the door back so I can shoot through it and leap down the two porch steps. I don't turn around even once, running barefoot through the desert until I reach Caroline's house. As I hightail it down the pavement of her street, I can see her mother and father loading suitcases into the trunk of their maroon Cadillac. They both look up as I reach them, and I'm huffing and puffing so fiercely that they stare at me as it takes me a moment to catch my breath. I bend over and place my hands on my knees to keep myself from passing out. Mrs. Mack doesn't remove her sunglasses but just watches me coolly behind her dark facade, not saying a word. Mr. Mack looks at me with a combination of alarm and a hint of a smile until I've calmed down enough to say that my cousin is trying to kiss me.

"Let's take her with us," Mr. Mack says.

"It's supposed to be a family vacation."

"We can't exactly leave her here. Go call her father and say she's coming with us."

Mrs. Mack turns on her high heels and enters their house. Mr. Mack places his big arm around my shaking shoulders. "Don't you worry," he says with the kind of confidence that makes a girl like me feel like she never has to worry. That's how I get to visit Disneyland. As I ride in the back of their Cadillac to California, sandwiched between Caroline and her brother, I wish I didn't have to worry about so many things. It would be so wonderful to be just another kid in the back of my parent's Cadillac heading to Disneyland, but I my life is nothing more than a total sham. I go through the motions of having a good time at Disneyland with Caroline and her family. Though I certainly appreciate their including me on their family outing, I feel like an outsider. I'm getting older and just beginning to recognize that it doesn't feel so good to be the rescued one anymore. I can understand and interpret the thoughts and actions of adults. It seems the more Caroline's father goes out of his way to include me, the more Caroline's mother resents me. When he hands $20.00 bills to his children he hands me a bill too, Mrs. Mack makes a clucking noise with her mouth and I prepare to hand the money right back but Mr. Mack places his big hand over mine and closes my fingers over the bill.

"You enjoy yourself, Marlayna. Buy something you need. Hell, buy something you don't need."

"My dad thinks you have cute chi-chis," Caroline says to me as we walk away.

"Chi-chis? What are those?"

"Boobies!"

"Yuck! He talks about them?"

"Oh yes, and my mom just hates it."

And what pit have I stumbled into?

Chapter Forty Four

RFB: High rollers are comped with free room, food, and beverage.

Eighth grade begins. For the first time since I was a small child, I have all the clothes I need. My cavities have been filled and I have shiny new braces on my teeth. My hair is cut with regularity. My medicine cabinet is filled with all the things a teenage girl needs: Noxema face cleanser, SeaBreeze astringent, Crest toothpaste, dental floss. I like the new shell I've grown, and see no reason to talk to anyone in a way that discloses my life is anything but perfect.

Therefore, as I'd grown accustomed to doing with my mother, Dean, and Mr. Nice, I hide my father's drinking problem from everyone as best as I can. My closest girlfriends certainly can't miss his drunken behavior but I don't discuss his problem with them. I go to great lengths to ensure no one knows my dad is an alcoholic. If I'm fast enough to grab the ringing phone before he answers slurring, I quickly tell callers he's sick, has the flu or has just returned from the dentist. I meet friends outside on the street rather than risk the embarrassment of them knocking at my door and finding my father passed out in his chair in the living room.

Unlike my mother and her other husbands, my father is a solitary drinker. He doesn't invite a single friend to the house. He doesn't talk on the phone. I don't think he even has any friends. When he returns from work in the evenings he quietly opens his pint of VO whiskey and pours a large glass, lights a cigarette and flips on the television, and there he remains. Late in the evening after he drains and refills his glass of VO, he dips a spoon into a tub of Rocky Road ice cream for dinner. It's easy for me to pretend I'm living the life I want because he provides everything I need. Except guidance. He doesn't lose his temper or his job when he drinks. He seems content with his solitary life. I'm just too young to know that silence doesn't necessarily equal contentment.

I can't deny that initially it hurts to see him sit there and drink himself into oblivion night after night. I do care about him, after all, and feel so helpless watching him kill himself. I'm so joyful when he stops drinking for short periods of time and maintains sobriety for a few days, a few weeks and sometimes a few months. During these times he faithfully attends AA meetings, drinks coffee and makes steak and salad dinners instead of driving to the McDonald's drive-through. Every time without exception I get my hopes up that this will be the time he quits drinking for good. The subsequent letdowns never get any easier. Each blow feels just like the first.

He is very particular about his food when he's sober, especially about his salads. Explaining to me that a salad must have as many colors as vitamins, he shreds carrots, chops lettuce and tomatoes, and slices hard boiled eggs into the big salad bowl. "I know you grew up with that mother of yours eating TV dinners and junk food, but it's important you know how to feed yourself properly," he often preaches as he chops and dices. Dinnertime is lecture time during the periods of sobriety. He lectures me on the state of the world. He lectures me on how the niggers and chinks and gooks are taking over the little that's good about the world. He lectures me about politics and my ignorance of the political process. He lectures me on my mother's poor lifestyle choices. He lectures me on everything about me he finds wrong, including the fat calves he says I inherited from my mother and how much money he has to spend to make my teeth right again. Whenever I hear, "I told her to stop feeding you that sugar, but she just wouldn't listen," it usually signals that I'm in for a long dinner.

At times I wish he was drunk, if only to end the psychological form his hatred takes. Instead of the salad, mother, diet and racism lectures, I would prefer my father lecture about the world of boys, a kingdom I find truly inexplicable. The kids around me - the normal kids - instinctively know how to behave around boys. I find this part of my world strangely confusing. Boys terrify me. I both want and abhor them. As soon I learn that my latest crush has an interest in me I fight an undeniable urge to run away from him as fast as I can. I usually lose this fight and am becoming known for being flaky, a prude and hard-to-get.

That winter I learn that a boy named Mark likes me. On the bus I eye the big cowlicks his hair makes over the center of his forehead, deducing he isn't entirely unfortunate looking. That evening a group of friends gathers in our local park, including Mark. Someone suggests we play Spin the Bottle. It's winter and very cold and although I'm shy, I won't be the one to shoot down the idea. We form a close circle on the grass in the dark park, and the February wind howls through the trees around us. Someone has pulled a discarded coke can from the trash to use as the bottle. I'm already plotting how I will remain clothed. There's no way I'm going to let any of these boys see me undressed. Every time the coke can points to me I remove an article of clothing from underneath my windbreaker. By the time the boys are eagerly down to their boxers and my girlfriends are in their bras and underwear, I'm still wearing my pants and my windbreaker. I haven't broken any rules of the game. Nor have I become unclothed, and as much as the boys complain or tease, I just smile. One thing I've learned from my time spent with Dean is that I don't have to do anything I don't want to do.

The following day Mark takes the seat next to me on the school bus and asks me to be his girlfriend. I instinctively say yes and later wonder why I did so as I know the pressure will begin. And two nights later I'm sitting alone in my living room eating a frozen dinner and doing my homework when I hear a knock at the door. Mark is outside in the dark on his bike, and he is alone. I say hello and we stand there listening to the crickets until he laughs and asks if I'm going to invite him inside.

I open the door and let him in. I'd never been alone with a boy before outside of those few tense minutes in the art room with Kevin Oliver. Paralyzed by shyness, I can't do anything but smile and nod my head in response to his faltering attempts to make conversation. I'm not really listening. I'm thinking of the family unit I fantasize about having. I imagine Mark entering the warmth of my home to a well-furnished living room with a dad and a mom and other siblings and how he would fold into our mix like eggs into pancake batter. The conversation would flow through the group, and the pressure on me to perform would be absent. After a few minutes of awkward silence, Mark announces he's going to leave. "Can I have a kiss?" he asks, his voice breaking.

I feel no better knowing he is just as nervous as I am. I tell him no, he can't have a kiss because I've just eaten rice and it might be stuck in my braces. He gives me an odd look and says goodnight. I wonder how many things I don't know about human interactions…am I not supposed to be honest? After I shut the door, I lean my back against it and imagine how different my life could have been had things just been normal in my household. If Mark had just left the home of my fantasy family, there would have been no mention of a kiss. He would have shaken hands with my fantasy father, said goodbye to my mother and winked at me as he walked down the pathway to his bike. I would have returned to my family, wishing and hoping I could have been alone with Mark so that we could have kissed.

I break up with him two days later when I'd finished pressuring myself to be someone other than how I view myself. I resist the same pattern as I had with Kevin, and Danny before him. A few days later I realize I do like Mark after all and want to at least try to make the effort to be normal and to have a normal relationship.

Mark will have none of it. "I'm not a toy, Marlayna. I'm not a yoyo," he says to me when I tell him I've changed my mind about being his girlfriend.

I am stunned. In the year I'd lived with my father, I'd made the cheerleading squad, excelled at school, and was dressed as fashionably as anyone else. How could he not want to be with me now? I thought money and popularity was the guarantee that I could have anything I wanted. Mark will not be swayed, regardless of what I say or do.

Our large group of neighborhood friends spends every day after school together and I join them whenever I don't have cheerleading practice. Since Mark is a part of this group it quickly becomes a little difficult for me. When I know he's unobtainable I want him that much more. He plays around with me from time to time by starting an impromptu wrestling match or good-naturedly putting his arm around me, but goes no further. I figure all I have to do is find a way to get him to like me again, as if he's some sort of puzzle and I just need to twist the little pieces around to find just the right fit. It doesn't occur to me that I'm so accustomed to laboring within an impossible situation that's entirely out of my control that I take Mark's rejection as normal. Since I've spent much of my life managing rejection, Mark is just another personality I need to find a way to 'manage.'

One night after a group of us have spent the day together, I open my front door and see Mark sitting alone outside on his bike. "Listen, Marlayna," he says in his slow drawl, "I just don't want a girlfriend right now and you need to know that. I'm sorry. There are other boys out there, you know. I know we kissed today, but I don't want you to get the wrong impression…"

Heartbroken by his brutal honesty, I thank him for coming over and solemnly shut the door. The next day I have to face him again and my discomfort is so palpable no one can ignore it. Mark sees this and leaves. I burst into loud sobs. The other boys look surprised and stunned. No one has witnessed emotion of this kind over a boy or a girl yet, and none of them know what to do. I don't even know what to do. As much as I try to be normal, it's clear to me then that I'm different from the other kids. It's no secret that my parents have addictive personalities and their choices of addictions are alcohol and cigarettes. I realize that I have an addiction of my own now. I have transferred their addictive behavior to my own object - Mark.

God, how I love him. He is my obsession. The chemicals of puberty band together, enslaving me to him. When our friends are at his house and I walk up the drive to meet them, I close my eyes and inhale that particular intoxicating smell of him. I feel drunk when he passes close to me. The pitch of his voice vibrates a rhythm in my heart. His laugh is an invitation to nirvana. While I can control my emotions much of the time, sometimes I can barely speak around him. I'm often shy and silly and goofy and tongue-tied when he's near. While my feelings for him are no secret to any of our friends, I'm continually frustrated when I both annoy and honor him in no predictable way with my feelings for him.

One day he kisses me impulsively. Another day he just as easily reminds me that he isn't interested in me at all. A big joke in our neighborhood grows from the time I run down the middle of the street crying at the top of my lungs after Mark. All the boys laugh good-naturedly at me, but I couldn't care less. I am in love. I don't yet know that my feelings for Mark are a source of great annoyance and confusion for the boys in our group. I won't know or understand for many more years that Brett, Tom, Steve and Tony would lie in bed at night and wonder why a girl didn't love them the way I loved Mark. My loving him put him on a pedestal no one understood, not Mark, and not even me.

The worst part is this sets a pattern for my future relationships. I think it's normal to yearn, to want, to teeter on the line between safety and chaos. Free room, food and beverage becomes the norm, regardless of the odds or if I have a definitive losing hand.

Chapter Forty Five

Royal Flush: In poker, an ace-high straight flush; the best possible hand.

During one of the times Mark is 'being selfish,' I meet Rebel. The ability to attract those that will shape your life in major ways can be as simple as opening a friend's door one afternoon and finding him on the doorstep. I am fourteen years old and imagine that he's just fallen from the sky and landed in front of me: a gift, an offering, a boon from the heavens. One look at him and I am weak with the chemicals of puberty flooding my body. He throws his head back and laughs from where he sits on his bike, and his long, feathered hair falls across his shoulders and lays down the length of his back. He smiles at me and the sun glints across his teeth. Although I stand in a cluster of girls on the porch that warm autumn day, it's as if the two of us are alone in the universe. The birds fall silent. Traffic stops. The murmur of conversation falls to a dull underwater roar. We can't stop looking at each other.

From that day on we are nearly inseparable. Although he lives in a different neighborhood and attends a different school, he faithfully rides his bike to my bus stop every day after school where he greets me with his downturned smile as I exit the school bus. "Check out my thighs!" he says, lifting his leg and flexing, "Riding four miles uphill every day to see you is such a workout!" Once inside my apartment we waste no time collapsing on my bed in a heap of hormones, grabbing and pulling at each other as if the skin between us is too much of a border. I take a job babysitting for a doctor's family several nights a week which cuts short our time alone together. He walks me to their house, grabs my face and kisses me hard before the Mrs. opens her front door. I float into their home, high on oxytocin.

Every evening is spent on the phone, often falling asleep with the receivers in our hands. I'm enthralled with his experience in the world and the variety of his many stories. He's a fabulous story teller and loves to talk. He's so outgoing and self-confident that it makes it easy to hang on every word of his every story. Like me, he too is being raised by a single parent and has experienced his own share of dysfunctional stepfathers. His last stepfather regularly smoked pot, and had showed him how much pot to add to brownies and pizza to get stoned. He spends his summers with his real father in Hawaii, smoking pot and surfing. His life is much crazier than mine, and he is much more accepting about the details that I don't feel the need to apologize to him for the fact that we don't live in a house or have as much money as the families of my other friends. I can just be me…for the first time in my life.

He is so full of life and experiences and not afraid to try anything. When he smiles, the corners of his lips turn down instead of up in a way that I find endlessly endearing. Lying next to him on my bed in the afternoons, I direct, "Smile again!" and trace my fingertips along the corners of his downturned lips. "Now again! And again!" To say that one falls in love completely and totally denotes my experience with Rebel. I fall so hard and fast in love with this boy, it's like tripping and stumbling into a pit without giving a single thought to the consequences. I'd never felt loved before and his attention is nourishing, life-giving. I'm entranced with the fascinating idea that he loves me. This gift of his love is powerful, incomprehensible and absolutely addicting.

One evening on the phone he tells me he lost his virginity at the age of ten with a neighbor girl. I mentally add this detail to all the others that build my idea that he is the most fascinating human being that has ever lived on the planet.

Overlay – A Tale of One Girl's Life in 1970s Las Vegas

The loss of my virginity is not entirely unexpected considering how much unsupervised time we spend together. Although I'm not allowed to have boys upstairs, my dad works until eight PM each night and this leaves us hours together alone. During Christmas break, my father works all day and I'm alone. So it happens a few days before Christmas, when I'm home in the afternoon. I'm packing for a ski vacation I'm taking with Caroline's family that afternoon when Rebel appears unexpectedly at my door. I open the door and we smile at each other in that space of silence and joy. He's sweating from his ride to my house and says he's leaving for Arizona the next day for Christmas break and had to see me one last time. We race upstairs and fall back onto my bed in a tangle of limbs on neat stacks of underwear and sweaters and ski socks and mittens.

Pat Benetar belts her latest hit from my record player as Rebel whispers that he loves me and his lips are so close to mine that we trade the same air back and forth between our mouths. He cups my face in his hands and says he doesn't want to spend Christmas break in Arizona away from me. I can't imagine two weeks without him either, and the thought of this separation naturally pushes us into territory I hadn't imagined entering until I was married. I lose my virginity on top of my glove warmers, and ski gloves and wool socks. At the front door I hug him fiercely, burying my face in his chest and ask, "Am I still a virgin?" My question is muffled against his sweatshirt.

"To everyone but you and me, you are," he replies and then he is gone, a blurred figure on a bicycle fading into the afternoon gloom.

Once I'm alone, I rest my back against the door and slump down to a fetal crouch. Hugging my knees to my chest, I wonder at what I've just done. I'm being raised by a single father whose negative views on sexual activity are already well known to me. I have no other adults in my life to talk to about sex, and none of my friends have taken the leap yet. My friends are protected by their families I peevishly think, again cognizant of the vast distance between me and everyone else I know. If I didn't have the continual opportunity to be alone all the time this wouldn't have happened to me. I feel utterly alone and terrified. What if I'm pregnant? I know very little about the reproductive system as our health class at school covers little real-life material. I run upstairs and throw myself on my bed, sobbing hysterically into the now-rumpled piles of clothing that smells of him, of us.

And then it happens. I sense before I smell the presence of someone in my room with me. Thinking Rebel has returned to kiss me goodbye again, I lift my swollen eyes, sit upright and turn around, but I'm still alone in my room. An overpowering aroma of roses slowly fills the air, thick and cloying. Next I feel a cool hand and slowly brush the top of my head and continue along the length of my body. A sense of calm, peace and serenity settles over me. I reach for my journal.

"The strangest thing just happened this very second! I was about to write down what happened when I suddenly experienced déjà vu. I pictured myself leafing through this diary when I'm older. I read it and started smiling because I was so scared for no reason. Something told me everything would be alright and I had no reason to cry. Now my room is almost chokingly filled with a very sweet smell of roses! Isn't that strange? Now I'll finally write down what happened. R came over today for about four hours. I'd promised myself a million times that I wouldn't make love to a guy until I was sure I loved him and I was completely ready. All the other times I refused.

All except this time.

Now that stated what happened, didn't it?

Overlay – A Tale of One Girl's Life in 1970s Las Vegas

At first, after Rebel left, I cried and cried, worried to death of pregnancy, ashamed of myself because I'm only 14 years old. A thousand other thoughts ran through my mind. But now a peaceful feeling has settled over me and that strange smell of roses is still in my room. I don't know what to feel. I'm not crying anymore, but I feel a million different feelings including an unexpected sadness. Shouldn't this be a happy day?"

Caroline's family decides not to go skiing after all so later that evening I'm able to attend a cheerleading party hosted by our instructor, Mr. Grafton. The other cheerleaders laugh and joke around me. They are young and silly, just teenaged children. I'm unable to participate in their mirth in any way. I am different from them now, different in even more ways than I had been before. The chasm between me and everyone else has grown. The noise of the cheerleader's laughs and screams cocoons me in my own head. I can't stop thinking about what happened. Every time I think of the afternoon a worried, sick feeling comes over me and I struggle to keep my food down.

During the subsequent weeks, my confusion grows. While I can now exert such fierce control over myself and accept I have no governance over other people, this curious lack of control over my own person now frightens me. I'd always been the one on the sidelines, fiercely judging and condemning the acts of my parents and others. I felt what I was doing now was wrong, yet I felt powerless to stop myself. If I can't control myself, what level of control can I possibly exert in the world? I talk to no adults about my sexual activity, but ask a few what I believe to be surreptitious questions when the opportunities present themselves. I ask my father what he would do if I were to become pregnant.

"Give you $50 and tell you to hit the road."

Next I ask my cheerleading advisor, Mr. Grafton, what he would do if he had a daughter my age and she became pregnant. Since he's 27 years old and happily married with an infant boy, I feel certain he will have a good solution to this troubling possibility.

"I would sit down and talk with her and figure out what our best options are," he responds, eyeing me carefully. I say no more, and file away this detail.

If I do get pregnant it will have to be Mr. Grafton I approach for help.

A Royal Flush can be the sound of a toilet.

Overlay – A Tale of One Girl's Life in 1970s Las Vegas

Chapter Forty Six

One-armed Bandit: Slot machines gained their universal appeal in casinos because unlike the other games, they were played at the pace of the player and didn't require the player to have any skill. They are commonly referred to as one-armed bandits.

January of 1980 doesn't have an auspicious beginning. My father starts drinking again which ends a two month period of sobriety. Rebel and I argue frequently, and I begin wrestling with the thought that the end of our relationship might be approaching. One cold and windy afternoon at the end of the month I open my front door to find him sitting on his bike on my front porch. When he makes no move to come inside, I fight the urge to rush forward and place my fingers across those downturned lips before he can speak. Silently I will him to be silent. I'm not entirely surprised when he says he wants to break up. He says, "Just for now. Just for a while."

When he leaves and takes his friendship with him, I fall to the floor, crushed and beyond angry with myself. I'd given away my virginity, thinking it was some sort of guarantee that we would be together forever. I run upstairs and throw myself across the hateful bed where I lost my virginity and grab my journal:

All day today hot and cold feelings about Rebel came and went. I cried one minute, laughed the next. Everyone says not to call him but if he wants to get back together 'after a while' he can call me. So I'm going to follow everyone's advice and just blank him out of my mind for a while. I'm dying to talk to him, but for once I will listen. I feel I've come to some logical conclusions. First, it's clear I love Rebel for what I thought he was but really is not. I really thought he loved me and would have done anything for me, as I would have for him and that sex really meant something to him. Maybe I was wrong. Maybe I was right. Who knows?

While I was on the phone with him today, clearly upset, he was normal, perhaps even angry that I was so upset. I think he needed a change, new scenery, or maybe I'm trying to think up excuses for him being so cold. The truth was that he was brought up in a different neighborhood. Getting high a couple of times a day is nothing; getting laid every day is nothing, stealing from houses is nothing. Everything considered big in my neighborhood is not a big deal in his.

He was my first love and I really got burnt because he was just the wrong person. I don't know what to think if he really loved me or not. I think he did. I'm positive he did because the look he used to get in his eyes sometimes – ooh. I think it's good we broke up now because he's going in the wrong direction in life and I'm planning a successful life. I'll miss him, of course, and he will be on my mind a lot. God watch over him while we are apart and when I think about him, let it be to remember our fun and not to curse him for hurting me. I still love him but I will always wish him luck.

The first few months are very difficult. Navigating the pain of heartbreak, I throw myself back into my studies, and in private moments continue to berate myself for having sex with Rebel. My lack of self control continues to perplex me. I wonder if we would have stayed together if I had not had sex with him? Yet when later Rebel calls to say that he might want to get back together with me, amidst his talk of drugs, fighting and riots, I realize that I've already changed. I hang up the phone after telling him I'm not interested anymore, feeling thankful for unexpected events that are out of my control.

Karen from Jefferson Street calls me around this time. She asks if I remember Max, an older boy who lived with his little brother and his grandmother in a dirty white house on the corner. I don't think I ever spoke to him, but I remember him.

In pig latin, she whispers into the phone so her little brothers can't hear her, "We-the-gee too-the-gook L-the-gel S-the-gess D-the-gee an-the-gand bu-the-butt fu-the-gucked."

"What!"

"We snorted acid and butt-fucked."

"What is THAT?"

"Acid or butt-fucking?"

"Either one."

"Don't you know anything?"

"Not about those things. They sound horrible."

"They're not. You're just a baby."

After that conversation I no longer fret about the fact that I'd had sex. With Karen's admission I realize I could have been doing more destructive things and it makes my own choices not seem quite so bad in comparison. I think of the eleven year old Karen that I'd known and how impressed and envious I'd been with the way she effortlessly managed to take care of her household. She never complained about the cooking or cleaning she did for her siblings. I guess I'd incorrectly assumed she liked how she lived and would grow up to be the perfect mom she already was at eleven. Snorting acid and butt-fucking were two things I hadn't seen in her future (or even imagined existed until that day).

Life could be lived with no skill.

I never speak to her again.

Overlay – A Tale of One Girl's Life in 1970s Las Vegas

Chapter Forty Seven

In poker, strict rules govern the betting order, which also varies with the type of poker game played. The betting order is important because the player who bets first has the disadvantage of providing other players with information about their hand before receiving any information about any other player's hand. The player who bets last has the advantage of seeing how everyone else bets before deciding whether or not to play their hand.

My last year of middle school ends in May, I turn fifteen years old in June, and while most kids I know are planning summer vacations and choosing summer camps, I become homeless. My father announces he's moving into a halfway house to battle his alcoholism and this leaves me with nowhere to live. He doesn't seem particularly concerned about where I will go so I start making phone calls. Caroline's family agrees to take me in for a time, so I pack the back seat of my father's yellow Chevy Nova with my clothes and ride with him across town to an isolated suburban development outside Las Vegas city limits.

My father is still a very handsome man in spite of his drinking, and I'd long ago learned to tolerate the inevitable fawning and flirting of my friend's mothers – it was part of being my father's daughter. Mrs. Mack is no exception. Thin and vampirishly pale, her skin is so flawless it seems as if she purposely tries not to use her face to avoid wrinkling her smooth facade. Her makeup is always perfect, her eyebrows expertly penciled in above her heavily mascaraed lashes. Her jet black hair is unnaturally shiny and still. There is no muscle tone at all to her body. She appears to be so soft if you were to touch her your hand might sink in until it reached a bone.

My father delivers me to Mrs. Mack's doorstep and she fixes her eyes directly and only upon him as if I don't even exist. Taking languid drags on her cigarette, she smiles and giggles at everything my father says, exposing the softest part of her neck when she throws her head back to laugh. My father doesn't react. He is stiff and polite, answering her questions with short, succinct answers. He probably has too many years of VO in his system to have much of a libido. Instead of responding to her fluency in body language, he tucks a wad of folded bills into Mrs. Mack's hand, turns on his heel and walks down the sidewalk to his car. Caroline's family has a lot of money and I'm a little taken aback that Mrs. Mack even took the proffered cash instead of pushing it back into my father's hands and wishing him to get on his feet quickly. When she doesn't hand the money back to him, I think she might hand the money to me but she doesn't. The folded bills disappear into her ample cleavage when she closes the door at my father's back. Then she pads down the heavily carpeted hallway toward her bedroom without speaking a single word of welcome to me.

I've never lived in a house as beautiful as Caroline's, so in trying to make the best of my situation I get really excited about the big rooms, dark plush furniture and the swimming pool in the back yard. The first few weeks of the summer with Caroline's family crawl by regardless of my surroundings. I'd erroneously assumed they'd take me in and treat me like a second daughter. Instead it's as if I'm on an extended sleepover at Caroline's house. The only family treatment I receive is to be governed by the same strict rules Caroline follows. I'm used to exercising daily, as my friends and I often wandered the neighborhood where I'd lived, visiting friends and jumping in swimming pools. Caroline isn't allowed to leave the house very often. Nor is she allowed to snack, and is never allowed to eat after 8:00 p.m. at night. For reasons I can't understand, no matter how often I entreat her to do so, Caroline never wants to swim in their beautiful backyard pool, even though it is an unwaveringly hot summer.

215

Caroline's parents go out of town one weekend during my stay with her. Mark visits with a boy Caroline is dating. Once they'd Caroline and the boy disappear into Caroline's bedroom, Mark and I find ourselves alone in the big game room.

"You're different," Mark observes.

"I am?"

"Quieter."

"Because I'm not crying over you, you mean."

"That too, but no, that's not what I meant."

"What then?"

"You slept with Rebel, didn't you?"

"Why do you ask?"

He puts his head down, taps his thumb against the soda can in his hand. "I'm sorry....it's not my business."

"I guess I'm just surprised that you care."

"Oh, I care all right. I just don't understand why things are so complicated sometimes."

"What's complicated?"

"Just things. Anyway, it's great to see you again. Here you are, living in this mansion now..."

I move closer to the familiar warmth of Mark and snuggle under his arm. I feel safe. Protected.

"I miss you, and I'm sorry things are the way they are for you," he says next.

A lump forms in my throat. What can I possibly say to him, knowing he is witnessing the poor state of my life?

"It's not too late for us you know." He draws me tighter into his arms.

"I'm... I'm just so lost," I say before biting down hard on my bottom lip so I won't cry.

"I know. My father is an alcoholic, too."

"I didn't know."

"Not many people do. Since he lives in Arizona, it's easy to hide. Unlike your situation."

Mark's confession floors me. Who knew there were so many people wandering around hiding secret sorrows? Perhaps once you broke through the surface of a person's life you could always find a dark and secret rot the deeper you dug.

Betting order could make all the difference in divulging secrets.

Chapter Forty Eight

Handicapping: The term "Handicapping" refers to the assessment of relationship between the speed of the horse and other factors that affect a race's outcome.

The morning sun of an already overheated day in July breaks through the blinds and wakes me. Wandering down the long hallway toward the kitchen, I turn the corner as Mrs. Mack says to Caroline, "She never does anything around here. She's so lazy!"

I stop walking when I stupidly realize she is talking about me. My cheeks burn with color. Hurt and embarrassed, I enter the kitchen anyway. Mrs. Mack turns her dark eyes and gazes pointedly at me, her cigarette smoke trailing circles around her pale face. Although I would later learn in life that you could make an instant enemy by being direct with a person, I don't know this yet. I think honesty is the best policy, as they say. Too young to realize that Mrs. Mack dislikes me for reasons that have nothing to do with me, our fate is written as soon as I ask what I think is the next logical question.

"What would you like me to do?"

Clearly angry at my challenge, she rattles off a quick list of things I should be doing, including sweeping the pool and doing yard work.

"But Caroline doesn't do any of those chores. You have a maid and a gardener." From the corner of my eye, I see Caroline shifting her weight from foot to foot.

"That's not the point." Mrs. Mack lowers her cigarette and holds it to the side like a weapon. She is stiff, poised to strike.

"What is the point? My father paid you to help him, to help me, while he sobers up. He didn't pay you so I could be your maid."

Her perfectly red lipsticked lips fall open.

"And we've appreciated your help," I add. All the weeks I'd been staying as a guest in their home, Mrs. Mack hadn't once hugged me or welcomed me, or asked what I needed or sympathized with me in any way. For the most part, she'd completely ignored me. Although I'm homeless, I don't consider myself a beggar. I'm simply a human being who had the misfortune to be born to alcoholic parents. I can't understand why Mrs. Mack doesn't see the same. My unfortunate circumstances certainly don't give her or anyone else the permission to treat me poorly.

I run from the kitchen, wishing desperately I could just open the front door and keep running, but I have nowhere to go. I throw myself face down on Caroline's bed and cry angry tears into an expensive silk pillow. While Caroline later apologizes to me for her mother's behavior, I don't feel any better. You can't apologize for someone else's actions. It's about as meaningless as brushing your teeth and expecting someone else's to be clean, too.

When the sun sets that evening, the neighbors gather for a block party in Caroline's neighborhood. Groups of adults gather outside in the warm darkness of the Vegas night, drinking cocktails. Their children race around the yards, screaming to each other, back and forth across the wide lane. I stand apart and drink a glass of Seven-Up, watching the homeowners and their children interact. I have no place here. I'm crossing the street to return to the emptiness of Caroline's house when Caroline's father approaches me. "I love you," he whispers.

I look up at that big Irish man and my stomach drops into my sneakers. I figure he's drunk and I nervously giggle. A fierce blush spreads across my face as I mumble, "Thank you," and feel grateful that we're in the middle of a public street, under the warm, dispassionate blanket of black sky.

"No, you don't understand. I really love you." He grabs me with one big, rough hand, wrapping his thick fingers all the way around my skinny arm. When I look from my arm to his eyes all I can see is that he cares about me at a time when no one else seems to. I want to believe him. I want him to love me with an intensity I'd never felt before, straddling this world between child and adult as I am. I want him to provide for me in the way he does for his family. I want to live in their big house with its fine furnishings and closets full of clothing. I want a game room full of pinball machines and exercise equipment like they have. I want so much I don't know where my wants begin or end. My wants are a circumferential band of desire that wraps around me and everything I think and say and do. My wants define me. The road to achieving my wants is not clearly defined...all I desire can arrive through a father, a lover, a friend, I don't care about the vehicle. An adult expressing the desire to love me is enough in itself. The definition of the relationship is meaningless in the giant face of my desires.

Mrs. Mack's voice echoes across the street, calling her husband back to her.

The words autonomous nervous system run across my brain, a remnant of a phrase from science class. I hope my autonomous nervous system continues to function as it is supposed to, providing the breath and blood flow that I can feel is about to fail me. Loneliness and isolation has broken from my ocean floor where I'd pushed them, and now they've risen to the surface of my skin to pattern themselves around the odd members of Caroline's dysfunctional household. Mr. Mack releases his grip on my arm and returns to where Mrs. Mack stands with her arms akimbo. A heated argument looks to be beginning between the two of them, judging by the flashing arm movements of Mrs. Mack. I sneak into Caroline's house and crawl into her silk-sheeted water bed, closing my eyes against the world and the complications of the people around me.

The next morning I wake early with a solid plan. Determined to win Mrs. Mack over and improve my immediate circumstances, I don my white bikini and head to the back yard. I really do want Mrs. Mack to like me and her antipathy both hurts and confounds me. I want her to see that I am smart. I want her to acknowledge that I'm a good friend to her daughter. So I go to the backyard and sweep the entire pool, enjoying the morning sun on my body and the satisfaction of a job well done. When I finish, I return the pool broom to its place in the pool house and quietly walk through the side door into the kitchen so as not to disturb anybody.

"Yooooooooou!"

Thinking I'm alone, I jump at the hiss. As my eyes adjust from the bright outdoor sunshine to the dim of Mrs. Mack's kitchen, her outline grows visible from where she stands near the window where, apparently she'd been watching me.

"Don't you EVER wear a bathing suit in MY home in front of MY husband again." Mrs. Mack has lost her insufferable cool. Her hands are actually shaking, the cigarette vibrating back and forth between her fingers.

I think this has something to do with my body. Perhaps I'm not attractive enough to be viewed. I numbly offer, "Okay," because I'm not sure what else I can say. I turn and run down the long, carpeted corridor to Caroline's bedroom where I call Angel's mother directly and ask if I can live with her and will she mind picking me up as soon as possible? In surely what is one of the longest hours of my life, I wait to be whisked away from Caroline's house forever.

Wishing to reach back through time and place my own arm around my shoulders, I want to offer my younger self the love that had the power to eradicate the hatred of the Mrs. Macks of the world. If one is loved, the inexplicable hatred is so much easier to bear. Those of us who were not loved were therefore all the more vulnerable.

I think maybe the sheltered ones of the world can be surprised to learn of the large-scale liberties adults take with children who are unprotected.

Then again, maybe not.

Handicapping is a thing we all do, even if we don't consciously realize our actions.

Chapter Forty Nine

The American Quarter Horse: The American Quarter Horse may be America's most consistent athlete. American Quarter Horse wagering favorites finish in the money (first, second or third) 71% of the time, while winning 35%. Those are figures that can't be claimed by Thoroughbred or Standardbred racing!

Living with Angel and her mother is like living at home with my father with the added bonus that Angel's mother doesn't drink. Unlike Caroline's, their house has very little furniture….only beds and dressers in the bedrooms. The dining room houses one lone ironing board so we don it the 'ironing room.' The living room holds a few moving boxes stacked in one corner. "Did you just move in?" I'd asked a few years before when first entering the house.

"No!" Angel had laughed. Now that I am living with them, we both occasionally wonder when her mother will get around to unpacking the two boxes in the living room. It's already been five years.

It is 1980. I anticipate the start of tenth grade – high school at last! I search beyond my homeless state to create little pockets of success for myself. I start a regular exercise routine of running and sit-ups. I focus in school and begin considering the prospect of attending college. I'm eager to meet more friends and expand my opportunities. One evening a friend of mine named Reggie invites me to double date at the drive-in with him, his friend Frankie and Frankie's girlfriend, Janet. I'm completely struck by Janet's loveliness when I sit down in the back seat of Frankie's car. Janet has long, beautiful, curly blonde hair that frames her impish face in charming tendrils and ringlets. She looks like an angel. Even the high pitch of her voice sounds angelic and I am instantly envious. However, as we sip beer in Frankie's car at the drive in, Janet gets drunk and my envy quickly dissipates. Soon she becomes obnoxious, talking about reoccurring acid flashbacks in her high-pitched angelic voice.

"Like one morning, I was just getting ready for school, completely straight you know, and all of a sudden I'm like wow, on acid again, and when I went to pick up my blow-dryer I became really scared, because like I thought it was going to blow me away."

Frankie is extraordinarily good-looking and athletic, I consider from my vantage point in the back seat. He is a senior, and wrestles on the wrestling team. I sneak a few looks at him during the movie, and as he turns his head to pay attention to Janet, I admire his chiseled cheekbones and the line of his jaw. I wonder what he sees in someone like Janet, particularly as she consumes increasing amounts of beer throughout the movie. It's hard to concentrate on the screen, because Janet keeps talking in an unpleasant way that reminds me of my mother, fluctuating back and forth between exhilaration and feistiness in a singsong, drunken way. I wonder if Janet is interesting when she's sober. Maybe she's clever. Or warm and endearing. Surely there has to be something Frankie likes about Janet besides her lovely hair. For the millionth time in my life, I wonder how people stand people who change personalities when they drink alcohol. I'm relieved when the evening ends and the trio drops me back off at Angel's house.

A few weeks later our group of friends piles into Reggie's old white car to make the circuit of the parties held at the homes where parents are out of town. I find myself at a party where I know no one, being new at high school. It's a senior party, held by one of the wrestlers. I recognize one person but the smile dies on my face when Janet spots me and says, "Bitch" in a rather loud voice.

Overlay – A Tale of One Girl's Life in 1970s Las Vegas

It's clear by the slurring way she addresses me that she's already been drinking so I ignore her, hoping she will just go away. As the hours pass and the party becomes crowded, Janet has more to drink and becomes increasingly belligerent, just like my mother. I do my best to ignore her name calling for the first few hours. Janet becomes bolder, finally approaching me with a group of her friends and surrounding me. At her insistent badgering I finally lose my own temper and quietly whisper, "Fuck you."

"What did you say to me?" Her face is suddenly so close to mine that I stare at her perfect little white teeth. I realize I've just handed her the opportunity to fight me she'd been angling for all evening.

"I said, 'FUCK YOU,'" I repeat and the party noise around me grows quiet.

With the palms of her two hands, Janet shoves me so hard in the chest that I'm instantly back in time facing Dean in my bedroom. As I fall backwards I punch forward and hit Janet so hard in the mouth that my fist skips across her face, pegs her eye and then and slides in a graceful arc over her head. She flies backward against the wall behind her, her long hair billowing about her head in a curly blonde cloud. I hope she's too drunk to take it any further, but that isn't the case. Someone reaches under my arms from behind and pulls me off the ground in a headlock. I lift my feet to kick Janet as she lunges at me, shrieking hysterically. My feet are all I can use since my arms are pinned over my head.

"Put me down!" I yell to whoever it is that holds me, and am unceremoniously dropped to the floor when they release their hold.

I immediately leave the party with Janet drunkenly screaming in pursuit of me. "Come back here! I'll kick your ass right now!"

"Grow up," I yell over my shoulder and duck into Reggie's car.

Janet runs at Reggie's car like a rabid dog and lunges at me again. Through the open window she tries to land a final punch to the side of my head. Reggie drives away as Janet's friends restrain her. Her screams are still audible over the sound of the engine as we pull away and drive down the street.

"Jesus," Reggie turns to me, his eyes wide. "I didn't know you had that in you."

On Monday, Janet walks the halls of our school sporting a blackened jaw and eye. Word travels quickly throughout our high school that it was me who gave her the shiner. I'm stopped in the halls, and people crowd around the lunch table to ask why I beat up Janet. "She hit me first," is all I will say. A few days later, Janet offers me a sullen apology through a friend of hers. I have no more issues with Janet or anyone else at school after that.

People respect you when you stand up for yourself. This much is clear to me now.

Show up and be a consistent athlete. That must be the key to winning.

Chapter Fifty

Keno: Keno is such a popular and exciting pastime because it offers the possibility of winning spectacular payouts on relatively small wagers.

While most of the teenagers in the neighborhood have loose rules and few responsibilities to their parents, there are several notable exceptions in the motley crew of ours. Angie lives in a home governed by her strict Italian father. While we are always welcomed at her house to dine on pastas and sauces and meats and other Italian culinary treats, Angie is very rarely allowed to spend much time with us outside of her house. While her family is kind enough to invite me to have holiday dinners with them (knowing I would otherwise be spending them alone), I often feel her father is looking at me as if I am a dangerous science experiment. He isn't quite sure how I will turn out if Beaker A is added to Beaker B, but seems to be reasonably sure I will end up pregnant, on drugs and on welfare before I'm out of high school. Although I won't admit it even to myself, I want him to like me and think I'm a good kid, as I had before with Mrs. Mack. Would I forever be paying homage to this perverted vestige of anticipated judgment?

As the summer ends before eleventh grade begins, we are all surprised and elated when Angie is at last given permission to spend the night away from home. In true celebratory fashion, we quickly plan for a blowout evening to mark Angie's evening of independence. In the afternoon, she exits her father's white Cadillac at Angel's with a hesitant smile and an overnight bag slung over one shoulder. After a slight hesitation, her father slowly pulls his shiny car from the curb and drives to the end of the street and out of our view. The van of high school boys immediately pulls into the spot Angie's father had vacated and the boys eagerly jump out to help us load our sleeping bags and groceries into the van. With the new Devo cassette tape blaring "Whip It" from the speakers, we head to Lake Mead to spend the night.

It's an innocent night marked by voluminous beer drinking and ridiculous behavior from teenagers lacking the experience to handle the effects of alcohol. There's singing. There's vomiting. There are no drugs. There is no sexual activity. Late that night, I find Angie sitting at the edge of the lake by herself and take a seat next to her. She tosses rocks into the dark water.

"What are you doing?"

"Do you know that I've never slept outside of my parent's house before? It feels strange, like I'm doing something against the rules."

"You are doing something against the rules."

She laughs. "Yes, that's true, but it still feels strange."

"I bet."

"You're all so lucky. You have so much freedom. It's like I don't even know how to behave like a teenager. I don't know what to do. All the things you guys are learning, I don't know. I have no experience."

"You're the lucky one, Angie."

"Lucky? I'm fifteen years old and I can't even go to the movies without my parents! Do you know why I'm not allowed to go to the movies? Because my dad is afraid some creepy stranger is going to put his hand up my skirt in the darkened movie theater. As if!"

As Angie vents her frustration, I recall a time at the movie theater when I was ten years old. One of the other Cambridge Apartment kids and I had walked to the movie theater alone to see a Steve McQueen matinee. Matinees cost $1.00 in those days, and we had roughly $2.00 each for the movie and snacks. After paying for our movie tickets, I bought popcorn and she bought candy and we took our seats in the mostly empty movie theater.

We were surprised when a large man sat one seat away from me. Most of the theater was empty and yet he chose to sit close enough to me that I could smell his unwashed body. When the movie started, my friend and I turned toward each other and swapped our snacks back and forth. We'd forgotten all about the man until we heard the sound of a coin hit the cement floor underneath our seats. Looking next to me, I saw that the man had adjusted his position so that his massive back was to me, with his outside arm dangling toward the floor. He dropped another coin. Sneaking a quick look at my friend, I handed her the popcorn and crawled under his seat to pick up the two quarters. Eagerly, I turned to my friend and in the dim light of the theater, unfurled my fingers to show her the two quarters in my palm. We giggled and whispered over what to buy with this newly found treasure.

Deciding on a three pack of Reese's Peanut Butter Cups, I handed the quarters to her and she left for the concession stand. While she was gone, I heard another quarter hit the floor. Placing the popcorn and candy in my friend's seat, I crawled under his seat again to pick up the quarter. My friend returned, and we tore into the Reese's Peanut Butter Cups, munching and smiling as we each ate one cup and divided the third in half. Since we had one quarter and needed a second to buy more candy, we forgot about the movie and kept our eyes on the man to wait for another quarter to drop to the floor.

This time, however, he took his palm and placed it on his lower back with his beefy fingers. The dim light from the movie screen revealed the glitter of the quarter lying in his palm. I grabbed the quarter. It was my turn to run to the concession stand, and I returned with a bag of MnMs. My friend whispered that while I was gone, the man did not drop any more quarters, and as we swallowed the MnMs we kept looking at him, waiting for our cash cow to pay. He didn't drop another quarter for a while though, and when he did I eagerly crawled under his chair and picked it up and we again began watching him for the next quarter.

This time he placed the quarter between two fingers he held behind his back, and slowly lowered his fingers until they rested at his rear waistband. As we watched the progression of the coin, we saw the quarter reach the upper crack of his butt. Then he removed his hand. My friend and I stared at that quarter for all of a minute before I grabbed it. This time we both went to the concession stand to buy ice cream. When we returned to the movie theater, we took different seats. We were full. I was sick for the rest of the afternoon and when I later complained to my mother about my stomach ache from eating too much candy and she asked where I got the money to buy all that I said I ate I didn't tell her.

Sitting on the edge of Lake Mead as Angie talks, I think of this story but don't tell it to her. In truth I'm thinking that there are much creepier things a stranger could do in a movie theater other than put his hand up your skirt. Keeping the thought to myself, I just repeat, "You are lucky. At least you know your parents care about you. I can't say that."

Angie is quiet. I know she wants to be annoyed with her parents, but there is no arguing with my logic. Her parents watch over her because they care about what happens to her. I'm not watched, because, well, no one cares about me. We hear the unmistakable sounds of someone stumbling toward the water and the splat of vomit hitting the pebbles. Angie and I smile at each other in the moonlight and return to the campsite.

The next morning we load the van and Tim starts the drive to the cliffs where we plan to spend the day cliff diving. I sit silently in the back of the rocking van, my head spinning from the beer I'd drunk the night before. I'm tired and hung over and so when Tim stops and rolls down his window and a hand reaches in and slaps him hard across the face, I'm not sure I've really seen what I think I saw. Then the driver's side door opens and someone reaches in and pulls Tim from the driver's seat. A woman jumps in the driver's seat and peers at us from under a halo of wild hair. "I hope you girls are on birth control!"

A collective gasp rises from all of us as she continues, "And which one of you is Angie?"

Angie raises her hand as she is accustomed to doing in class when she always knows the answer to the teacher's question as a sob bursts forth from her throat, "I am! Oh, I am!"

"You're in BIG trouble, young lady! Your father is worried SICK about you. He called the police, the lake patrol, the highway patrol. This whole night EVERYONE has been looking for you!"

"Nothing happened!" I say and Tim's mom shoots me a look in the rear view mirror so evil the devil would have approved.

"Don't tell ME nothing happened! I didn't just fall off the turnip truck! You girls ought to be ASHAMED of yourselves!"

Angie sobs hysterically. Tim's mom yells at us the entire time it takes for her to drive us all to Angie's house. When Tim's mom pulls the van into Angie's driveway, we see her father standing out front with his arms crossed over his chest like Napoleon about to take over the nation.

"Out of the van, all of you!" Tim's mom orders.

We scramble out of the van as Angie's father yells at us to line up and face him, one by one. He holds a small notebook and a pen in his hand. "NAME!" he barks at each boy.

Although I'm close to tears from sheer mortification, I quickly gain control over myself when I hear the first boy say, "Robert Plant," before scurrying back to the van.

"NEXT!"

"Jimmy Page."

"Jonathon Lennon."

"Mick Jagger."

"Rod Stewart."

By the time it's my turn to face Angie's father I'm trying to stifle a horrifying surge of hysteria. I don't know whether to laugh or cry. When I see the disappointment in his eyes as he looks down at me, I crumble at the realization that he thinks he's been right about me all along. He says nothing at all to me, dismissing me forever with his eyes.

We're no longer allowed at Angie's house and she is not allowed to spend the night at anyone's house for the remainder of her high school years.

I can't say I blame her father. He isn't about to allow a spectacular payout on the small wagers neighborhood boys are offering.

I wish someone felt that way about me.

Chapter Fifty One

Class: Class is probably the most important factor in handicapping. Analyze everything you see, hear or read in the context of class. In the most basic sense, class refers to the ability to win, produce winners and develop high quality, competitive races. Class not only involves racehorses, but sires and dams, owners, breeders, trainers, jockeys, races and even tracks.

Confident in his sobriety, my father moves from the halfway house and rents a new apartment in November of my sophomore year. I move from my happy existence at Angel's house to live with him again. Really, he announces he is going to be leaving the halfway house and I volunteer to search for an apartment so I can move back in with him. I try to feel happy about this transition, but when he starts drinking again at the conclusion of the first week after his release, it sends me quickly spiraling down into the helpless depression I'd successfully kept at bay during my time at Angel's house. We don't have any furniture or lamps in our apartment, so we sleep on the floor in our separate bedrooms. Our living room has a weight bench and a small television on top of a cardboard box. Since it will be two months before we get telephone service, I spend much of my time at the pay phone near our apartment.

It grows colder as winter progresses. John Bonham overdoses. John Lennon is shot and killed. Ronald Reagan is elected president. I pay a form of limited attention to the news to pull myself from the increasing misery of my own existence. Since my father works evenings at the casino, I am alone most nights, left entirely to my own discretion. I am adrift, free-falling without the support and familial structure that others around me have, and it begins to bother me with a searing intensity. I just want someone to tell me no, to create some sense of boundary. It isn't so easy anymore to ignore all I don't have, as I was able to do when I was much younger. The kids around me live in houses with furniture, and are now driving cars bought for them by their parents. My friends have new clothes and take vacations with their families. They are planning their applications to colleges with their parents. I feel increasingly helpless, disconnected, isolated and alone. The rift between me and everyone else is not just growing, but multiplying exponentially.

I write to Ana in hope that something in her life will have changed that will enable her to take me in. I receive no response. I date Mark again, off and on according to his varying whims. Sometimes I sleep at Mark's house and don't come home at all. My father doesn't notice whether I'm home or not and eventually I stop checking in with him at all. Mark and I break up and reunite many times, which causes me an immense amount of stress and angst when I'm already feeling overextended and overwhelmed. At one point, Mark says he just can't keep hurting me and we need to end our relationship. Two nights later he is again underneath my window, tossing pebbles and waving for me to come downstairs and take a ride with him.

I spend Christmas Eve and Christmas Day of my fifteenth year alone, with only the company of my journal.

Today was so sad. I really don't like Christmas anymore. It's no fun for me. It is depressing. I don't spend any time with my father. He's drunk anyway so I don't want to be with him. It's so lonely. I just sit here by myself on Christmas Eve and cry. There is no dinner, no presents, no family, no hugs or kisses. Just one scrawny little Christmas tree with my father's present underneath it. He'll let it sit there for another year for all he cares. I didn't even get one surprise or anything. I don't want to be by myself anymore. Please God – it's not that much to ask and it means so much to me. I wish I at least had someone here to hug me and tell me that everything will be alright.

Overlay – A Tale of One Girl's Life in 1970s Las Vegas

Several days later I call my sister Linda. She now lives with her husband and infant daughter in Colorado. In all likelihood my father is not ever going to remain sober, and I recognize I can't continue to live on the roller coaster that he's chosen for his life. After suffering some intense stomach pain, I've recently been diagnosed with ulcers, no doubt brought on by the immense stress and instability of my living situation. My sister tells me she thinks I need to live peacefully for a while because I had to grow up too fast. She says at my age I shouldn't have to worry about rent, food, and my parent's health while compromising my own. She urges me to move to Colorado and live with her, but the thought of abandoning my father again is more than I can bear.

I'd already had to abandon one parent. How could I possibly abandon another? So instead I take a job at the local Burger King when my father's drinking problem becomes so all-consuming he can no longer hold a job. He has lost three jobs, one after another. Though I'd taken a job so that I could buy my clothes and personal items, instead I often pay the rent. My interactions with my father deteriorate into a pitiful semblance of a relationship.

As if dealing with the stress of hormones, high school, and an addictive love affair isn't enough, I have no patience left to deal with my father and what I perceive to be his incompetence as a parent. Most nights I walk home from work at the restaurant to find him sitting on the living room floor with his back against the wall, sipping a glass of VO, and smoking Kool Menthols. He is usually so drunk he can't hold a conversation, instead mumbling incoherently at anything I ask of him.

One evening in utter frustration I empty his bottle of whiskey down the sink. When he hears the liquid gurgling down the drain, he jumps up from the living room floor and runs at me in a surprisingly fast drunken gait. He grabs the bottle from my hand and slaps me hard on the back of the head.

My chin slam down into my chest. I must have bitten my tongue because the thick, metallic taste is flooding my mouth.

It's the first time he's ever been physical with me.

Whiskey before kin runs through my head that evening.

As if this isn't enough - there is the gambling. There are periods of time when we have no money if he's on a losing streak at the crap tables. I'm therefore very careful to save every penny I make at the restaurant, because I never know when I will need to buy groceries. Between my grocery purchases and my paychecks, I go to my friend's houses in the afternoons where unbeknownst to them, the snacks I eat often serve as my dinner for the evening.

There are occasional peaks to these valleys. One morning I open my eyes to find a stack of bills next to my bed, evidence of my father's winning streak at the crap tables. I count out $1,000.00 in crisp one hundred dollar bills. I go to the grocery store that afternoon and prudently buy food and deposit the rest in the bank in case my father doesn't pay rent the next month.

I take small solace in the fact that I am not the only one riding the waves of parental alcoholism and gambling. A big family of boys attends my high school. Their father's wins and losses are much more evident than mine. Each boy receives a new car and has a few months to enjoy it. We all envy the Camaros and Trans Ams before they are traded in for used mini trucks and Datsuns. The used cars disappear next, and the boys became regular passengers in their friend's trucks. Then the new cars arrive again and the cycle begins anew. Though we all know about their father's gambling problem, we would never have dreamed of bringing it up to his sons. Just like no one ever talks to me about my situation.

I wonder how much the other kids know about my own situation.

It is a lonely classless state.

Chapter Fifty Two

Track Condition: Weather can change a track's condition quickly. Dirt tracks are rated as follows: ft-fast; sy-sloppy; m-muddy; gd-good; sl-slow; hy-heavy; fr-frozen. Horses that perform well in conditions similar to today's could have the edge.

"Let's go."

I'm talking to Mark in my bedroom when my father opens my bedroom door. I tell Mark I have to go, and once I hang up I tell my father I refuse to go anywhere with him. I say I have friends to talk to, homework to do, and the last thing I feel like doing is spending any time with him.

"Now," he interrupts. While my dad is usually quick to turn his back and walk away, he stands still in the doorway. "Right now."

The reptilian part of my brain raises its head, instantly alarmed. His tone of voice is bad news indeed. My father is sober. He is angry. Something is horribly wrong. So without saying another word, I obey his directive and follow him out of our apartment and downstairs to his car. Wordlessly, he steers the car onto the highway leading out of town. He doesn't light a cigarette. He doesn't speak. Both of his hands are clenched firmly in the ten and two positions on the steering wheel, so that the whites of his knuckles rise up against the brown of his hands.

I watch him from the corner of my eye, noting his extreme concentration. I ask where we're going.

He doesn't answer. Thirty minutes pass in this way. I try not to notice that we are headed into the desert. I stare out the side window, watching the desolate scenery tick by. The late afternoon sun drops low in the sky and the shadows of the scrappy bushes grow long over the desert sands. We are well out of the city now, so I ask again where we're headed. In answer he pulls off the highway, steers the car along a dirt road and heads deeper into the desert. Dust rises in response to the tires' disturbance, floating around the car's windows. The rocks crunch underneath the tires. My father flicks on the headlights and slows the car, continuing toward the darkening, colorless mountains. I know there is nothing located in this direction other than desert. If he was simply interested in talking to me, he would have driven to the Sizzler restaurant. I imagine that we are driving to Sizzler, and I'm going to sit across from him at the table, and he will talk about his problems at work, and his difficulty remaining sober, as he used to do. We haven't held a conversation of any kind in many months, and I realize with a burning sensation in my stomach that I have no idea how troubled he could be.

Then he stops the car. He flicks off the headlights. Breaking the ensuing silence, he says, "This is the end."

"The end?"

"I'm finished. I can't do this anymore."

"You can't do what anymore?"

"Be a parent."

Overlay – A Tale of One Girl's Life in 1970s Las Vegas

"Dad, I'm really sorry you've been having such a hard time lately." I struggle to keep my voice from shaking. If I panic he might panic, so my success depends on how oblivious to my situation I can appear to be.

He eyes me. Deciding what to do. "You don't understand."

"Maybe I don't, but I want to."

"I can't go on like this anymore, Marlayna." He doesn't use one of my nicknames.

"That's why we'll make some changes. Changes that will be good for both of us."

"I can't see how any changes will help the root of what's wrong."

I clench my inner thighs together to stop my shaking knees. I make grand gestures and twirl my hands around for emphasis as I talk as if saying through my movements: 'Look at me – I'm alive!' "Maybe you want to go back to the halfway house. I could find another friend to live with."

"There is so little you understand. You don't know how much strength it takes to raise a child. How hard it is when no one has taught you the right thing to do. How impossible it can be to know what to do. You don't understand that alcoholism is a disease. It kills you. It kills everyone around you. And it's not a quick death unless you're lucky. It takes a long time, which makes death so much more painful."

"I do know this can happen, but it doesn't have to happen," I say. The sun has set. My palms are wet. I am only fifteen years old, I think. That's not enough time!

"I don't know that I can wait this out any longer. I don't know that I can leave you alive here on your own."

Please God, it's not enough time! I think of all the things I still want to do. Attend college. Marry. Have children. Have a career. Have grandchildren. Know love.

My father's voice is filling the car, replacing the dust with a sinister, impending violence. I stop trying to control my shaking knees, as I know he can no longer see them in the inky darkness. It's now completely dark on this moonless night and my eyes flick back and forth and my breath quickens as I plot my break from the car and run through the desert. Looking down at my feet, thankful I'm wearing tennis shoes, I wonder about the odd absence of light from the stars when the idea comes to me.

"Dad, remember a long time ago when I was about five, and we had a party at our house on Flamingo?"

"No."

"John and Karen and Jess and Phyllis and all the kids were over and everyone was swimming?"

"Hmmmm."

"And you went out to the front yard and lay down on the grass to look up at the stars? Do you remember that I followed you, and lay down next to you?"

"Yes."

"I asked you all kinds of questions that made you laugh, like what do flies eat for breakfast, and do cats have best friends? What I remember most was your answer when I asked you where butterflies went when it rained, because it had rained earlier that day and I was really worried about the butterflies. I knew when their wings got wet that they couldn't fly anymore, so I wondered where they went to stay dry since they didn't live in houses. You told me that butterflies were a lot stronger than we knew. That when it rained, they would find a safe place to hide, and tuck their wings up and over their bodies to stay dry. You said they didn't need houses, because they were strong enough to protect themselves with their own wings. You said the weakest part of their bodies became the strongest when they needed protection the most."

I stop and take a measured breath. "I never forgot what you told me, Dad. Later when I experienced rough times with my mom, or Mr. Nice, or Bullfrog, or Dean, or anyone else, I remembered your words. I looked for ways to turn the weakest part of myself into the strongest. Your words saved my life. Probably more than a couple of times. I took my size, which was the weakest part of me, and used it to my advantage. People thought I was weak because I was small, and they were wrong. My small size was my greatest advantage, and it was all because of you....because you told me the story about the butterflies knowing how to protect themselves."

I wait. My right hand firmly grasps the inside car door handle for safety. This is my insurance. My odds behind my bet. He is silent and I imagine what's going on in his brain. The key to my survival is to bargain for my life without letting him know.

When he turns the key to start the engine, I exhale a slow, shaky breath.

I know my dad probably sees me as a selfish and self-absorbed teenager, and I only wish I had the luxury to really be so. He's underestimated the extent to which I pay attention to my surroundings. I had to learn to do so to survive the men my mother brought into our lives, but I'd never imagined I would have to survive my own father.

I don't consider myself safe until we near our apartment complex. My legs don't stop shaking until he pulls our car into the parking space. Adrenaline dissipates from my body, replaced by a terrible fatigue. My legs are weak as I walk up the stairs to our apartment.

As physically exhausted as my body is, my brain is operating on overload. My first step upon returning to my bedroom is to call Mark and tell him that our relationship is over. I say it's unhealthy for me. Trying to maintain control, he replies that he agrees, and perhaps we should put our relationship on hold for now. I tell him I'm ending it forever. I hear his stunned silence on the other end. His efforts to sound agreeable rather than try to change my mind reinforce my decision. I tell him I will miss him, hang up the phone, and begin sobbing. I resist the urge to call him back and tell him what just happened to me. I know I have to be strong enough not to go down that path again.

I don't call anyone else that evening.

In truth, I have no one else to call.

M - muddy.

Chapter Fifty Three

Luck: Luck may be a deciding factor in the outcome of any single game. It will inevitably go against you on occasion, but it may balance out in the long run.

I turn 16 years old. My friends are given cars for their summer birthdays but my gift is homelessness. My father moves to the Good Samaritan rehabilitation home again. I call my friend Josie and ask if I can move in with her and her mother. Since my dad hasn't offered to contribute to my room and board, I feel very fortunate to be welcomed as a guest in Josie's home. I take a job at the mall, working the 3-9 shift at a shoe store to buy clothing and personal items. Since Josie's family eats dinner while I work in the evenings, Josie's mom sets aside a dish of food for me in the oven each night. It's a small gesture, but after all the times I've gone without dinner, the sight of the oven light highlighting the foil-covered plate has a nightly warming, powerful effect upon me.

Josie's Italian family is like nothing I've experienced. Her grandparents and mentally challenged uncle live nearby and often eat dinner with us on the weekends. I sit quietly in their ornately furnished formal dining room while the chattering group of back-east Italians continuously talk over each other. I couldn't squeeze a word in if I tried so I don't, and frankly I'm content to sit silently among them and bask in the energy of their competing conversations.

"Doesn't she look like Barbara Mandrell, Dad? Doesn't she look just like Barbara Mandrell? Dad? Dad? Dad!" Josie's uncle repeats until her grandfather tiredly replies that yes, yes I do in fact look just like Barbara Mandrell.

"What does she do, this friend, and where are the parents?" the grandmother asks about me to Josie's mother as if I'm not at the table. I know she isn't being rude, but trying to learn from her daughter a story she can make sense of, a story she can understand.

"Doesn't matter, Ma, we're helping her out and she's Josie's friend."

"She's a pretty girl, isn't she Dad? She looks like Barbara Mandrell doesn't she, Dad? I think she looks like Barbara Mandrell, Dad. Dad? Dad!"

"Yes, son, she does look just like Barbara Mandrell. Just like her."

"Where's the mother? Where's the father?" Josie's grandmother persists.

"I don't know, Ma, they're around. They can't take care of her."

"Can't take care of her? What kind of parents can't take care of their own child?"

"Barbara! Hey Barbara! Barbara, you look at me! You look just like Barbara Mandrell!"

"Ma, I don't know about these kinds of parents, but she has them so she's staying with us. I've never met them."

"Never met them and their kid is staying with you? You could be maniacs for all they know!" Josie's grandfather says, twirling spaghetti around his fork.

"Dad, we're not maniacs," Josie's mother says. "What are you gonna do?"

Overlay – A Tale of One Girl's Life in 1970s Las Vegas

"Hey, speak for yourself," Josie's younger brother says as he smiles at me. In addition to this brother from her mother's last marriage, Josie has older sisters from her mother's first marriage. Some live in town and some live back east, and I can't keep their names straight to save my life. They all look the same: tall, brunette and all share their mother's fabulous Sophia Laurenish smile. It is simply awesome to be in Josie's house. Sometimes I lie in bed at night and listen to all the talking and bantering going on downstairs and fantasize that this is the Italian side of my family. When I imagine the Irish and Italian sides of my ancestors together, it's almost too much to bear. When I can afford to do so, I think about what I'd lost, or even worse, what I never had to lose in the first place.

As the weeks pass during my stay with Josie's family, I feel increasingly comfortable. Her mother is kind and sincere, and includes me in all conversations and interactions with her family. "If your rooms aren't cleaned today, I'm throwing all of yous out!" she yells up the stairs in the mornings. A great, secret thrill travels down the length of my spine that she feels comfortable enough with my presence to include me in threats and potential disciplinary measures.

Josie's brother, John, who lives back east with his father, stepmother and stepsister, is staying with us for the summer. He is tall and handsome, with an eastern accent that thrills me to no end.

"Say water!"

"Watuh."

"Say river!"

"Rivuh."

"Coffee!"

"Coughee."

"Say my name!"

"Mahlaynuh."

"HAHAHA!"

"Hey, quit busting my balls already!" But he's smiling, and I fall secretly in love with his innocence. John isn't like the other boys I know around Las Vegas. He is serious and sincere like his mother, and means what he says. I'm not used to this degree of reliability and confidence in a person's word, and feel rather conflicted about whether I like it or not. Truthfully, it scares me.

By the time the day arrives to take John to the airport for his return to New Jersey, he and I both feel so heavy we can't hold a conversation with each other. When I hug him goodbye I don't want to let him go, yet I understand it's only good manners for me to allow his mother and sister more time to say good bye than me. Watching him board the plane leaves me feeling bereft and empty inside. After my experiences in the last few years, I'm already operating at an emotional deficit. Saying goodbye to John after our time together is much more painful for me than it should have been. So many goodbyes in this life. One after another.

When Josie's mother announces that she is selling her house and they will be moving into an apartment, I go apartment shopping with them. "Marlayna's going to share my room, Ma. She doesn't need her own room," Josie says as we tour the rooms.

Her mother looks at us and it's clear to me she's weighing just how to handle this delicate situation. "No, honey, our apartment will be too small for three people," she finally says, and my stomach drops into my sneakers.

My stomach rolls and churns for the rest of the afternoon. When we return home I call my aunt Ana in Hawaii. I must bide my time through her long, drunken greeting until I can get to the purpose of my telephone call. "Aunt Ana, do you think I could come and live with you? My dad's in rehab, and my friends where I've been staying are moving and won't have room for me anymore."

"Oh darling," she says, and I already know I'm about to hear my second piece of bad news today. "Chuck isn't well, and it's just not a good time."

"Who is Chuck?"

"Chuck is my new husband, darling."

"But Ana, I don't have anywhere to live." I choke back the anxiety and sobs that are rising in my throat.

"I'm sorry darling, I can't help."

"I don't have anywhere else to go."

I see it's useless to talk facts. My aunt's not going to help me. I hang up the phone.

"What did she say?" Josie asks when I walk back into the kitchen. She is sitting at the kitchen table eating grapes.

"She said no."

"What are you going to do?"

"I'm not sure yet."

"Shit."

"Exactly."

The next day at school I look carefully at all the people I pass in the hallways between classes. I've known some of them since elementary or junior high school. Surely one of them has a family that can take me in. I only have a little over a year and a half until I graduate from high school. I feel certain I should be able to find someone to let me stay with them during what doesn't seem like a long amount of time.

I move in with Violet's family after her parents agreed to let me stay in their guest bedroom. I continue working at the mall to earn enough money for my personal items, but I'm unable to contribute anything toward their household. My dad is still unwilling or unable to help, and the reason doesn't really matter. I don't feel as welcome in their home as I had at Josie's home. Not through anything they do or don't do, I quickly begin feeling like a burden. So I try to balance my time by spending the week nights at Violet's and the weekends at Lisette's house. This doesn't work as I'd hoped it would, as I can feel that Violet's parents feel like I'm using them during the week so that I can enjoy freedom at Lisette's on the weekends. One afternoon Violet's mother uncharacteristically yells at me in a burst of emotion, "I just don't understand how someone can have a child and not care about them at all!"

"Either do I," I answer numbly, and walk upstairs to call Lisette's family.

I move to Lisette's that evening and live with her family in their guest bedroom until the end of my junior year when I officially and finally give myself permission to fall apart.

Emotionally, I begin slipping in at first an almost imperceptible way. Only someone who was paying close attention to me could have noticed the subtle differences in my outward behavior. I skip homework assignments. I stop studying. I don't return phone calls as promptly as I once had. I gradually stop talking to the several family members I had because I question the point of remaining in touch. The answer to anything I need is always a firm NO. The instability of hopping around from home to home has taken a tremendous toll on my emotional health.

Lisette drinks and smokes cigarettes and since I'm now spending most of my time with her I pick up both habits. Having easily been able to hide her addictions from me in short bursts during the weekends, I'm shocked to learn the extent of Lisette's dysfunctions once I start spending every day with her. Developing a close friendship with Lisette during one of the weakest periods of my life is one of my more unfortunate choices in life. Lisette's mom thinks I am the bad influence. Lisette takes me straight down with her when I am the one keeping the two of us from falling completely apart.

Ironically, Lisette's parents are stricter than most, so Lisette has devised a variety of ways to get around their rules. Since she has to be home by eleven o'clock on weekends while most other kids are able to stay out until one in the morning, Lisette routinely lies to her parents and tells them we plan to sleep at a friend's house. After the parties are over, Lisette parks in a shopping mall parking lot and we crawl drunkenly into the hatchback area of her Toyota Celica to sleep. When we don't ask to sleep out, we sneak out Lisette's bedroom window after her parents fall asleep. Apparently they never check our bedrooms because we're never caught. We return in the early mornings, wearing sweat pants and acting as if we'd been out exercising.

Lisette smokes many cigarettes and hardly eats. During her early teen years as an Olympic hopeful gymnast, she'd developed very strange eating and purging habits, gorging one day and then not eating for the next six. I learn that one of her primary meals consists of a pound of bacon and a tube of Pillsbury biscuits. Otherwise she subsists on a steady diet of cigarettes and sugar free sodas. Since we spend all of our free time together, I pick up her bizarre eating habits. We spend our evenings driving around in her Celica, smoking cigarettes and listening to the cassettes of punk rock music she'd brought with her from California. I quit my job and when we can scramble enough coins together, we go to the arcade and play Ms. Pac-Man. I stop reading books. I stop thinking about college. I stop planning.

Lisette's sexual activity directly opposes her restrained eating habits. Lisette has a beautiful figure as a result of her years of athletic training, and subsequently attracts attention from the boys. Curious to me is the fact that as much attention as she attracts, it's never enough. Lisette is always desperate for more attention. One more boy. One more phone call. One more date. She sleeps with nearly any boy who pays the slightest bit of attention to her.

"You're too uptight about sex," she says to me. "You ought to relax and do it more often."

I don't see her feeling very good about herself when the boys she's had sex with don't call again. It seems most boys are willing to have sex with a willing participant once or twice, but generally not a third time. From what I see sex certainly isn't the way to become someone's girlfriend, the solid relationship I crave even more than a home of my own.

Luck has nothing to do with sex and love.

I don't know what does, but it isn't luck.

Chapter Fifty Four

Sports betting is a game of skill. The challenge is to gather and analyze as much information as you can about a game, weigh the probabilities of each team winning, and subsequently compare your opinion to the oddsmaker's. Make the right judgment and you win. It's as simple as that.

Make the wrong judgment and you lose.

My life isn't the way I want it to be, and I know I'm slipping further and further away from the possibilities I had once envisioned. Attending what is the nicest school in the city, I am surrounded by good kids from supportive families. While the kids around me take the SAT and evaluate colleges they hope to attend, I work off and on for my next paycheck to pay for my food and clothing.

Even buried deep within my own teenage angst, I can't miss Pat Lizotte. No one can. Greasy-haired, lanky, his pimpled face partially covered by large glasses, he is difficult to miss. He hugs his books in front of his chest like a shield as he navigates the halls of our school. You can hear his labored breathing well above the din of yelling, laughing and shuffling that echoes throughout the hallways. His jaw looks as if he clenches it so tight that the sound of his breath is the resulting forced whistle past his teeth.

Angie thinks it would be amusing to make fun of Pat, so she jumps behind him one day as he labors down the sloping hallway that leads to the cafeteria. Mimicking him, she hugs her books to her chest and emulates his loud, hissing breathing. Her long, curly hair swings back and forth behind her in glorious half-arcs as she makes exaggerated, stomping steps behind Pat. She wears the fancy purple mini skirt that I secretly envy, as I don't have the money to buy the fashionable faux-punk 80s wear that's currently popular.

"Stop it!" I whisper to her, my own anger at her mistreatment of Pat ignited by that purple mini skirt. The hair, the purple, that smile in thinking she is funny at someone else's expense suddenly makes my heart pound in ire. She has no good reason to make fun of Pat. Though he doesn't react outwardly, I can feel him all the way through my own body. I can feel the hell that every day of his life must be. I know it's much worse than my own.

Angie smiles and bounces away. I sneak a peek at Pat. He doesn't react in any way, not even to smile at me in gratitude. In the way that kids sense things, I know this isn't a good sign. It's a very bad sign.

Mr. Clarence Piggott is the psychology teacher who teaches the class everyone wants to take - Psychology. Wanting to be a psychologist, I had eagerly filled out my class choices at the end of each school year, carefully penciling in 'Psychology – Piggott' as my first choice. I am silently disappointed when I don't see his name on my class schedule each year.

On the spring morning the secretary announces unexpectedly over the classroom loudspeaker that school has been cut short and we were to go home immediately, the kids in our class burst into cheer. They are so loud we almost don't hear her next words, that Mr. Piggott has been shot and killed that morning. My mouth is still half open in a cheer and a smile when the guilt crashes down. How could I have been cheering about a free couple of hours while Mr. Piggott's dead body was lying somewhere in my school? I push my chair so hard it falls backwards, grab my backpack and run out of the classroom where I melt into the pool of streaming, jostling teenage bodies. In the parking lot in front of the school, kids are crying and hugging and rushing about and yelling while teachers rush among us screaming, "Go home! Call your parents!" I huddle in a group of friends. No one is really sure what happened and people are running from circle to circle spreading news.

"It was Pat Lizotte!"

"Pat killed Mr. Piggott because he didn't want to give an oral report!"

"He dropped down to one knee and shot Mr. Piggott in the chest!"

"I knew he was crazy!"

The newspaper publishes the grim details of Mr. Piggott's death the next day. Those of us who weren't in the classroom learn that Pat had walked into his psychology class room, set his books on a table near the door and pulled out a .22-caliber Sturm/Ruger single six, long-barrel revolver from his green army jacket. Since Mr. Piggott's classroom was always full of students, Pat had to call Mr. Piggot's name to draw his attention. When Mr. Piggot turned to face Patrick, he said, "No. No. Come on Pat, don't do it," and stretched out his palms. Patrick kneeled on one knee and fired a shot into Mr. Piggot, causing him to fall backwards and collapse to the floor. Then Patrick wounded two other students before calmly holstering his gun and leaving the building. As he passed a fellow student in the hallway, she heard him say, "Well, that takes care of that."

We learned that the teachers surrounding Mr. Piggott's classroom chased Pat Lizotte down the neighboring streets. He fired shots behind him as he ran, yet those brave teachers continued the chase and finally tackled him on someone's front lawn and held him there until the police arrived.

Pat was tried and convicted of the murder of Mr. Piggot and sent to a mental institution where he will likely remain for the rest of his life. An elementary school was eventually named in Mr. Piggott's honor.

In many ways, Mr. Piggott's death is the end of innocence for us. Collectively my schoolmates and I realize we are no longer children. Our actions are real. Our actions hold consequences. We are more somber. As the months pass after Pat Lizotte murders Mr. Piggott, it becomes clear that some things are permanent. You can make the wrong judgment and lose.

Some things can never be undone.

Chapter Fifty Five

Tapped out: Broke, beaten, busted, a common result of pressing.

Right before my senior year of high school, I move into an apartment with Lisette when her parents transfer to Hawaii for her father's job. It's Lisette's first year of college so her parents pay her rent. Considering I don't have a job, I have no idea how I will finish my senior year of high school and simultaneously pay for my half of a place to live.

Lisette and I throw a party, and Mark shows up. Although he has a new girlfriend, I'm so happy just to see his face again. He says that out of the blue he had dreamed about me the night before and woke up with the realization that he cared about me more than he did when we were dating. With horror, I witness him cry as he apologizes for how he'd acted when we were dating. He says he didn't realize how much damage he'd done, how much angst he'd caused me. "I was spoiled, and selfish, and I'm so sorry for anything I ever did to you, Marlayna."

I don't realize that he is witnessing my breakdown and attempting to take responsibility for what he believes is his contribution. I think if I had known this, I would have started crying too, and would have likely been unable to stop. Mark's confession weighs heavily on my heart, and the next morning I awake feeling lower than I'd ever felt before. I am seventeen years old. I live in an apartment and am supposed to be responsible for my expenses. I have no job and no money. I often go days without eating, living on diet soda and cigarettes as I'd learned to do from Lisette.

I take a job as a canvasser with an aluminum siding company. The manager is a tall portly man with a receding hairline. Rick tells me that although competition for the job was stiff, he interviewed 20 girls and decided to hire me. I swell with pride at his words. I just know this must be the break I need. My first day on the job we drive around together and map neighborhoods we will then canvas over the next week. I am to go door to door, repeating a script designed to entice the homeowner into allowing Rick to visit next, close the sale and put aluminum siding on the home.

While we drive around on the second day, Rick casually mentions he would enjoy taking pictures of me and making a portfolio so I could model. He says that I'm pretty enough to model. He says I should be in my own apartment. He offers to cover my rent. I can't understand why he offers such a thing. After all, he's married and I have a roommate, so what difference does it make where and with whom I live? I thank him politely for his offer, but don't accept.

Some days we work with another canvasser named Stephanie, and the two of them smoke pot as we drive from neighborhood to neighborhood. Late one afternoon I get in Rick's car after having canvassed an entire neighborhood in 110 degree heat. Perspiration drips down my forehead and runs off the tip of my nose. Rick grabs my forearm and says, "You incredibly sexy creature! Let's go to a motel and I'll lick off all your sweat."

I'm still trying to think of a way to deflect his suggestion while attempting to stem the tide of running sweat from my face when he continues, "Come on! Let's leave Stephanie to work and you and I go to a motel."

Stephanie snorts from the backseat. "Jesus, Rick, the kid's 17. What are you thinking?"

Rick pulls into a fast food restaurant and I quickly escape the car without having to utter a word.

Overlay – A Tale of One Girl's Life in 1970s Las Vegas

While we stand in line, Rick leans into me from behind so that I can feel his erection against my back. He whispers into my ear, "I'm going to keep you for my personal mistress. I won't require much time, just two nights a week, and the rest you can spend with your boyfriends. What you really need is a good head job. It'll relax you. I'm very good at it and I'd like to do it to you."

I feel his hand pull the back of my shirt open so he can peer down my back. I stand unmoving underneath the shine of the fluorescent lighting, watching the cashier take the order of the family in front of me. I tell myself that I'm in public for God's sake and things like this can't possibly happen. I know I should turn around, stomp on his toe, kick him between the legs, elbow him in the stomach, but I do no such thing. I order a diet coke from the cashier when it's my turn and politely pay for my order. I wasn't expecting Rick to be another in a series of predators, and his actions leave me feeling even lower. There just seems to be no end to the long line of predatory males.

Even though I am very far away from my apartment, I take my soda and walk out the front door of the restaurant. The sun sets. The temperature drops. I keep walking. I hear the car slowing before I see it, so I have a moment to compose myself. I'm careful to walk with strength, pride and self-assurance, my head held high, my arms swinging with determination.

"Hey," a man's voice calls through the open window of the red sports car next to me, "would you like a ride?"

Without stopping my purposeful stride, I turn nonchalantly to my left, look the young man driving the car in the eyes and say, "Nah. I'm almost home. Thanks."

"Well, okay, then," he says after a moment and pulls away.

Stupid. So incredibly stupid. What was I thinking to cut through this neighborhood at night? I am furious, more with myself than anyone else. Besides I reason, I should be home in 45 short minutes if I keep walking at the pace I've established. I'm not safe. I know this, but I'm too mad to be scared. Until I hear the car slow down next to me again, and see the man from a few minutes earlier.

"Hey, I really don't feel safe with you out here," he explains, slowing his car down to keep pace with me. "I won't be able to sleep tonight knowing I didn't help a beautiful girl out. Just get in, let me give you a ride, even if it's only to your general neighborhood. You don't even have to tell me where you live."

I fall for it.

In one of those inexplicable moments where one does something so completely out of the realm of their ordinary common sense, I open the door of his red sports car and climb inside. His car smells like a mixture of leather conditioner and cologne and I think that anyone who spends time trying to smell good can't be bad. When I shut the door, and he locks the doors with a click, hits the gas and guns the engine, I know I'm wrong. I turn to look at him in horror as the realization hits me that absolutely no one in the world knows where I am. No one knows I'm walking on this road. No one knows I'm alone. No one sees me get into the red sports car. I will leave no trace if I vanish. Just another missing teen. My history will certainly make me look like a runaway.

He doesn't look like a serial killer, I think as my head is thrown back in the seat by his acceleration. He doesn't look too much older than I am, so how could he be bad? His mousy brown hair falls across his forehead in an innocent way. He seems so young, I think as the car hits 30 mph, 40 mph, 50 mph, 60 mph. Someone young can't be bad. Perhaps he is just a fast driver. It is a fast car, after all. Perhaps he is just showing off. I see movement from the corner of my eye and ask what he's doing.

"Come on! You didn't think I'd pick you up for free, did you? Gas, grass or ass, baby. You're gonna put out for this ride," he fumbles around with his zipper, until he's able to pull his penis out of his pants.

I can't help but look at his stroking hand. "If you don't slow down and let me out of this car, I'll jump."

He speeds up, "Go for it." He laughs.

As we approach the first major intersection, I demand that he let me out of the car. He doesn't slow. From the side window, I watch the street corner come and go, as a sinking feeling spreads in the pit of my stomach. He makes a quick left and my body slides and hits the interior door as he turns into a darkened subdivision. We speed down a friend's street and I watch her house as we pass, the windows dark, the blinds drawn. I once slept in that house. My friend's father made scrambled eggs for breakfast. We looked at yearbooks. Mr. Peterson was inside sleeping, right now. Perhaps if the driver stops soon I can break away. I will be close enough to run back to their house. Maybe Mr. Peterson would wake up if I started screaming as I ran down their street. Maybe he would come outside, see me running from this man and save me.

But the driver continues along the dark streets, winding slowly, turning corners. I know eventually we will have to stop, and I have to be prepared for whatever is coming next. I have no idea what is next. Will he pull out a gun? Or a knife? Will he grab me by the hair? Is he going to kill me? Or does he plan to just rape me? I know this neighborhood, and from the way he keeps turning corners, he doesn't. I say nothing. I just wait. I don't jump from the car as long as we are still near the darkened houses because I know the likelihood that he will be able to chase me down before I can get someone to answer their door at this hour is great.

Perhaps my strange silence unnerves him. I don't panic. I don't scream. I just sit in silence and wait for what is coming next. I experience an extremely heightened sense of 'fight or flight syndrome' and am ready for anything. Without explanation he suddenly slams on his brakes and yells, "Get out!" I open the car door and fly out of that red muscle car so fast my legs are pumping before I even hit the ground. His tires peel with an alarming screech as he guns his engine and I realize he's heading straight for me. He isn't letting me go, after all. He's going to run over me. I race off the street and head straight into the desert. He guns his engine and hops the curb to come after me. Thinking better of it I guess, I hear his engine rev as he backs up and the sound of him and his car fades as I move further into the desert.

I run all the way home without stopping, though I want to stop.

How I want to stop.

I am tapped out.

Chapter Fifty Six

Stuck: Behind, losing, buried, down for the count.

Time is flying by so fast and I don't feel like I'm doing anything important. I go through each day without appreciating it or doing anything substantial. I don't want to just be alive. I want to live and do things. Day after day passes bringing along more problems, and most of them seem insurmountable. I am really at my wit's end with everyone right now. I don't know what is happening to me. Life used to be so simple and easy. I don't want to grow up yet. I used to be such sweet, innocent girl. I wish I could just get away from everyone and everything right now. All my friends ever do is try to be so damn cute and I hate it. Everyone wears a mask, and I am myself all the time. I guess if I can't stand it when people don't act like themselves I should lock myself in a closet or something because no one seems to be themselves anymore. Everyone is trying so hard to be something else. I despise the very hypocrisy of everyone around me.

My attitude sucks. My life sucks. I'm tired of worrying about my father and his job and our money and my getting a job and dieting and my friends and not eating and where I'm going to live and every other thing that is wrong.

I would just like to lie down, go to sleep and not wake up. Nothing is humorous to me anymore. No one makes me feel any better. Everything around me is dark and terrible, even though I try to tell myself that it probably isn't as bad as I feel it is. I am frustrated and bored with everything around me and don't find excitement in anything.

So I slit my wrists one evening when Lisette isn't at home.

The next morning I rise to consciousness much like I did when I was a child in the back seat of my parent's car. My awareness starts in the familiar space on the bottom of what feels like the ocean floor of my consciousness. It travels slowly up, until it reaches the surface and I open my eyes. I'm not sure which part of what I am remembering is a dream. I am indeed alive, and I am no small child in the backseat of my parent's car. I am 17 years old and this is no dream. I've survived a suicide attempt. I pull my wrists before my bleary eyes to see the thick scabs and dried black rivulets along my arms. I sit up and look around at my bedding, like a princess surveying her mini kingdom. The bedsheets are smeared with dried blood.

Oh, God.

Oh, my God.

In the silence of that November morning, it seems there should be a sound for what I'm experiencing: some soundtrack to my slide off the face of the earth as I scrabble and scratch around for traction and find none. The worst part of it all is that I am awake and coherent, and know this latest turn of affairs isn't anyone else's fault – only my own. I am consciously falling, and failing to find a single handhold during this tumble into uncertainty. It would have been a relief to no longer be faced with the arduous task of living. The rent, the food, the boys, my senior year, my father, my mother – the thoughts circulate in my head as I sit alone in my bedroom, covered in my own dried brown blood.

I raise the window blind and feel the gentle early morning sun warm my face. I feel a tug in my chest, evidence of my conflict about remaining on this earth. Evidence that I am still alive. My heart still beats. I ask myself if I really want to live, and find I can't honestly answer the question. The apartment is silent, empty except for me and my multitude of thoughts..

I ask myself the most difficult question of all: should I just finish the job?

The hours tick by on the first day as I consider the answer to this question. The thought that any single moment I can end my life is nothing short of overpowering. Just one good slice and all my struggles would be over. It would only take one second to erase 17 years of pain. It would be so quick. So easy. But what if there is something good ahead of me? I would miss it. Then these past 17 years would have passed in pain for absolutely no reason and with no gain or benefit to anyone. Surely there is no sense in such a pattern. The horror of my thought process sinks into my consciousness. What have I done? What am I thinking? Instead of washing the blood from my sheets, I could be lying on a slab in the hospital morgue, my skin blue and pasty. I imagine Lisette struggling to contact my mother and my father. I imagine the phone calls going on across the city as friends call each other asking, "Did you hear the news?" I imagine the ones that thought they could have stopped me, could have done something, anything, one thing, ten things that would have made the difference and kept me alive. I picture the tears of the ones who had walked through my life, wondering if somehow they were at fault. I would have never been able to tell them that the fault was my own. That the action was my own.

I remember Matt, a boy I'd known who committed suicide in tenth grade. Angel and I had danced and skipped past his house on a rainy afternoon a few years ago. I saw in my mind his little wave from his porch as we passed. He'd been sitting outside smoking a cigarette, and looked up as we ran by. He had smiled at us. I remember hearing that Matt had liked me. When I heard that he'd killed himself, I wondered for a long time if I had had the power to save Matt. What if I had agreed to date him? Would he be alive today? Would the time I spent with him have helped him past the difficult period he did not survive otherwise? Perhaps I never had the power to save Matt. The action, after all, was his own. He wanted to die and he made it happen. How could I ever have explained to anyone that my action had been my own? I realized that I had slipped so far down that I felt as if I wouldn't be able to crawl back up again. If I didn't save myself and do it right now worse things than death could happen to me.

"Help me," I mutter and bury my face in my bloodied pillow. 'Help me, please, somebody, anybody, please, please, please, please help." With each word of my prayer, I pound a weak fist on the mattress beside my pillow. I want so much more for myself. My dreams of attending college and of having a family of my own seem so far away on this cold November morning.

It is then, for the second time in my life, I smell the roses.

As before, a hand brushes down my body, starting at the back of my head and slowly moving down the length of my spine.

You will be okay, I feel more than hear. We love you.

This moment never strays too far from my memory.

Overlay – A Tale of One Girl's Life in 1970s Las Vegas

Chapter Fifty Seven

Take A Price: To bet the underdog and take the points.

"I think I'm having a nervous break down," I say to my mom on the phone. "Can I come live with you in Los Angeles?" I sense the happiness in her being before she even responds with yes of course there is plenty of room for me to live with her and Denny, and she will find out how to get me registered for high school. This is a time for amends.

A day at a time, I tell myself. Treat this break like you would recover from a cold or the flu. One thing at a time.

On Monday, I go to school and withdraw myself, wearing sweatbands around my wrists to hide the scabs.

On Tuesday, a used furniture company arrives at my apartment to buy my bedroom set for forty dollars, which incidentally is the cost of a bus ticket to Los Angeles.

On Wednesday, I spend my last evening in Las Vegas with Mr. Grafton, my cheerleading and math teacher from ninth grade. Over Mexican food he does his best to try to talk me into staying in Las Vegas, though his efforts are futile. I know what I have to do. When he takes me back home he hugs me for a long time, and kisses the top of my head. He says he wishes there was some way he and his wife could take care of me. "I've known you for five years and you were always one of my favorite kids. I've always worried for you as if you were my own daughter. I knew your situation at home was rough, living with an alcoholic father."

"You knew?"

"Of course I did honey, we all did."

"I didn't know anyone knew about my dad and about my life."

"It's hard to keep a secret from people who care about you."

It's the first time in a long time I feel someone loves me. I take that feeling and seal it in my heart: a present to myself. It gives me the hope I need to move forward in my life, to seek the happiness I hope I can obtain.

On Thursday, I board a bus for Los Angeles and to a new life in California. I end my journal on the bus ride: *Character:*

1. Take yourself seriously!

2. Develop a clear sense of self-respect and stick to it!

3. Define to others what you will and will not put up with.

4. Tact is a part of character too.

5. People with character are people who defend their territory with skill, determination and tenacity.

6. Do not forget you are your own territory, too.

7. Above all, defend yourself. Defend yourself. Defend yourself.

EPILOGUE

Active Player: One who is still in the pot.

Although I've taken small liberties, the details on the preceding pages are true. In real life I'm known for my memory and long journaling history. This story is a natural outgrowth of both sources. Some of these tales were not revealed until I wrote this book, for reasons you may understand. The characters I have introduced to you are real people who lived during the1970s Las Vegas era.

It is not my intent to offend anyone but such offense may be inevitable. I've changed the names of nearly everyone in this book to preserve their anonymity. I've tried to portray the characters that have crossed my path in as honest a light as I can. I've also tried to be kinder than reality presented in some cases, primarily out of respect for living family members.

Cousin Robert is a father of four and lives somewhere in California. That's all I know and all I want to know.

Cousin Marie (Robert's sister) lives in Maui with her four grown children and more than a few grandchildren. I haven't seen her since I was ten but I would sure love to. We keep in touch on Facebook.

Aunt Ana is alive and lives somewhere in California. I understand she is married to her fifth husband. She just keeps outliving the men as the women in our family do. I haven't seen her in many years. I prefer to remember her as young and blissfully happy with my uncle.

Mr. Nice is dead. He remarried after my mother and had a listing in the phone book for many years with his next wife. Yes, I checked because I desperately wanted to show up on his doorstep and say, "I know what you did." Unfortunately I never took the opportunity to do so. He died in 1997, three days after my mom's sixty-seventh birthday and a few months before the birth of my fourth child. None of us noticed or cared.

My childhood friend "Christine" has been lost to obscurity. Wherever you are, Christine, if you read this book and see yourself on these pages, please know I am sorry for what happened to you at the hands of Mr. Nice. I wish I could have prevented what happened to you. I wish social services had been in place back then so I could have alerted them to help you. I hope you've found peace and happiness in your life.

In trying to find my childhood friend "Angela," I have found someone with her exact name and bearing a striking resemblance to my friend on a very prominent and popular website. This young woman is a porn actress, stripper and model. Angela's real name was unusual, so I might assume this young woman is her daughter. Angela, if you read this book one day and see yourself on these pages, I am sorry I did not do more to help you. I'm also sorry I kicked your ass, though I still feel you had it coming.

Dean Parker was stabbed to death in a bar fight in the late 1970s. I understand that none of the patrons moved to help him and he bled to death on the floor before the phone was even lifted to call the police. He found the killer's bar on his own.

The bully Diana has a long history of drug problems and has been in and out of prison. She looks exactly as she did when I knew her: a scrappy twelve year old boy. Though we are not friends on Facebook, I occasionally click on her page just to remind myself that things that once seemed truly frightening can become benign and meaningless with the passage of time.

Cute little Donna is also lost to obscurity. I heard that her brother was murdered some years ago and instantly remembered him walking through the living room in his Dyn-O-Mite tee-shirt. I hope she is doing well and think it's safe to assume she is dancing happily somewhere, surrounded by children and grandchildren of her own.

The last time I spoke to Mark, he told me he was in line to inherit 76 million dollars. He also apologized for being so mean to me when we were kids. His apology still warms me and makes me smile. He is married, though he never had any children of his own. His wife is a lucky woman.

For all of his wild beginnings, Rebel has done quite well for himself. He has been married for a long time to a girl he met after me. They have two children and live happily in Australia. We still keep in touch from time to time, although I've not seen him in many years. He has never apologized to me, but he should. He knows why.

Caroline has a very prominent career and has done well for herself. When she said her father passed away a few years before, I was surprised it left me feeling sad. I appreciated his kindness when I was a lost and lonely child. If I were to run into her mother, I would have difficulty being kind to her. Still, I am grateful for the safe haven they offered me during my runs through the desert and homelessness.

Angel is married to a dentist with three children. They live a safe existence in a small Texas town. When her mother died a few years ago, I bawled like a baby but I did not attend the service. I have a thing against funerals, having suffered enough loss in my life.

Angie has done well for herself. She married a much older politician and seems to have crafted a life that works for her. While in town for our twenty year high school reunion, I stopped by her family home and visited with her father. I'm happy to say he was more than pleased to see I did not turn out to be the mess he thought I would. He died of cancer shortly thereafter.

Josie is a strikingly beautiful woman with two children. She married a famous sports figure, but seems to have found her real peace since the divorce. She wanted to name her daughter after me, but her husband said no.

Reggie did name one of his daughters after me.

Josie's brother, John, is now famous in the fashion world. He is married with two children. I'm happy to say he calls me once or twice a year to check in. He is The One That Got Away.

I am still in touch with Violet and appreciate the time her family took me in. I know her mother did not mean to be cruel to me. As a parent I now understand her frustration when she exploded and asked how a parent could not care for their child? She passed a few years ago from cancer. I am happy to be in touch with her father, and still able to enjoy his phenomenal vocabulary.

I am not in touch with Lisette, but have heard she is married with children. I've met many women like Lisette over the years and have done my best to avoid them. I hope she settled down and found peace and self-acceptance.

Overlay – A Tale of One Girl's Life in 1970s Las Vegas

Pat Lizotte is serving two life sentences without possibility of parole at the Southern Nevada Correctional Center at Jean.

In contrast, Clarence A. Piggott Elementary School opened in 1993.

My sister has been married for many years and I am blessed with two fantastic nieces and one amazing nephew. Though my sister and I have lived very different lives, I am often warmed by our similarities.

My brother has also been married for many years and they now live in her native Japan where he teaches English and rides his bicycle quite often.

My eighty year old father turned up nearly a year after his disappearance into a nursing facility. He tells a fantastic story of being held hostage by an armed guard at the nursing facility. "How in the hell were any of us going to escape from that hellhole?" he asks. "We had no money, no shoes and were forced to wear paper gowns and diapers!" I wish him well. I do not keep in touch with him. He did call in 2012 and ask what was new in my life. When I told him I'd written a book, he asked two questions: "Am I in it?" and "Was I a good parent in it?" I answered, "I think you were the best parent you knew how to be."

My mother is still married to Denny, her fifth and final husband. A few years ago I called her and apologized for blaming everything on her that had gone wrong in my life. She said I didn't need to apologize as it really was her fault. I said that I'd had plenty of years to make my own choices, and that I took total responsibility for all that took place in my life. She still insisted that it was her fault. I wish we would have had that conversation years earlier Now there isn't a conversation we've had that I don't feel thankful for the presence of Denny in her life. They have no savings and aren't in great health. Living in a retirement apartment community in the high desert outside of Los Angeles, they have only each other now. This my friends, is love. I'm glad she finally found what was once such an elusive state for her.

As for me, I have four teenage children that continually teach me something new when I think I know it all. I have three college degrees and have had several different careers. I speak three languages, some better than others, and can say hello, thank you and goodbye in many more. I have lived, loved, traveled the world, wrote, drawn, photographed and accomplished many, many other things.

But those are other stories for other days.

Just know that I am still in the pot.

Overlay – A Tale of One Girl's Life in 1970s Las Vegas

Close to my heart is the phrase, "If you save one life, you save a whole world." It is my wish that my tale of challenge and survival will serve as inspiration to you if so needed.

Marlayna Glynn Brown is a mother of four, an author, screenwriter, actress, producer, yogi and photographer. Marlayna was born and raised in Las Vegas, Nevada but now lives wherever she lays her head.

In addition to Overlay - A Tale of One Girl's Life in 1970s Las Vegas, she is the author of:

City of Angeles
Big as All Hell And Half of Texas
Forty-Something Phoenix: A Travel Memoir of Love and Rebirth

Her 2009 short film, People That do Something, is based upon a chapter from Overlay and can be viewed on Youtube.

She is currently planning her next set of experiences on this wonderful planet we share.
Connect online!

www.marlaynaglynnbrown.com

Facebook: Marlayna Glynn Brown

mailto:marlaynaglynnbrown@gmail.com

Overlay – A Tale of One Girl's Life in 1970s Las Vegas

Preview from City of Angeles – the next sequel from the trilogy The Memoirs of Marlayna Glynn Brown:

Alex is the leader of the Los Angeles Death Squad, a charismatic good-looking kid with extraordinarily white teeth. He looks more like a Spanish movie star than a gang banger. After one of the shows the crowd empties into the parking lot where I stand silently next to Chris. Boys are stumbling around, having had too much alcohol or too many drugs. I am sober, watching all that goes on around me.

Alex stumbles toward Chris, balancing his perfect smile on unstable footing. Although it's a warm summer evening in Hollywood, they're all wearing thick leather jackets with the LADS skull and cross bone arm patches. Alex looks uncertainly down at me, weaving slightly.

"You're pretty," he says and smiles. The streetlight reflects the white of his teeth and lights up his face. Alex is the leader. The cool guy. The untouchable one. Everyone loves Alex. Just standing in close proximity to him is causing me to feel a little weak. I smile a small smile up at him.

"What the FUCK?" a girl suddenly yells and the crowd around me shifts in response.

Alex takes a step backwards and slowly turns around as a green-capped girl is doing her best to push her way through the crowd. He places one black jacketed arm around me for stability.

"Alex, what the FUCK?" she repeats. She is closer and louder now.

I attempt to take a step back to try and get behind Chris, but the heavy weight of Alex's slack arm holds me in place.

"That's Alex's girlfriend," Chris whispers to me. "I think you should run."

But she is close now and frantically elbowing through the last several kids that stand in her way and I don't run because I'm like a looky-loo at my own wreck and have to see what's going to happen next.

"Who are YOU?" she yells and someone reaches out and grabs her chest from behind, effectively blocking her from moving forward any further. She is thrashing her skinny body around, violently trying to get out of the grasp from behind. Her pregnant belly protrudes from beneath her thin tee-shirt, and although I should probably be running, I can't take my eyes from her belly.
Alex is laughing, his arm still holding me in place. Chris moves in front of me just as Alex's girlfriend breaks from the grasp and lunges toward me. Her body hits the solid mass of Chris instead of me, and he easily grabs both of her skinny arms and prevents her from moving forward.

"Get the FUCK out of the way!"

"I didn't do anything," I say, but I think I'm whispering and no one hears me. The words fall from my mouth in the form of a prayer rather than a response – a plea for sanity.

Alex stumbles away to the side, still chuckling. He is either completely oblivious to the situation he's created for me or simply doesn't care enough to watch the outcome. His girlfriend takes no notice of him and continues trying to get to me while Chris holds her firmly in place.

"Marlayna, run," he urges over his shoulder. "Now."

I've not yet seen Chris even slightly disturbed, and the edge to his voice finally slices through my mesmerization. I turn and make my way through the crowd behind me. Her screams follow me, cutting through the bodies and echoing against the dirty buildings around us all. Since I've walked away from the group and Chris has driven me to Hollywood, I'm not sure where to go. I head down an alleyway leading off to the side in case she breaks free and sprints after me. I hear footsteps and turn quickly, expecting to see the pregnant girl followed by the crowd. Instead I see Paul – the one I don't know very well. He is walking toward me, his face shrouded in darkness. "Hey," he says as he nears me.

"Hey."

"Dawn's crazy," he laughs as he takes a seat on the ground and props his back against the wall. He pulls a bottle of whiskey from the inside of his LADS jacket. He pats the ground next to him.

"Is she dating Alex?"

"Yes, and has been for a long time." He takes a deep swig from the bottle and hands it to me.

"And that's his baby?"

"Most likely."

I'm quiet and take a swig of the whiskey.

Paul says, "You've made an enemy for life. I wouldn't come around here no more."

"Because her boyfriend smiled at me?"

"She will hurt you."

"I didn't do anything wrong. I don't know Alex. I don't know her."

"Doesn't matter. Nothing does except reality."

I feel the burn of the whiskey warming my throat, my stomach and relaxing my body. I take another drink. "And what is the reality?"

"This group includes very unstable and violent people. Dawn is one of them."

"Why do you hang around with them?"

"Because I've known them forever. We grew up together."

"Are you're like them?"

"I suppose I am. Alex is the leader of the LADS. It's his life. His girlfriend will have his baby and

256

they will continue the violent relationship they have. Kevin will continue shooting up drugs until he's dead and Chris will continue providing the drugs."

"Chris provides drugs?"

"Come on, you can't tell me you didn't know Chris sells drugs?"

"I didn't."

"Did he tell you the story that he has family back in the Philippines that support him?"

"Yes."

"And you believed it?"
"Why wouldn't I?"

"Do you believe everything you hear?"

"Why wouldn't I?"

Paul laughs and hands the bottle to me and I take another healthy swig. I want to dull the thoughts of the earlier part of the evening. At some point he puts his black-jacketed arm around me. The skull and cross bone arm patch catches my eye until my reactions are dull and slowed to half-time reels in a black and white film. We continue laughing but the thought forms in my brain that he is not laughing with me, but at me. I am embarrassingly naïve compared to him. I don't have the social experience he does. I can feel this through the haze of the whiskey but when I try to think I'm no longer sharp enough to complete the thought process. We continue sharing swigs from the whiskey bottle and by the time he pushes me down I'm so numb it's as if my body is existing separately from my brain. My brain is a part of my soul, ethereal and tenuous, and now separate from the heaviness that is my physical body. I think my mouth says no to him. I know I try to form the words. But my body is lying prone on the alley against the wall and his fumbling around could be anything, really. It could be rape. It could be misinterpreted acceptance. I black in. I black out. Questioning thoughts drift in disconnected bubbles across my consciousness. Each time my brain reconnects with my body, it slithers away, abandoning me and all that I am in the gray murkiness that is the horror of consciousness and the sublime beauty of imagination.

2880887R00139

Made in the USA
San Bernardino, CA
13 June 2013